WHAT SHALL WE DO TOMORROW?

Mary Hayley Bell has also written:

PLAYS	Men in Shadow Duet for Two Hands The Uninvited Guest Angel Foreign Field Dear Enemy Feathers on the Water *etc.*
BOOKS	Avolena Whistle Down the Wind Far Morning
TELEVISION PLAYS	Hermit Crabs Dollies
FILMS	Sky West and Crooked

WHAT SHALL WE DO TOMORROW?

an autobiography by

MARY HAYLEY BELL

CASSELL · LONDON

CASSELL & COMPANY LTD
35 Red Lion Square, London WC1
Melbourne, Sydney, Toronto
Johannesburg, Auckland

S.B.N. 304 93264 7

First edition October 1968
Second impression October 1968

Printed in Great Britain
by Ebenezer Baylis and Son, Ltd
The Trinity Press, Worcester, and London
1068

To the
source of the river
and the streams that sprang from it

CONTENTS

PART ONE BOM JESUS

1 Hayley Bell's Children 3
2 Mysterious Gateway to the Sea 22
3 The Unforgiving Garden 30
4 Goodbye, Bom Jesus 35
5 'Outcast Children of the East' 44
6 A Web of Schools 56
7 That Boy 69
8 The Japanese 80

PART TWO THEATRE

9 Bye Bye Blackbird 87
10 Hell's Bells 105
11 These Flowers Need Watering 120

PART THREE JOHNNIE

12 A Sudden Spring 133
13 Ships that Pass 147
14 Johnnie Comes Marching Home 153
15 The Sugar Plum Fairy 157
16 The Men in the Shadows 164
17 King of the Open Sky 171

PART FOUR JULIET, HAYLEY, AND JONATHAN

18 Hayley 179
19 The Boy with Red Hair 186
20 The Garden by the Water 196
21 Over the Dim Blue Hills 207
22 What Shall We Do Tomorrow? 226

ILLUSTRATIONS

My mother and father *following page* 52
Me and Amah (*Ah Fong*)
The Commissioner's House at Macao
The Tiles
Steps to our mother's garden
Beak, Hooky Walker, Bebe, Brownie, me and Wee Willie Winkie
Aylmar House, Sherborne
Johnman, our father, and Dennis
Johnman

The cast of *Vintage Wine* at Blackpool *following page* 68
Lady Jane in *Victoria Regina*
As Johnnie saw me on 15 May 1939
Johnnie in *Of Mice and Men* (*Angus McBean*)
Janet Johnson (*Universal Pictorial Press & Agency*)
My father and Johnnie
Pilot Officers Francis Hayley Bell and Dennis Hayley Bell
Johnnie and me, married (*London Society Photographic Service*)

The Oast House (*Pictorial Press*) *following page* 164
The Mills family (*Pictorial Press*)
Johnnie as Scott of the Antarctic
Fernacres
The Mills family in Richmond Park (*Star Copyright Picture*)
Letters from the children

Juliet's wedding day (*Kent and Sussex Courier*) *following page* 180
Sussex House Farm
Jonathan, Hamlet II, and Hayley (*Denis Hughes-Gilbey*: *Studio K*)
Jonathan and me
Hayley
The Wick (*Odhams Photographic Studio*)
The garden by the water (*Odhams Photographic Studio*)
Johnnie and me, 1967 (*Gene Ray*: *Bermuda News Bureau*)

Will you ever let us, Fate,
Sit quietly again upon the gate
In the evenings, and say, 'What
shall we do tomorrow?'

PART ONE

BOM JESUS

I

HAYLEY BELL'S CHILDREN

He towered above me, a lean, taut figure, chiselled from the granite rocks themselves.

'Go away and sit by yourself until you can show a proper spirit to Bebe,' he said evenly.

Eyes blazing I faced him.

'It's my birthday!' I sobbed. 'And Nosey Parker is *my* rat!'

'That is no excuse for making her cry,' he replied quietly. 'If you don't learn to control that temper, you're going to store up a lot of trouble for yourself.'

'I might *die*—and then you'll all be sorry!'

I paused long enough to see the fear on my sister's face, and then wrenching myself away from the small knot of children on the grass among the ponies, I snatched up the bewildered black and white rat, stuffed him into my shirt, and stumbled away through the lacerating undergrowth with tears of humiliation streaming down my cheeks. Flinging myself face down upon a huge slab of rock, I gave myself up to heavy self-pitying sobs, unobserved.

It was my ninth birthday, and it wasn't fair! I was only trying to show her how to put knickers on Nosey Parker! What did she have to go and blub for? They'll never understand me, never . . . Nanny Day's voice echoed in my ears: 'Don't be such a plaguey nuisance'—and my mother's, soothing, gentle: 'Quiet, Baba, don't get so excited! Oh dear, you do remind me of Auntie Alice!'

As I had frequently heard Auntie Alice referred to as being 'cracky' and having a screw loose, my misery deepened. The remembered picture of Auntie Alice in an old album floated before me, her smiling mouth hanging half open, a garland of flowers between her hands, and I howled aloud, aware at the same time of the warm comfort of the rock beneath me, the cracks full of long dead insects, the humming of wings close to my ear.

A large praying mantis alighted on the slate-blue rock beside me, its forelegs folded in prayer, its hypnotic eyes turned warily upon me. With pleasure and wonder, I regarded the palely green creature, transparent as a blade of grass. Slowly my hand crept towards it. Could I catch it? It would undoubtedly put me back into favour with the others; but in one gigantic leap, it was lost among the cactus bushes.

I sat up, chewing the ends of my long red hair thoughtfully, staring out across the Praya Grande to the Bay of Macao. The fishing junks were hanging out their amber and red nets in the late afternoon sunlight. The distant Islands of Ladrones across the sea thrust out their headlands like grim warriors, bold and defiant, guarding the secrets of the Chinese pirates who lay beyond. Brown sails of junks turned as if by magic to burnished gold in the fiery rays of the departing sun, gleamed and glistened as they emerged from the molten sea, and the sky above turned suddenly from duck-egg blue and lilac to amethyst and rose madder.

I rolled over on my back with a sigh of contentment and well-being, and stared up into the growing darkness of the banyan trees. My ninth birthday had come and nearly gone, for I could hear the distant angelus from St Joseph's church drowning the cries of the bean curd seller in the street below. The garden around me was full of whispering evening noises, the creaking of crickets, the laughter of a child. . . .

'There's nowhere like this in all the world,' I thought, although this had been our only world, through all our formative years.

Macao. 'City of the Name of God'—this slumbrous old world of pink, discoloured churches and monasteries; silent witnesses to the splendour of the bold seamen of Portugal, once masters of the Southern Seas; and this enchanted garden under a spell, this Eden of fascination and wonder.

The Garden had always been known as Bom Jesus for as long as anyone could remember, and its history never ceased to entrance us. On this very hill, behind its wall, now a tangle of trees, faded grasses and cactus bushes, there had once existed, centuries ago, a temple dedicated to the sea and sea rovers.

When the Portuguese began trading from Macao over four hundred years before, the men of Albuquerque had sought to dominate the peninsula and clear it of the pirates who ruled the Southern Coast, but the Chinese under the Manchus fought desperately to hold it and it was many years before the Portuguese, with their long swords, won their way to this temple on the crown of the hill.

'With the last of the Sea Gods, died the Priests of the Sea,' my father had told us. 'And the story goes that the aged "Bonze", with his last breath, laid a curse upon any man who should so much as break the soil in this Holy ground.'

Hugging ourselves with anticipation and excitement, our eyes alight, we rolled ourselves into four small balls of silence as he talked.

'Many attempts have been made, because it stands in the best part of Macao, but centuries have stolen through the city and the Garden has become untrodden, inviolate. . . .'

The Garden now belonged to the Chinese Imperial Maritime Customs, of which my father was the Commissioner. Years before, a former Commissioner had bought the unwanted place behind the high walls for a song, thinking it to be a splendid site for a new Commissioner's house. It was never built.

An architect came from Hong Kong, and enough of the undergrowth was removed for retrenching in order to determine the nature of the subsoil and the foundations which would be required. A clerk of the works came from Canton with his men—since no one in Macao would take part in the building—and even the coolies came from the Pearl River, sixty miles away.

Not a single stone was ever laid; for one reason or another, six white men and thirty-five Chinese died within a few weeks of each other.

There was nothing unearthly for us: mysterious, yes, especially at night, when the night-scented moon cactus filled Bom Jesus with the possessiveness of incense. The 'Kanmenti', our night watchman, had another tale to tell, that spurred us into an endless, hopeless search.

Fighting our way on hands and knees through the dense and obstinate tangle of creeper under the banyan trees in that ghostly garden of grey stone, scratched, bleeding and incredibly dirty, bringing Nanny's wrath down upon our heads, we crawled daily in our quest for pirate treasure. Once, we had found a flight of narrow stone steps, leading from nowhere to nowhere, half buried in the accumulation of age old moss and leaf mould. To my father it suggested a building now walled up.

'You're to go no farther!' he said, and refused to share our excitement.

There was something else we had found; but we kept this to ourselves until much later. . . .

*

I sat up, pushing the long, tiresome hair out of my eyes, and looked across the garden at the others, now rubbing down the ponies. My father was sitting on the grass beside them, laughing at something one of them had said, and I was reminded of another birthday, when with one of his sudden secret smiles he had summoned me into the street outside our house to see my present. Wee Willie Winkie, a white Yunan pony, stood by the gateway, a grinning 'Mafoo' holding him by the reins. My shriek of delight brought tears of disappointment to my brother's and sister's faces, but as if by magic and a clap of my father's hands, round the corner trotted Brownie and Hooky Walker!

'You'll all have to fall off a hundred times before you can ride!' he said.

He was right. As an ex-cavalry officer, he taught us like troopers. No bridles, no saddles, our arms folded before us, driven round and round a circle on a long leading rein, reliant entirely upon the pressure of our knees to remain vertical. Falls were followed by tears, protests and intercessions, but at the end of it we could ride! A bucking buffalo wouldn't have shifted us. . . .

There were five of us, all saddled with those comical, bizarre names with which children reinforce themselves. The eldest, I had the greatest variety of names. To my mother I had always been Baba, to my father for some unexplained reason I was Muggins, possibly because he enjoyed the alliteration; and to the Chinese I was 'Oong deu', 'Red-head'.

Bebe was Winifred, with the two blue bows in her brown hair, her missing front teeth, and an everlasting forgiveness for those things I had done and those things I had left undone.

Beak was Dennis, his wing of white hair hiding eyes so often clouded with tears he struggled to hide.

Beattie was Elizabeth, a child with gazelle-like eyes, and lastly there was Johnman, the baby, from whose quick observation and unprejudiced wisdom so much was expected, but who was the first to leave his 'uniform' in a sailor's grave overlooking Plymouth, where some of his forefathers left the coast of England for America in 1666.

We ran more or less wild. Our mother, Nanny Day, and the Chinese amahs between them managed a pretence at cleanliness. Our long hair shone with brushing, and so did our teeth, and under Nanny's tyranny we went to the bathroom morning and evening, these requirements being the only ones of importance in their eyes. When Nanny was in Hong Kong on one of her weekends off, the Number Two Boy took the responsibility upon himself, and Nanny's morning cry of 'Quickly do your duties and come to breakfast', translated into his pidgin English with complete ignorance of its meaning, became 'Quick do stews go beliefossay'.

We were the only English children in Macao and the few friends we had were Chinese or Portuguese. Oscar, the son of Dr Schmitto, was one, and Yvonne Lebas, daughter of the Portuguese Governor, a willowy, cinnamon-coloured girl with sorrel hair, another. None of us had ever seen a film, or been near to the theatre.

Lovely, long, loitering days! Days of sapphire and turquoise seas, and mother-of-pearl skies; shimmering mornings, and shadows of evening creeping along the narrow cobbled streets like tallow-faced ghosts when the sun had vanished in the West, and doors that had stood open all morning were barred and shut against the evil spirits.

*

The light was dying rapidly; no twilight here with its deepening blacks and greys stealing across the faded city, but sudden lavender everywhere, the moment the last of the sun has fled the sky.

I saw my father coming towards me.

'Hallo,' he said and grinned. 'Big thoughts, Muggins?'

'I don't want to lose any of this. I want it to go on for ever and ever, and never grow any older or bigger.'

He regarded me seriously.

'Nothing is ever lost, Muggins. We're a great big storehouse of everything that's ever happened to us. The important thing is to enjoy every moment of it *now* . . . you never know.'

'Never know what?'

'When it might end.' He picked up a stone and wrote the word in capital letters: N O W.

'*Now* . . . always remember that word, then you'll miss nothing! Today and now are yesterday and tomorrow, but sometimes tomorrow never comes.'

'I was eight yesterday, nine this morning, and now I'm on the way to ten. . . . I don't like it,' I said.

'Why not? Most children like the idea of getting older. It's only when you *are* older, that you want to stop!'

'Don't want to get older and go to a beastly English school—and that's what'll happen,' I said darkly.

'*Now*, Muggins! Don't let go of it for one second, and all your life you will have no regrets.'

As we walked towards the others, I squeezed his hand. He looked down and wrinkled his nose at me, and I knew he understood.

'We want a stable,' said Bebe, in her high, small voice. 'Even a mat shed would do, for rainy days.'

He frowned. 'Better out at grass.'

'The Kanmenti says this is a magic garden,' I said suddenly.

'What else?' he asked quietly.

'Things weren't put back in the right place,' Bebe said.

'What do you mean?' He turned his eyes to her.

'You can't build, he says, because it's already full of houses,' Beak chipped in slowly.

'Yes,' I added. 'Chooldren can use this place in daytime, but in the night, it's theirs.'

'Whose?'

'He didn't say. He just said it would be too crowded, 'cos sometimes things aren't put back in the right places.' I put Nosey Parker round my neck like a scarf; his loose legs scratched and made me laugh. 'That's why we didn't find the steps at first,' I added.

'It's the Night People,' said Bebe.

My father didn't reply. He was busy securing the ropes that tied each pony to a stake. Nanny's voice floated from far beyond the garden. 'Bath tiiiiime!'

'Oh bother!' I said irritably. 'How I hate bath time. Why can't we eat and sleep when we want to?'

'And *never* wash,' added Beak hopefully.

'Because when you're small there have to be rules.'

'Bother rules!' we chorused, and followed him out of the gate.

We padded along the cobbled road on our bare feet, until we came to our home, the Commissioner's house on the top of the thick, four hundred years old unwelcoming wall of the earliest navigators to China. A sentry guarded the door, and innumerable stone steps led us to our mother's joyful garden of colour and scent. White marguerites and Easter lilies stood in huge green and blue glazed pots. A sheet of mesembryanthemum now closed and sleeping, but a burst of vermilion in the sunlight. Drooping bamboos, bananas, an elegant frangipane, and great drifts of bougainvillaea over walls and up pillars: it was surely this place that imbued me with my love of flowers.

It was an exceptional house, even for Macao, standing alone in the garden a few yards away from the servants' quarters. In style it was early colonial Portuguese, its façade supported by four white pillars. Lofty rooms looked out across the top of the wall to the Bay of Macao. Stained floors, high windows, folding half doors, rattan matting . . . long bamboo chairs, a profusion of flowers everywhere, and in the dining-room, overhead, solemnly, gracefully, a white punkah swung, worked by pulleys and ropes and hauled at by one of the coolies, 'giving a delicious sense of relief and cool air', I wrote in my journal.

The most significant part of the house and the best remembered by all of us, was the wide veranda known as 'the Tiles'. It swept out from the bedrooms, and ran the length and breadth of the whole building, entirely open to the sky, with a balustrade of peacock blue porcelain, copied years and years before from the Temple of Heaven in Peking. It was here that night after night, in any weather, the four of us slept under the stars. The mattresses lay on a groundsheet, and in the event of rain or storm, we automatically in our half-sleep pulled a tarpaulin over our heads or retired to bedrooms.

Our father had the odd idea that not only should our heads be out of the bedclothes, but that it was healthier for our feet to be out too. To this day, I sleep with my feet out, and in Chelsea in 1944, during an air-raid, it was so that my father died.

Here, guarded by three Chow dogs, Wang, Pongo, and Tootles, with Nosey Parker tucked under my pyjama jacket, the four of us lay, staring at the empurpled vault above us, showered with a million stars, and watching the moon grow from a slim silver dagger to a full yellow balloon; playing games and making up stories of galleons crossing uncharted seas through the Milky Way to the Southern Cross. The notes of the Last Post from the Portuguese Fort were our nightly lullaby.

'That's the most beautiful sound in the world,' I said sagaciously. One day I was to discover it to be the most mournful.

The other three were forced to listen to my tales of adventure and terror, and if anyone so much as dared to fall asleep I was up and clambering over them, prodding and pummelling them awake to hear the end.

'Bebe, remember this line and tell it to me tomorrow, so I can put it in my journal.'

'Oh, what is it now?'
And solemnly I said:

> 'Here the Tartar Horseman stood—
> And bowed to Buddha, who must be obeyed.'

'All right,' she said sleepily. 'Why can't you remember it yourself?'
'I'm too busy with the next bit.'

*

As we reached the top of the steps, we saw the short, sturdy figure in clerical black, with dog collar and thick silky white hair above the fiercely blue eyes set in a brown face.

'Grankapa!' we shrieked and fell on him as he flung open his arms. Grankapa, my mother's father, Dr John MacGowan, was a missionary in Amoy for fifty years until he died, aged ninety-two.

He was a writer of some repute, who knew more about China than almost anyone we had met, except my father. The first, most prized book that I ever owned or read, was his collection of fairy tales, *Beside the Bamboo.*

His friendly arguments with our father amused and confused us; for though Grankapa carried the Gospel of Jesus Christ, my father lived by the Philosophy of Buddha, and the two of them were nearer than either liked to admit.

'Gautama Buddha, Confucius, and Lao-Tze, bequeathed human doctrines that dignified the human spirit! Confucius, moral nobility, and Lao-Tze, humility.'

The old man would smile gently as he stroked Beattie's head.

'And Christ, the universal brotherhood of man, Hayley! He laid down the rules for the most perfect world order!'

For myself, at that age, the Religion, or Philosophy of Buddha, already appealed to me the most, probably because of my father's teachings. The religion of Buddha was altruistic, it dovetailed its transmigration into Ancestor Worship, and as it had captured most of the East so it captured my imagination.

'Chia chia yu Kuyanyin'—'Every place has its Buddha, every home has its Kuyanyin'. The Home with the Buddha—mother and baby—the Buddhist anticipation of the Virgin and Christ. . . . 'When Matthew, Mark, Luke and John were writing their gospels, Buddha had been dead for five and a half centuries!' my father told me, his eyes alight.

'My duty to God,' said Grankapa, thoughtfully, 'is to love my neighbour as myself. One religion for North, South, East and West, a religion which shall know nothing of assumption, prosecution or ban, a religion that shall stand with its temple doors open for every truth to enter, every falsehood to flee away. . . .'

A dear, remarkable man, one of thousands who came full of Faith to China, his life in his hands. If he fell, he fell of his own free will; if he succeeded, to God the Glory. His safe-conduct was in the words 'I am with you alway', for in his youth, in the early days of the first missionaries, no consuls, no gunboats, accompanied them, and uncomplainingly they put up with every possible hardship, with death and torture. St Francis Xavier had died in Macao in 1552, and many others had followed him, sometimes violently, in the centuries which followed.

'What about Grandmama?' I asked. 'Tell us about Grandmama. . . .'

On both sides of our family there were families of twelve, fourteen and sometimes seventeen children, fanning out like flights of geese, from Scotland to Ireland, and England to America, India, and finally China. One characteristic persisted from both sides: red hair!

Among the early tortuous branchings of my father's family, William Hayley, the poet and biographer of Romney and Cowper, sprouted, and later, by marriage and other slips, came Rudyard Kipling, Stanley Baldwin, and Burne-Jones, the painter.

In 1424, the Earl of Douglas granted a Charter to William Bell in the lands of Kirkconnell in Annandale, under the seal of James I of Scotland. He built a tower, called Bell Tower, at Blacket House. They were brave and war-like men, 'standing firm' to the 'Black' Douglas to whom they were allied in blood. Though they lost their lands in the rebellion against James II, they kept Blacket House for several centuries. We were always told that 'Fair Helen of Kirkconnell' was one of the 'ladies'.

They moved eventually to Ireland, the family splitting up, some drifting away to the South and embracing the Catholic Faith. The coat of arms which hung in a disreputable frame in our nursery, was azure, three bells and a hand holding a dagger. A bad drawing of this haunted most of my school books.

Hugh Bell, born in 1761, married a lady named Bethia. Little is known of her, but she did produce my great-grandfather William. He in turn became enslaved by a forceful lady, Elizabeth Kinnear of

Edinburgh, whose portrait by Raeburn hangs in the Scottish National Portrait Gallery. He moved to London and joined a firm of silk and tea merchants belonging to Jo Mackrill Smith, who lived at the time in Canton on the Pearl River.

William and Elizabeth Bell had fourteen children, several of whom died, and although the ninth child could never have been called lusty or vigorous, he, Frederick Hayley, found himself by his father's orders on his way to Shanghai to join the House of Mackrill Smith.

This was a powerful family. Jo Mackrill Smith, one of the early settlers in China, had gone out to Canton in 1818 in one of his own tea clippers (or 'tea waggons' as the East India tea clippers were called). His wife, Mary Ann Lefeaux, daughter of a Huguenot, was one of the first women to step ashore on the Bund at Shanghai. She was, we were told, an irresistible creature with the rare combination of red-gold hair and violet eyes and a collection of amusing sons and daughters, one of whom riveted the attention of Frederick Hayley. This was Elizabeth Mary, a replica of her mother, and though Frederick was fifteen years her senior, in due time they were married. He was a quiet man, more immersed in music and playing the organ in the Anglican cathedral than in silk and tea, but Elizabeth Mary was a chip off the Mackrill Smith block, and when she wasn't peering out of her sedan chair at the silk and brocade, she was amassing a good collection of rare Chinese porcelain.

I remember my grandmother in her later days. She moved before me like a galleon in full sail, on her head a vast hat of osprey feathers tilted on red hair which remained that colour unaided till she was sixty, and clothed from head to foot in violet to match her eyes.

When she died, she left me her splendid Siberian amethysts and jade, but alas they found their irrecoverable way to the pop shops during my early struggles in the theatre.

She had eight children. The youngest, Francis Hayley, was my father. He was born in Shanghai in 1877. His parents were wealthy, and he thought so little of money all his life that at the end of it he had none. Like all children in the East, he was sent home to school at the age of seven. His schooling at Oakfield, the preparatory school for Rugby, was only significant because of his great friendship with the Headmaster, who, although the boy was a nonconformist from the start, understood him, loved him, and was more of a father than his own, who died while he was at school.

Music, which he had taught himself, languages and literature, were the only things that interested him. School he considered a waste of his life, and at the age of fifteen he begged his mother to allow him to return to the sun. Back in China, he was left much on his own. Although he adored his mother secretly from afar, there was never any communication between them, for she had other favourites. She had remarried, a rich and gentle man, Edward Jenner Hogg, several years her senior again, who idolized and spoilt her. 'Angel one moment, fury the next,' my father told me. 'You remind me of her!'

He wandered from Shanghai to Chefoo, to Hong Kong, working with various firms, his mind in his books, his eyes on the mountains and undiscovered places of China. In 1896 he joined the Imperial Maritime Customs under Sir Robert Hart, and for the first time he was happy, but even during this period he was always alone, and on one three months leave he walked from Hong Kong to Burma. In 1902 he was to find himself in a state of exhilaration, caught up in the Boxer Rebellion, where he looted with the best and the worst of them, bringing back rare treasures to Unkaza, his family's beautiful home in Shanghai.

He went to South Africa in 1905 and joined the Natal Carbineers as a trooper, and in his diary of January 1906 there is this entry: 'Anchored at Table Bay at last after the longest twenty-four hours voyage in the *Braemar Castle*. Had a good clean tiffin at Mount Nelson with Baden-Powell. . . .'

He explored Madagascar, Egypt, Ethiopia. He went to Russia, and Jehol. He was mauled by a tiger in Pakhoi and carried the scars to his grave. The mountains like the sacred Tai Shau that he had stared at and read about, he had now climbed. Kilimanjaro, Kanchenjunga—and years later he stood with his friend the old Dalai Lama at the Rongbuk Monastery watching Leigh-Mallory make his ascent on Everest.

His knowledge of China had become enormous; he spoke with the dialects of seven different provinces, Kwangsi, Szechwan, Kiangsu, Yunnan, Honan, Kiangsi, Chekiang, as well as Mandarin and several other languages including Russian. . . .

He thought it was time he settled down. Sir Robert Hart agreed and sent him to Amoy to study Fukien as well! In Amoy he met my mother.

*

My mother's family were descended from a wild extrovert called

Recompense Sherrill of Plymouth, who in 1666 followed the *Mayflower* to America. He was shipwrecked off the coast of East Hampton, Long Island, and swam twenty miles before he was rescued. A tall, powerful man with a mane of auburn hair, a book on the Sherrill family declares that he 'Set all the girls in a fine twitter concerning him'.

From the Sherrills, eventually, a girl, Clemence. She fell in love with Lyman Peet, who had recently graduated in Divinity from Middleburn College, Vermont. He had his dark brown eyes set far away beyond the horizon to the mission fields in China, in the footsteps of the celebrated Dr Peter Parker of the American Mission.

Against fierce opposition, and with a tenacity which would have warmed the cockles of old Recompense's heart, they were married and set sail in a Baltimore clipper in July 1839.

It was a journey of many mishaps, including the occasion when that ill-omened bird the albatross took a header through the main rigging in the Indian Ocean. Many died of sunstroke and dysentery, but the Peets weathered every storm and 'Tai fung' that came their way.

'Down the Atlantic and round the Cape of Good Hope', Clemence wrote in her meticulous hand. 'Across the Indian Ocean to the Golden East. Pictures of hospitals and dispensaries, scattered through China, where crowds of sick can be healed, and where the Gospel of Great Salvation can be preached, never cease to wander like a fairy procession before our eyes. The prospect is an alluring one, fascinating and most thrilling.'

One hundred and fifty days later, to their mild surprise, they found themselves in Siam, where they remained for seven years!

Early in 1846, my grandmama, Jennie, was born. In the same year, still determined to reach their goal, Lyman and Clemence set off again for China, with baby Jennie in a clothes basket.

*

Of the 300,000 inhabitants of Amoy in the Straits of Formosa, there were only sixty Englishmen and five Americans. They were referred to as 'Fung Yang', Foreign Devils, for they wore no pigtails; worse, one of the Peets had *red* hair. Both facts were a source of amazement, and red hair was an undoubted mark of barbarism—but the real wonder was that she had the face to appear in public with hair of such a colour. Nevertheless, they laboured unstintingly in the mission field of Amoy for twenty years, and during them had two more daughters and a son.

Jennie, a tranquil, contented creature, was captivated by the short sturdy figure and intensely blue eyes of young John MacGowan of the London Mission. His interests became hers, and in 1869, at the age of twenty-three, she joined his Mission Hospital, and her hand to his for forty years.

They had a son and seven daughters. The fifth daughter was Agnes, my mother. She was unforgettably beautiful. With her dove-grey eyes and an abundance of dark red hair handed down from Recompense, she was the most diverting companion, her ringing laugh echoing down the passages of the hospital in Amoy where she worked as a young woman. When she was not on the wards, she was on a horse, a slender figure in a tussore, side saddle skirt, a green tam o'shanter perched on the top of her long coiled hair. Was it by chance that she so frequently cantered past the bungalow where the young Customs officers were studying? Did she turn her eyes his way, or was it his imagination? Was it by chance that he, too, took to riding at the same hour? A raising of the hat . . . a courteous exchange of the time of day, which lengthened not only into conversations, but became a relentless pursuit, until one day he chased her from Telegraph Hill to the White Stags Temple, where he proposed to her among the joss sticks and Buddhist priests, and was accepted! They celebrated with a cup of thin 'oong cha', sweetened by candy. Two years later they were married from Unkaza, with its flying Chinese roof, its conservatories housing rare plants from all over Asia, and its lawns paraded by strutting peacocks—a house which is now Jessfield Park, a university for students in the new, Communist China.

Hayley and Agnes went to live in a small house in Love Lane and one night a year or so later, when they were at the opera, my mother leaned across to my father during the first act of *I Pagliacci*, and said in her soft, half American voice: 'Hayley. Mary's in a hurry to arrive. I'd better withdraw.'

So, one cold 22 January, with undeniable signs of Mary Lefeaux's and Recompense Sherrill's red hair, I, Mary Hayley Bell, was born, under the waving yellow flag of the Green Dragon of China.

This flag has been one of the few valued possessions of my life. It hangs on the billiard room door in Richmond today, a torn, tattered talisman of yesterday.

*

I sat up in the bath and peered at myself intently in the mirror. My father's eyes stared at me from the mirror and I sank back into the water. The smell of rice rose from the servants' quarters. . . .

My memories of babyhood were nearly all smells. The smell of cigars and horses; the upholstery of my grandmother's carriage in Shanghai; Chinese drains and Chinese food; bean shoots and dried fish; frangipane and English roses. . . . My grandmother and my mother had their own individual smells; so did my father and my uncles and aunts . . . saddles and smell of heat . . . morning coffee, and the heady delight of Lapsang tea when the teapot was open. Fur and perfume; elderly Chow dogs; wood smoke, tweed and wild azaleas. . . .

My father's eyes regarded me solemnly from the mirror.

He was tall, thin as a Ghurka blade, with piercing dark blue eyes and a nose like Wellington's—which unfortunately he has handed down to all of us. A strange, complex man, spiritually proud, with the heart of a lion; sometimes *too* strong, and in his early years viewed with benevolent intolerance or amusement by many; though the friends he had, he kept always. Only my mother knew his private heart. To Francis Hayley Bell, love was the mainspring of his life; susceptible, he was ever in search of the *ideal*, and demanded and was dependant upon unstinting affection. He idealized those in whom he placed his affections, clothing them with the reflection of himself, often suffering the searing pains of disillusionment. Yet he never looked at himself for the cause of any failure, but blamed it elsewhere!

There were stormy scenes with me sometimes, for even as a child I would stand up to him, and though he punished me there was a flicker of admiration which I recognized instantly and cherished.

He was my first teacher. He taught me to read at an early age. He showed me the magic world of books through Spenser's *Faerie Queene*, Tennyson's *Collected Poems*, and Scott's *Marmion*—I decided to change my name to Marmion, but it was not always easy to refuse to answer to Mary, and Marmion never caught on. He gave me my first diary and in his handwriting in the now faded brown journal are Drake's lines: 'There must be a begynyng of any great matter, but the continuying untyl the end, untyl it is thoroughly ffynyshed, yeilds the true glory . . .' which my impatience has found a difficult axiom to follow!

I can remember an occasion when the question of courage arose. At five years old, my brother Beak was terrified of deep water, and refused to learn to swim. We were out at sea in one of the little armed Customs launches *Lung Tsing*. My father was in the water and repeatedly called to Beak to jump. Naturally, being the big Show Off of the family I was already in, squeaking 'Look at me, Daddy, look at me!'—but it was his son he wanted in the water. He climbed aboard, and threw Beak in, hoping his instinct would make him strike out. It didn't and my father had to leap in immediately and get him out. My mother burst into angry, frightened tears, and so did we. The day was ruined and we returned to shore in silence.

Beak's voice comes down the years: 'I don't like him much, I *hate* boxing gloves and the sea and always wanting to be away somewhere on some Adventure.'

My father's gay, towering personality reacted on all who came into contact with him. Passionate; emotional with a thundering temper; sometimes arrogant and self-indulgent; selfish on his own admittance; never amenable to censure from others; slightly ostentatious and grandiloquent at times, with a splendid rhetoric: 'I must know everything of something, Muggins, and something of everything.' His vitality was unbounded. His laughter filled the house, for he could and did laugh at himself continuously. Yet I have looked up into his face in church when he was singing, seen his lips trembling and the tears splashing down his cheeks, but if I dared to slip my hand into his, he would draw sharply away.

There was something distinctly feline about his unleashed claws when angry: 'Take care, Hayley,' my mother's voice. 'Tread warily!' And his answer: 'Oh bosh!' He saw himself as a figure of Destiny. 'We whom the Gods love are hunted in the end, Muggins.' In the end Destiny itself turned away from him, and he only emerged as a glorious failure.

My mother, on the other hand, lived for the most part in an aura of smiling detachment. She was deeply religious, modest, and unemotional, a shade over-critical perhaps, with a desire for exactitude and perfection which she endeavoured to instil into us. Beneath her calm assurance, I believe she had a sense of inadequacy, yet she was fiercely intolerant of any backslidings.

Unlike father, she had no inspirational, no really creative ability, except in her gardens, which seemed to bloom and flourish at the very sight of her. 'What are you doing, you naughty Japonica, coming out so early?'—and I do believe the wretched plant closed its eyes in shame and embarrassment.

If there was passion, it was in the possessiveness of her family: 'Too many generations of us in China have perhaps injected into me the Chinese loyalty of "Family only",' she said; 'Smotherlove' one of us said, years later. She clung to us with her small, birdlike hands, and try as we might, she never would, and never did, admit any son-in-law or daughter-in-law to the magic kingdom of her nursery, where all her geese were swans!

Of us all, perhaps she loved Johnman the best. I would see her staring at his short red curls, a little frown between her eyes, as though in her strange, psychic way, she knew he would be taken from her first.

*

'Come on, out of that bath.' Nanny's voice smashed my meditations.

'Why?'

'You can't lie there forever! It's bad for your skin, and it's bedtime.' Then, 'Your grankapa is waiting.'

That got me out quickly, too quickly for Nosey Parker, who slipped on the soap and fell in.

Grankapa was sitting on the end of my bed when I arrived with the wet rat tied up in a face towel. Through the windows I could see my mother dressing for dinner, and down in the drawing-room below my father was playing the piano, the strains of a Chinese boat song, which he had written down and added the harmonies to, a sad and plaintive melody which has haunted me down the years.

'You're very late, Oong deu,' Grankapa said. 'What have you been doing?'

'Thinking,' I answered. 'I wish I wasn't "Oong deu"—the village kids laugh at me and point.'

'So they did to your great-grandmother!'

'I wish I could have seen Jennie,' I replied. 'Everyone who is interesting is always dead.'

'Yes. . . . Isn't it a curious thought, that somewhere in the world today are boys and girls, already born, whom one day you will meet and marry, and whom I shall never see.'

'Why not?' asked Bebe.

'Because I should be over a hundred,' he said.

'You *could* be,' added Beak.

Grankapa gave my hair a tug.

'A small boy, eh? A few years older, perhaps, running across an English field with a butterfly net. I wonder what he's like. . . .'

'A sailor, he must be a sailor,' I said firmly.

'His name . . . ?' He stared up into the night sky.

I paused, then wanting to please him, I said brightly, 'I *know*! His names begin with—J. M.! Like yours!'

'John . . . John and Mary. That's a good old-fashioned combination,' he said.

Bebe sat up abruptly. 'She only said John 'cos she's in love with the captain of that gunboat! John Millet!'

'I'm not in love with anybody!' I answered hotly.

'I'm in love with Captain White,' said Beak.

'He's got a red nose,' I said unkindly.

'Someone once said that every complete soul is half male and half female,' said Grankapa. 'And the one half must forever wander through the world till it finds its twin.'

We stared at him, round-eyed.

'I can't for the life of me remember who said it,' he went on, 'but I remember liking the idea that if your spiritual twin is living in Patagonia you are separated by Space, but if he or she is not yet born, they may, as Maeterlinck suggests, be separated by Time. . . .'

'I *like* Patagonia,' said Bebe.

'*I* like Maeterlinck,' said Beak, not to be outdone.

'What happens if one of the twins dies before he meets the other one?' I asked him. 'Does he go on searching for ever and ever and getting old with no one?'

He looked at me curiously, and got up.

'You think too much about death for a child,' he said jokingly. 'Say your prayers now and go to sleep', and he disappeared into the shadows.

We lay back on our pillows and stared up at the stars. Nosey Parker was still wet, so I stuck him under my pyjama top, the sudden dampness making me shiver as the misty figure of mother came out onto the veranda to kiss us goodnight. The cloud of her scented hair drifted across us, and then she was gone again.

My heart swelled with love for her.

'I hope she doesn't die in the night,' I said softly.

'Why should she?' asked Bebe.

'Because that's when people *do*,' I said with great authority.

As the mesembryanthemum closes its petals at the departing rays of the sun, one by one they were asleep, but long after that I lay, contemplating the heavens, with the exhilarating sensation of sunburnt legs and arms under my pyjamas, watching the Milky Way through a cloud of fireflies and considering Death, which in my child's mind was all mixed up with Buddha, Confucius, Christ and Captain Millet. . . . I could hear my father's voice below and my mother's infectious laughter. I put my hands together under the bedclothes: 'Please God don't let anybody die, or anything be different,' I prayed fervently.

*

My abiding obsession at that time was to be their favourite, and I would go to any lengths, however dishonest, to achieve it; to hear father say 'Well *done*, Muggins!' would give me the greatest joy.

'Anyone coming for a bit of Adventure?' He would be standing in the doorway of the nursery, looking round at us all. Before anyone had a chance to answer or accept I, disgracefully, had literally stamped upon their feet under the table—and being King of the nursery, no one dared to move.

'I will, Daddy! I will!' I shouted, springing to my feet.

'Muggins is the only one with any spunk, dammit,' he would say, turning to go, and as I followed him I turned wickedly to look at the silent, flattened faces of disappointment around the table.

'Just this time,' I pleaded.

Nobody answered.

Today, I look back with a sense of shame on such incidents; but those Adventures—'Just alone, with you'—took me through some unforgettable, secretly guarded experiences. Standing on the bridge of his little armed launch, beside Captain White of the red nose, when a volley was fired to stop an opium junk off the Ladrones Island. Boarding the great swaying hulk with them—for there was too much confusion and shouting for anyone to notice 'Oong deu'—and standing close by, watching as the sailors opened the wooden casks to reveal the precious contraband cargo, looking like hard, earthy balls about the size of a small cannon ball. They were packed in almost the same condition in which they were scraped from the poppies in the Yunan Province, and needed little melting to transform them into the glutinous mass, ready for the addicts' pipes. . . .

Another Adventure. Beyond the Barrier which separated Macao from the mainland of China, far beyond, after a long day's walk, to an evening in a Buddhist monastery, supping with the monks, listening to my father as he talked to them in their own vernacular, their saffron robes against the darkness of the room while they ate shark's fin, toadstools, and twenty-three-year-old eggs. 'Fishes maw' I wrote in my diary—the lower lips stewed in snail's broth; I put my handkerchief to my mouth and spat out the accumulated mouthful, which brought me raised eyebrows from my father. The endless diversion of the monks, applying their own chopsticks and shoving various selections down my throat, waving their long thin hands and indicating that I should wash it all down with samshu, a rice wine, heady stuff with a horrible flavour. Then the hard trestle bed under the sloping roof, the wooden pillow at my neck, while the whispers of the night closed in around me. . . .

2

MYSTERIOUS GATEWAY TO THE SEA

It was six-thirty when the sun glanced through the drooping bamboos at the four of us asleep on the wide veranda, under a pale lemon sky with the last two stars reluctant to leave.

We tiptoed from our beds and into our bedrooms, pulled on our shorts and, evading any duty visit to the bathroom, made our way to the servants' quarters to join the amahs at their early bowl of rice, sitting cross-legged among them in their short blue jackets, black trousers, tightly drawn-back hair, jade pins, and their tiny bound feet, a wicked sign of beauty which came down from the Manchus. It was once my displeasure to see these feet without shoes on them. The bone beneath the ankle was fleshless and shrivelled, thin as a chicken's drumstick, the parchment-like, purple skin stretched tightly over it. The heel and instep were clubbed into a hideous, shapeless mass of deformity, and the four lesser toes were stunted and twisted under the foot, so that three parts were buried in flesh, the big toe forming a mere point, on which they tottered.

Although we could speak Cantonese, the amahs often addressed us in their pidgin English, a language now hardly ever used, for unless well acquainted with the true pidgin English, it is difficult to follow. Grankapa's 'Feed my sheep' became: 'Chow chow me sheepee'. An American was 'Mellican' and a paddle steamer was 'Outside walkee can see'.

The amahs were determined we shouldn't be a nuisance to the late sleepers. Waving their chopsticks they admonished us, 'No makee bobberee Bom Jesus! Tao-tai velly angly.'

Having eaten our fill of rice, we fled to Bom Jesus with bare feet and flying hair, flung a snaffle over the ponies' necks and proceeded down the Praya Grande, where coolies squatted under the long stretch of banyan trees, making bouquets of green, scarlet and orange flowers, and selling lichees and pumellos.

On hot mornings, the world seemed full of crickets. Some people were worried past endurance by their never-ceasing chirp, and Nanny Day was one of them. 'Like the rasp of scissors!' she complained and locally they were referred to as scissor grinders. The cicada's noise is produced by the vibrations of the horny springs fixed to their stomachs . . . brown and large as a black beetle, we picked them off the trees and brought them back to the nursery just to savour Nanny's intense discomfort.

Today, Sunday, was a special day. It was the opening and dedication of the rebuilt Protestant Church, first erected in 1831 by the East India Company, and to be dedicated this morning by the Bishop of Victoria and the 'Chum Ping' (the Admiral).

On this day, my diary was full of names, the faces of which have long since fled. Lebas, the Portuguese Governor; Mrs Galloway, our Sunday School teacher (for Ministers came only once a month); Iresons; Underhills . . . but only Underhill is remembered, for it is connected with 'Other peeples trajedys' still to come. . . .

H.M.S. *Tarantula* brought them all over from Hong Kong in the pearly sunlight—the Admiral and Lady Stubbs, the Bishop, Bruce Lockhart, and a score of others. We had to wear our topees with the long pugarees down the back, our only hats. I wore my yellow dress with a big enough pocket to house Nosey Parker, and we set off in rikshas, bowling along at a rapid trot through the crowded streets of 'Hawking hemming and expectorating' bean curd sellers, dried-blood sellers, water carriers and bird vendors, past Portuguese women with their mantillas, missal in hand—on to the Protestant Church, already covered in creepers.

I knew most of the graves by heart. George Chinnery fascinated me, for we had many of his paintings on our walls. Sir John Davies, Governor of Hong Kong, Lord Napier, who 'died of a broken heart', crews of galleons, and whole families swept off in a few days of fever.

It was an endearing graveyard, with its twisted banyan trees and leaning gravestones. The little wind stirred the trees around as if the thousand faces who had died here, were standing about us, listening, smiling and nodding their heads in the wind . . . their tiptoeing feet shuffling through the old grasses, their unanswered questions reverberating round the old stone walls. . . . We had often tethered our ponies and rambled about there, searching for bones and skulls. I liked it considerably better than the Catholic cemetery which had written over its portals: 'Hodi mi cras tibi', Your turn next!

After the service the Bishop was supposed to come for 'tiffin', but he never appeared. The servants were bothered: 'What for he no come the Number One Topside Heaven pidgin man?'

*

Bom Jesus in the late afternoon sunlight, and the Colonial Secretary, Captain Andrade, whose family had been in Macao since 1517, talking to my father.

In the tumble of undergrowth I faced the Captain.

'Why is Bom Jesus haunted?' I asked for the hundredth time.

'Why can't we build a stable?' asked Bebe.

'Too much talkee talkee,' he laughed in his precise, sing-song Portuguese voice with its influence of pidgin English: 'Many years ago, at the same time as in Europe perhaps—the black plague, bubonic—visited Macao . . . many thousands died, terror was extreme in the territory outside. Armed men blocked the land approaches to prevent the carrying of bodies for burial outside the wall. On this hill,' he swept his arm, 'in a part of the city not then much populated was a burial place. Large pits were dug and the bodies buried there by night, as so in your London plague, was it not?'

We nodded unknowingly.

'It became forbidden ground after such a time of horror, the word passed from one to another until it became, how you say, a tradition, a curse, an enchantment; myself, I do not believe!' He laughed at my father.

'The threat,' my father replied, 'that anyone who ventures to dig shall die within the year, is more than my Irish superstition can stand for!'

'The Kanmenti says different,' I told them. 'He says there are caves under the ground. He says there is a secret passage to the hills behind the town. . . .'

Captain Andrade looked at my father, took in a deep breath, and said nothing.

My father looked out across the bay.

'Anything can happen in Macao, in Ao Mun, the "mysterious gateway to the sea".'

'Ao Mun?' I said to Bebe. 'I must ask Miss Da Silva about that.'

Miss Da Silva was our teacher. A short Portuguese lady of indifferent years, with dark hair drawn tightly back in the manner of the Chinese, she had profound brown eyes, a large posterior, and long thin hands which she waved as she talked.

Our education consisted almost entirely of the war-torn history of Macao, which in a way was not surprising, as one of her ancestors, Pera Da Silva, Viceroy of Goa in 1680, figured largely in it. Of mathematics she admitted to knowing nothing, and indeed could not be bothered. She spoke in a high staccato voice, in three languages at once, all of which, as children, we picked up readily. Her Divinity was of the Jesuit and Capuchin teaching, and my mother, a strong Presbyterian and very averse to the Roman Church, was utterly dismayed on one occasion to hear us solemnly repeating the Lord's Prayer, 'Pater noster, qui es in coelis. . . .'

From those early years, the Catholic Faith has tugged at my sleeve. Three times I have taken Instruction with no end result, because of the wrenchings of inherited and bygone faiths.

Miss Da Silva's passion for the history of Macao went back to Kublai Khan, 'The only possible Emperor of the World', who founded the Mongol Dynasty in 1280.

Our knowledge was based on all its heroes and brigands from Marco Polo to Vasco da Gama, the first to reach Macao. Through the centuries there was Ricci, the famous Jesuit Priest, and the only foreigner ever to be mentioned in the Dynastic History of China; St Francis Xavier, buried so close to Macao; Padre Goncalves, whose sinologues were printed in Macao, and the great Amarel, the early Governor whose head and hands were cut off at the Barrier by assassins.

She abhorred most Englishmen. 'They were corruptionists; Bacon, Clive, and Warren Hastings, and your wicked Stuart Kings. Ugh!'

In answer to our endless questioning on Bom Jesus, she was little help. She believed it had belonged to the nuns of St Clara. 'Zay arrived in 1663, and sailed in ze same flagship like my ancestor from Manila, and were welcomed with perfumed flowers!'

'She doesn't know, does she?' we whispered among ourselves.

'Ao Mun?' she answered, speaking as usual in three languages. 'Naturalment, originalment la colonaie etait sapele Ama. You know ze 'istory of Tien How?—ze Goddess of 'eaven, non?'

We nodded heavily—she was getting away from the point as usual.

'Povacoa do nome de Dios do porto de Amacao na Chine—'

'Mais Mademoiselle . . .' I began.

She slapped the book on the table and the dust flew. 'Read, Maria, from *Christiana Expeditione* . . . it is Ama's bidding to ze Capitaine of ze junk.'

I took a deep breath. I wished I'd never asked her in the first place, and started laboriously reading aloud. 'In ea peninsula idolum erat hodieque visitur cui no nomen Ama. . . . Mais la question de Bom Jesus, Mademoiselle,' I began again.

She waved her ringed hands. 'Bom Jesus is of little importa now, except one day it will rise again with ze Jesuits. Zer are ozzer sings to learn of. St Paul's par example. . . .'

We used to leave our ponies at the bottom of the stately flight of granite steps and wander about the ruins; the beautiful east façade was all of St Paul's that was left to record the early work of the Japanese Christians. We were more interested in pieces of stone than the high grating voice behind us.

'Ze style is Greek. Look at ze Ionic columns ze upper tiers Corinthian, and *zer*!—beatified is ze glorious St Francis Xavier.' At some point in history someone had removed his nose.

'Zer is ze glorious Virgin,' and she crossed herself hurriedly.

The Virgin seemed to have suffered the same humiliation as the glorious Xavier. 'Nobody, but nobody here has a nose,' I said, absorbed in the thought. 'Not even *one* angel!'

'Because it was destroy by fire,' she replied evasively.

Sometimes 'la grippe' or 'la rheum' seized and strangled Miss Da Silva, making it impossible for her to struggle up the long flight of stone steps to the house, and mother took our lessons. Mostly they consisted of reading, so that she could continue with her petit point. *Pilgrim's Progress*, naturally, figured largely, as did *Gil Blas*, and for no particular reason a book called *Ships and Sailing Boats*, the author's name long since forgotten. Other lessons, and other readings, concerned tea and silk.

'The Great Tea Race of 1866 started at Foochow and ended 99 days later at London, covering 18,000 miles.'

'Silk was discovered in China by the Empress Si-Lung in the twenty-seventh century B.C.'

The names spun a cobweb of mysteries to us:

'Taysaam, great worm; and Yvenfa, garden worm.' And the tea:

'Same family as the camellia, there on the wall. Bohea, campoi, pekoe, Souchong, and oolong, the black dragon tea from Formosa where Grankapa lives. . . .'

*

There were some mysterious arrivals and departures at this time. Doctors appeared from Hong Kong with small black bags. Mother was endlessly in bed, and not to be disturbed, and to our constant, anxious enquiries, finally came this answer from Nanny: 'It was Edward, but he's gone now.'

'Who's Edward?'

'A new baby brother. . . .'

'Where's he gone?'

'Back to Heaven. . . .'

'Why?'

'Didn't have time to ask him.'

Edward! A new baby brother. Come and gone without a word without us even seeing him! Did he come in the small black bag? If so, how did he go back to Heaven? We hung about outside mother's closed bedroom most of the day, but no one either drove us off or addressed us.

Our baby brother Edward remained always an unknown imaginary boy of considerable wisdom who, on arrival, decided the whole issue of living was not worth while and returned immediately to the realms beyond the stars, at which we gazed nightly with such rapture.

*

Nine Islands, the Commissioner's summer bungalow, was our greatest delight, for here we stayed through the hot summer weeks, living in a primitive way and sleeping out on the biggest of the nine islands. The grown-ups and babies sailed round the point in one of the launches, but we three, accompanied by our father on foot, rode through the Barrier on our ponies.

'I'm King of the Open Sky!' shouted my father, and flung his hat in the air.

'To the Islands of the Blessed!' I yelled back.

'To the Land of the Ponomah!'

'To the Land of the Hereafter!' and digging in our heels, we cantered away through the sandy scrub to the sea.

The greatest game on these occasions, and never whispered of to our mother, was defying the water buffalo. This we did by getting as near to one as we could so that he could catch our scent. The water buffalo, though domesticated, is a sagacious animal who cannot tolerate the 'stink' of Europeans, and on their approach, and detecting their scent, becomes more savage than any English bull.

The idea, having got as close to him as possible, was to gallop the ponies away as soon as he tossed his head and charged; then, at the right moment, to turn suddenly, right or left, leaving the wretched creature either to hurtle onwards or, in trying to turn, fall over! Luckily for us, we never met the water buffalo who was able to turn at that speed, because for all their bulk their charge is very fast, and their great horns can be lethal.

*

Of the many people who came and went through the house, or joined us on those picnics, nearly all the faces have faded from my memory.

Mr Underhill, however, is not forgotten. Not that there was anything significant about him; he was a heavily built man, with a permanent twitch in the eyes behind his glasses. He worked with my father in the Customs, and his tall, faintly amused wife was about to have her first baby. We had been watching this growth with considerable interest. The day of its supposed arrival was getting closer, according to my diary, when suddenly there is the dispassionate entry: 'Mummy had to run to Mrs Underhill, becos she was ded.'

It was a black, whispering day. We sat up in the camphor trees in silence, watching the hurrying steps of Mummy, Nanny, and poor, confused Mr Underhill.

By evening, the baby, a pathetic, wizened scrap of flesh with a few rather touching black hairs, was installed in its brave little pink cot in our night nursery.

We were having our supper when suddenly we heard the Number One Boy's voice screaming: 'Snek! Snek! In nurserly.'

This brought us to our feet with a rush behind our father who ran to his dressing-room, picked up and loaded his gun and made for the night nursery. We tiptoed in behind him, peering through his arms and legs. A python was at the foot of the cot, its neck rigid, its eyes upon the sleeping baby. As my father moved slowly forward the python's head swayed round to face him; it emitted a sickening hiss and undulated towards the baby.

My mother stood in the doorway: 'Oh, Hayley, be careful. . . .'

There was a deafening report, and the python lay motionless, its tail slipping away from the hold on the cot.

'Hab killum . . . hab killum!' The Boy danced away from the room in his anxiety to tell the others.

That night on the Tiles there was a certain amount of apprehension.

'Poor Mrs Underhill,' I wrote, 'the funyral is tomorrow.'

'They won't let us go.'

'No.'

Suddenly Beak sat up in bed.

'They always have a wife, *always*!'

'Who do?'

'Snakes!'

'Where is she?'

'*Could* be coming out of the rock to look for him this very minute!'

Without a word the three of us rose from our beds and flew into the nearest bedroom, where we all slept huddled together in one large bed.

That bed was thereafter called 'Disarster corner'.

'Disarsters' are supposed to come in threes, and in threes they came, but the second was the worst as far as we were concerned and the best remembered incident, for all of us, of those Macao days.

3

THE UNFORGIVING GARDEN

It was another bright morning, when the earth was full of that aromatic fragrance of the East; we set off before breakfast as usual to Bom Jesus to collect the ponies, running, skipping, singing along the cobbles of 'Pancake Hill' to the gateway under the giant banyan trees.

'Winkie! Hooky! Brownie!' we called, expecting to see them trotting out from behind the shrubbery. There was no sign of them.

More calls, and no response. Anxiety made us hurry to the turfed terrace. They were there all right: Hooky and Winkie standing, Brownie lying down. Each of us scurried to his own particular pony, when a sudden shout of dismay from Bebe made Beak and I turn.

'He won't get up! He's dead, I know he's dead!' she sobbed.

There was no question that Brownie was dead. His once bright chestnut eyes were dull and expressionless.

'It's *them*!' I shrieked. 'It's the Night People!' and we fled shouting and crying back to the house and up the steps.

In a moment our father was there, wiping his mouth with his table napkin.

'What is it?'

'Brownie's dead! He's lying on the grass, dead!'

Holding Bebe's hand he ran back with us.

'He's been kicked in the stomach by one of the other ponies,' he said.

Beak and I looked at each other in wide-eyed guilt.

'But whose?'

'It doesn't matter *whose*, does it? Come back to breakfast, there's nothing we can do now.'

But we were inconsolable. Tears streamed down our faces, great lumps stuck in our throats. The rest of the morning was of such blank despondency that Miss Da Silva was sent away before she had reached the top of the steps, and for what seemed like hours we sat about in trees or on the wall, staring at each other, unable to speak, our imaginations shuttlecocking between melancholy and horror.

'This is the most garsely day of our lives. Death is a truly grimsome thing,' I wrote in my diary. In the afternoon, I had an idea.

'If you-know-who is still there we'll bury him in the place he loved best,' I said secretly.

The others agreed.

Telling the Kanmenti to keep out of the way we set off, carrying his garden implements.

Brownie was still there. Someone had thrown a couple of sacks across him, and for a moment we paused to collect scarlet poinsettia which we strewed across the silent hump that was once a beloved pony. . . .

It took several hours, for the ground was hard and dry and full of old dead grasses and stumps of trees. It was dark before we had finished a grave, a few feet deep and long and broad enough to hold Brownie. The long shadows thrown by the banyan trees had long since crept across the garden. In the distance, the soft angelus was ringing, and the last bird singing. We pulled the moonflowers from the cactus and threw them into the grave. It was to be a 'funyral befitting Lord Napier or George Chinnery'.

'You can come now, Kanmenti,' I called; but it was not the Kanmenti who came out of the shadows, it was my father.

His face gleamed white in the half darkness.

'Good God, Muggins!' he said. 'What have you done?'

'Dug a grave for Brownie,' I said. 'In our very own garden that he loved.'

'The sacred garden . . . *dug*!' His voice sank to a whisper.

'Now *they'll* take Hooky and Winkie!' Beak's high voice was full of accusation.

We stood in a small circle, staring at father, our hands blistered, our legs stained with the earth of the garden.

'You shouldn't have done it, Muggins! You *know* what is said about digging here, in this place. The "Fengshui", the destiny, is bad.'

Abruptly he started for the gateway.

'*She's* not bad—' I started to say.

He wheeled round.

'Who?'

'The lady.'

'What lady?' There was irritation in his voice.

Miserably, I led the way to where the lichee tree hid the face on the wall.

The phantasm stood out clearly, illuminated by the waning moon into the strangely natural likeness of a woman's face in profile. The brow was partly covered with a kind of wimple, or a veil that gave it a nun-like appearance. The face was not so remarkable in its beauty, though beautiful it was, as in some illusion of distance or movement, or whatever caused the shadows, which gave her a pure countenance, the impression of eyes that saw and gentle lips that trembled in a smile.

He bent down, staring at the face.

'We've known her a long time,' I said weakly.

'Aren't you afraid, children?' he asked suddenly.

We shook our heads.

'Why?' said Bebe.

He stared at us in silence, and we stared back.

'Shen chen wu chen,' I chanted in the high-pitched voice of the amahs:

'Chin yan yao fang
Ji jen cheuh che
Ko mo cheuh tai!'

'Where did you learn that?' he asked tensely. 'What does it mean?'

'It's poetry, only I can't say it properly in English. It means "Don't come near this forbidden place . . . the spirits watch here . . . if any man disturbs the ground he must be destroyed. . . ." It means more but I don't understand the rest. The Kanmenti told me, he said this is a spirit garden and no man must hurt it until the right time comes.'

'Knowing this—how *dare* you dig!'

'But it says no *man*, Daddy. The spirits won't hurt chooldren.'

He said no more. He took Bebe and Beak by the hand and led us away through the gateway, onto the cobbled road. Nobody spoke. As we went through the archway, he nodded to the Kanmenti, and for the first time, we heard the key turning in the lock of the gate behind us.

The next night we slept in 'Disarster Corner'. Our mother spent most of it trying to console us and stop our streaming, silent tears, the Requiem for Brownie, who had been buried that day beyond the Barrier, where he had so often joyfully jumped the coffins of the Chinese dead, and cantered away from the horns of the buffalo. For

Bebe and I, to this day, any funeral brings back poignantly, hauntingly, not the dead person, but the acute, childish imagery of a small chestnut pony called Brownie.

It was a strange night of distant thunder, dashing rain and lightning over the Ladrones. The lamentations, the groanings, the floods of tears and the sorrowing, stopped abruptly at the sound of an appalling crash. My mother caught her breath and turned her head to the door where a cloud of brick-red dust had seeped through the lintel. The appearance of my father was comforting for a brief moment in the ensuing silence.

'What was that, Hayley?' she queried.

'The door and part of the outer wall have gone. Come and look!'

My mother made for the door and we followed, afraid to be left alone. Up to the very sill of the doorway, the floor and all the contents of the bathroom had disappeared and crashed onto the terrace below. We stood staring in amazement. . . .

'Did the Night People do it?' I asked.

'Was it the digging, Daddy?'

He shook his head to reassure us. I clutched Bebe's hand.

Through the broken edges of the wall, standing out like a dark tunnel into the blue of the now quiet night, stood the distant trees of Bom Jesus.

*

It was the end of a period in our lives. The old building was even more in decay than my father had thought. The ravages of the white ants had endangered the whole structure.

A few days later, disconsolately, we repaired with all our belongings to the office of the Chinese Customs in the centre of the old town. On the top of it in a square tower was a huge room with ten windows. The only advantage from my point of view was the nearness to an extraordinarily varied library. It was during our time there that I read not only every book in a collected edition of Dickens, but also discovered, for a short time, the works of Freud, Jung, Adler, and the twelve volumes of Havelock Ellis! Though to my complete mystification I noticed that when I returned Volume V, Volumes I to IV and VI to XII had disappeared.

The enormous drawback was that not only did the whole family sleep in that same room of ten windows, but that for the first time, we were under a roof. It was a time when Bebe and I, who slept next to each other, went through our Terror of Death phase, and on more than one occasion we were discovered in the early hours of the morning by a sleepy mother, bending over first her, and then father, to see if they were still breathing!

'Baba! Can't you sleep?'

Slightly embarrassed, we stood limply in our rumpled pyjamas.

'We were afraid you might be dead,' I said simply.

Stifling her laughter under the bedclothes, her grave grey eyes met mine. 'Not yet darling. Not for a long time, please God.'

My father sat up immediately, propping himself on his elbow.

'What's the matter? Someone sick?' he asked.

'They're just going round all the beds to see that no one is dead.' There was a hint of hysteria in her voice.

He turned on the light beside him.

'There is no death,' he said solemnly. 'There is only an overcoat to be laid in the ground and remembered.'

'Do they have clothes on under the coat?' asked Bebe, practically.

'To be sure, and as they advance to a Higher life they shed each garment, one by one, until they have no further need for them.'

'Buddhist talk,' my mother said softly.

'They are the ghosts who cling round the people they have known and loved,' he went on. 'Given the right conditions and an awareness, you can still see them.'

I glanced round apprehensively.

'When your mother was nursing in Amoy, on night duty, she suddenly saw Grandmama Jennie. She walked right up to her chair and said—'

' "Don't worry darling",' put in my mother. ' "Everything is perfectly all right".'

'The next day,' went on father, 'your mother had a telegram from Grankapa, which told her that Grandmama Jennie had died at the very hour she had seen her in the ward. . . .'

The gooseflesh pimples burst all over me, and I shivered.

'Have you seen her again?' asked Bebe.

'No, but I often feel her very close to me.'

'Golly,' said Bebe, greatly impressed. 'She's taking a long time to shed her garments.'

That night, the muffled bells of St Joseph struck many hours before I was asleep, straining my ears to hear those unanswerable voices that no one can put a name to in the darkness.

4

GOODBYE, BOM JESUS

There was an infectious air of excitement in the house.

We were going to Hong Kong to stay with the 'Number One Topside Heaven Man', the Bishop of Victoria, for one night, and the Governor for the next.

'Why?' I asked the others.

'It's the Pincher Ales,' replied Beak with an air of superior knowledge.

Two nights later, after sweating chair-coolies had carried us to the Governor's residence, we stood with his children looking out to where wisps of cloud rose like smoke from the green slope of the Governor's lawn, dropping sheer in gloom to the harbour beneath, where battleships, dressed from bow to stern, stood out clearly in the sun against the sapphire sea.

I shall always remember that evening with delight.

We were in our pyjamas and had just brushed our teeth, when we had a quick vision of a slight, fair-haired young man in the doorway. We stood up, for we had been told to do so. The Prince of Wales came towards us, shook hands earnestly, and made some comment about the beauty of the harbour.

Full of jokes and laughter, he kissed us each in turn and pulled my hair. After he had gone, we remained sitting on our beds, each gravely conscious somehow that in spite of his boyishness we had been in the presence of a commanding personality. His gravity when in conversation with us children, not one more than ten years old, impressed us, and I have been a faithful adherent ever since!

A day later, after the Dragon Boat Festival and polo matches and hundreds and hundreds of people who milled around us in an endless noisy throng, we set sail again for the familiar quiet of Macao, where we had neither to wear shoes nor hats, nor sit quietly in a row upon an isolated seat away from our parents.

As we left Bias Bay and were into the Macao Roads, my father suddenly put his binoculars to his eyes.

'What is it, Daddy?'

'Pirates, I think,' and he swept the neighbouring islands with his glasses.

Pirates! How marvellous, I thought, and was immediately manning the *Lung Tsing*'s machine-gun and getting the Victoria Cross from the Prince of Wales!

In a bay not far away we could see what appeared to be one of the Hong Kong–Macao ferries. It had no right to be where it was, and there was a junk alongside it.

'*Sui Tai*, I think, sir,' said Captain White. 'Looks like she's being boarded.'

We hugged ourselves with excitement, though mother's face was apprehensive.

'Full steam ahead.' Father's decisive voice sharpened our conjectures.

'The children, sir?'

'Batten them down in the lavatory.'

Miserably angry, we were forced into the lavatory, and in an effort to prevent the door from being closed, Bebe broke her last front tooth.

Fighting for a place at the porthole we could see ourselves drawing closer to the *Sui Tai*. We heard the rattle of the machine-gun over our heads as it fired its warning burst.

'There's a gunboat,' said Bebe. 'Probably *Moth* with your old Millet.'

The *Lung Tsing* swung round and we could see nothing. Frustrated, we disobeyed orders, forced open the inadequate lock on the door, and crept silently to the companionway, and up the steps.

The *Sui Tai* lay silently, no signs of churning water from its propellers, while the junk was drawing rapidly away from the ship towards Lan-tao. The gunboat, hidden by the headland, seemed not to be moving.

'What in hell is going on with *Moth*?' asked my father. 'Send a signal: Suggest action. Commissioner Lappa Customs.'

Back came the answer from *Moth*. Captain White translated it slowly: 'Action impossible until radioed instructions from Whitehall.'

'Whitehall!' exploded my father. 'Whitehall! God dammit, what the hell do they know about it!'

The *Lung Tsing* moved in closer.

Sui Tai lay still, apparently devoid of humanity. Captain White hailed her through the loudspeaker, but there was no sign of life. We were creeping nearer. I saw him hand a holster to my father, and everyone waited as the ship inched towards the ferry.

'Shouldn't we make for the junk, sir?'

'We've got the damn kids aboard.'

The damn kids looked at each other and grimaced. 'And keep your heads down,' he added, noticing us for the first time and forgetting that we should have been in the lavatory.

'People in England wouldn't believe this,' said my mother, and I was to remember her words at my first school. . . .

Revolvers in hand, my father and Captain White leaped aboard the ferry as we came alongside. Then they disappeared below, and we sat waiting helplessly on the launch. The junk had vanished and *Moth* was steaming towards us.

'For once the Admiralty weren't at tiffin,' my mother said rather sarcastically.

After what seemed ages my father and Captain White reappeared with the Captain and officers of the ferry. They had, we were told later, been shoved in the baggage hold while several rich Chinese had been taken by junk to be held for ransom.

As *Moth* came up, a smart gig went to *Sui Tai*, collected my father and Captain White and went back to the gunboat.

'What now?' I asked mother.

'Pink gins all round, knowing the Navy.'

'Why don't they chase the junk?'

'All too political to explain.'

'I'm not a fool,' I said hotly.

'Don't understand it myself, Baba, but it would be called creating an incident. If they'd taken any Europeans it would be different, but it appears they've only taken Chinese, and we mustn't interfere.'

'What will they do to them?'

'Cut off their ears and send them to their relations!'

'Golly! Will they die?'

'Probably dead already.'

I was greatly impressed.

Once more the engines started up in *Sui Tai*, froth and foam kicking out from her stern. She had come to life again. Grabbing my father's binoculars I scanned the blue haze of Lan-tao. Not a sign of life. The whole scene was as peaceful in the noonday sun as if nothing had happened!

'Can we jump in and have a swim, Daddy?' I asked.

'Not today, we have a job to do.'

So, seated in comfortable chairs, we munched our cold chicken and tomatoes as *Lung Tsing* and *Moth* escorted the Hong Kong steamer into Macao harbour where the gravestones shone in the sunlight on the hills.

*

The end of our days in Macao was nearer at hand than we realized. Whether it had anything to do with the 'Diggin' in Bom Jesus, or whether it was a natural sequence of events is hard to say, but there was no doubt that the incident troubled my superstitious father, and started anxiety in his mind.

One night in the tower of ten windows, I heard him and my mother talking together. 'I think it's time they went home to school in England,' he said. 'Muggins is the one who troubles me most. She's too steeped in this visionary old world atmosphere . . . too much in love with native life and the language.'

'Does that matter?' she asked. I could hear the fear in her voice.

'Too much freedom, Agnes . . . too much self-development . . . it'll make it harder when she has to be with other girls who haven't had her kind of life. Pirates! Haunted gardens!'

'I hate the thought of it,' my mother replied. 'It's the end of all being together. You will be out here with the babies, and I'll be in England with Baba and Bebe—'

'And Beak!'

'He's *too* young!'

'No younger than I was when I was sent home.'

'Look what it did to you! No . . . I won't stay away from you. Life's too short.'

'We'll take a house in the country, and they can start as weekly boarders. I don't want it any more than you do, Agnes, but we have to do our duty by them. They can't grow up out here. Bebe is growing too tall already.'

It was my fault for digging, I thought. This 'being sent to England' was the 'Curse', exiled to a cold forbidding country, a country under a sunless sky.

I sat up.

'I don't want to go to England to any rotten old school and I won't and I'll run away!' I could hardly keep the sobs out of my voice.

'Ssh, Baba,' my mother said. 'You'll wake everyone.'

'I don't *care*!' I was beside myself, fighting for my life. 'They better know now. *Bebe! Beak!* . . .' My voice rose to a shriek.

'Be *quiet*, Muggins. How *dare* you!'

It was too late. My aide-de-camp and my soldier servant were bolt upright, their eyes wide.

'We're going to school in beastly England!' I howled.

'Why?'

'When?'

I was uncontrollably and unashamedly blubbering into my pillow, and seeing me, they started. Soon the room was in an uproar, for Beattie and Johnman woke and joined in.

'Why? Why? Why?' I moaned.

'Oh, my God! . . . Muggins, everybody has to go to school one day,' father said over the infernal din.

'England is a lovely country,' mother said soothingly from the farthest cot. 'We'll have a house in the country, a garden, chickens.'

'Chickens!' I screamed. 'I hate chickens. They haven't got any faces!'

'What about Wang and Tootles and the ponies?' Bebe was being practical as usual.

'What about Pongo?' added Beak.

The noise ceased. We held our breaths waiting for the worst. From the beds opposite it came, a distinct and determined shaking of heads.

'We'll get another dog.'

'Another dog! How *could* you!'

'What will happen to everything?'

An *embarras de choix* followed and a silence. They hadn't bargained on being heard, and were unprepared. 'We'll talk about it when the time comes,' my mother said sensibly.

'You'll see London. Piccadilly. Leicester Square.'

'What's Leicester Square?' I asked.

'It's full of theatres . . . we'll take you to see *Peter Pan* and *Where the Rainbow Ends*.'

'Will we have to wear shoes?' asked Beak sleepily.

'You see?' Father appealed to my mother with a hopeless wave of his hands.

'Everyone in England wears shoes.' She was emphatic.

'Sounds a horrid place.'

'Then there's the trip home, six weeks in a big ship—Singapore, Colombo, Bombay, Aden, Italy—'

'When can we come back?'

'When you're grown up—'

'How old is grown up?'

'Seventeen . . . eighteen. . . .'

'That's *years*!'

'It's not as long as you think, alas! . . .'

'There'll be new friends, new things to learn, games. . . .'

'Games?'

'Hockey. . . .' He laughed suddenly. I think it was a relief.

'Huh! Whacking people with sticks!' I said bitterly. 'I shall like that.' And I glared at him.

'Go to sleep, children. Tomorrow we'll go for a picnic, just us,' she said quietly, for she was not without imagination, and things were going too fast for her. I knew that.

I lay back with the tears of anger and sorrow trickling down my face, cold when they reached my neck. I was aware, deep within me, of a 'disarster' the like of which I had never dreamed. A picture rose before me of us all standing cold and unwelcome, barefooted strangers in a foreign land, rootless and restless, to be bundled up in hats and coats and hard unyielding boots. There would be frowning skies and the chilblain things that Nanny spoke of, where the only bird was a sparrow that never sang, and all dogs were on tight leads.

It was many, many weeks before our departure, but the misery seldom left me. I clung more fiercely than ever to Bom Jesus and to the garden on the top of the wall.

During this time I was continually sick in my stomach, often physically. The sensation was an unfamiliar one then, but I have since learnt that it is connected to:

Waving departures at railway stations, jetties and airports. . . .

Visits to dentists. . . .

Packing school trunks. . . .

Undertakers' parlours. . . .

Funerals. . . .

Marriages. . . .

Births. . . .

Sudden illnesses . . . and operations . . . and hospitals. . . .

Fear about money. . . .

Auditions in the theatre. . . .

First Nights. . . .
Critics' notices . . . and
Accidents. . . .

Curiously enough, in the years to come, things like hunger, poverty, loneliness and even the cold that we dreaded so much when we had to leave Macao, had the reverse effect, and became stimulants; but at this point the only thing I was actively aware of was that until now 'Life had been One Long Goldern Day', and it was drawing to its close.

The nights too were bad. Suffocated by the ceiling over my head, fearful dreams, and with a longing for the night sky, I wandered the long room, a pyjama-clad spectre of the future, muttering morose incantations to the watchful eyes of my brother and sister: 'The harvest is past, the summer is ended, and we, we are not saved! Not saved! Not saved!'

Finally, with Bebe and Beak in a state of nightly terror, my parents could stand it no longer, and we returned to the house behind the high wall and to our beds on the open Tiles. There, on the first night, inhaling the sweet air, I fell asleep at once—my last conscious picture the Chinese moon.

*

Relentlessly, it came at last, as such things must and will. Wooden crates, trunks, and suitcases; Amah insisting on taking her coffin in case.

'My *things*! Where are my *things* going?' I asked miserably.

'In one of the crates,' replied Nanny, 'or even Amah's coffin!'

'I'll bury them,' I thought. 'The things I love best shall stay here and be part of me forever, the real *me*, not the one I'm going to be made into.'

I tore my yellow dress into a hundred pieces and wrapped my small treasures in it, putting them all in a hole in the ground. A tiny Lohan Buddha, a small jade Goddess of Mercy . . . but I couldn't bury any books, and one, my favourite *Beside the Bamboo*, written by Grankapa, I never saw again.

A small cross was erected over the hole, and on it the words 'My things. M.H.B.'

We were told that Pongo, Wang and Tootles would remain as watch-dogs until our return from growing up. But even Tootles decided evidently the wait would be too long, for he was found dead at the bottom of the garden, lying peacefully among the marguerites. No one ever discovered why, unless it was something he had eaten.

'Rat poison,' one of the Kanmentis suggested.

'*Rat poison?*' I screamed. 'There's never been any rat poison here, not with Nosey Parker about!'

Mysteriously enough, though, Nosey Parker disappeared overnight, without so much as a flick of his tail.

'Why? Why? Why?' I asked.

'Simple, he didn't want to go to England,' Nanny said.

'Nor do I.'

'You wouldn't want to be left here alone, would you?' she said, and saw at once that she had said the wrong thing.

'Why didn't I know . . . why didn't he tell me?'

'How could he? Hardly expect him to leave a note like Oates: "I'm just going outside, I may be away some time. . . ." '

I never mentioned him again, but I thought about him a great deal. I missed his tail and his scratchy feet, his alert brown eyes and twitching cold nose—and I bit my fingernails to the bone instead.

TO NOSEY PARKER. A RAT

Like colour fading from the evening sky
You slipped away without a cry
And left me
Curiussley afrade. . . .

*

It was sunset when the Hong Kong ferry *Sui An*, with us all on board, blew her whistle for departure. Friends were weeping, especially the poor amahs—and mother, her arms full of flowers, was waving and waving to them all as we drew away—a chorus of hooting vessels in the harbour saluting my father as he stood on the ferry's bridge, waving his hat in reply.

I wanted to scream.

I could only stand on the edge of a child's numb despair, clinging dumbly to the salted rail till it bit into the flesh of my hands, my body shuddering with imprisoned grief; praying savagely that no one would lay a hand on my head or speak a single word to me.

Past Lappa Island now, and the fleet of junks with their nets, gold in the last of the sun. Beyond I could see where the Barrier Gate stood, guarding the ground where Brownie lay. . . .

Out into the Bay; Nanny was holding up Johnman and pointing: 'Look, darling, there's our house! And that's Bom Jesus.'

I ran blindly out of the range of her silly, comforting voice, and down to the stern of the ship with the last of the gulls.

The birds, I thought in a sudden panic, would come as usual to be fed at tea time and would stand waiting in vain for chocolate cake. The ponies would raise their heads expectantly at the sound of footsteps, but they wouldn't be ours. The whispers on the Tiles, father's piano, the creaking wheels of Johnman's home-made chariot, all would be silent tonight, and we no more than voiceless ghosts.

Suddenly I remembered a piece of paper that my father had slipped into my hand before we left the house. I hadn't looked at it until now, and scrabbling about in my pocket I found it, reading with difficulty by the small stern light, Tennyson's familiar lines:

> Come, my friends,
> 'Tis not too late to seek a newer world.
> Push off, and sitting well in order smite
> The sounding furrows; for my purpose holds
> To sail beyond the sunset. . . .
> To strive, to seek, to find, and not to yield.

The ship drew steadily away and the lights of Macao flickered and were lost in the soft loom above.

I turned my head, straining my eyes to catch a glimpse, just a glimpse, of Nine Islands and the white bonelike curve of the beach. 'I shall come back!' I shouted to the sea as the tears streamed down my face. 'I shall come back one day!' But I knew that nothing would ever be the same again . . . that it was the end of childhood.

A little slatter of cold mist blew in from the sea—and as I turned away, I remembered Amah's coffin in the hold.

5

'OUTCAST CHILDREN OF THE EAST'

The Japanese ship *Sua Maru* took us through five oceans, back to England.

Through translucent, pellucid, vitreous, muddy and turbid seas. Among deeply variegated flowers, vivid jungles and the gaudy dress of natives. Early sunrise flowed towards pearly evenings of beryl and indigo, when the masthead light swung through the canopy of only too familiar stars, and the phosphorescent flying fish fled helter-skelter from the sharp-pointed bows.

There were early mornings when the decks were washed down, and we stood on the dry teak, our feet sluiced by the exhilarating hoses. There was the smell of oil winches, of the sweat of Lascars, of Madras curry emanating from the hold; hot cups of consommé at eleven with small dry biscuits, and people lying on long deck chairs idly sipping and discussing 'the ship's run' in terms of a gamble.

The rough, unfamiliar, interesting feel of the canvas swimming bath against our backs. Children, who stared for a long time, and then edged their way into games, while we, who had known few friends other than each other, stood aloof, biting our lower lips, waiting, watching, unguarded, and slightly afraid.

My diary notes that we frequently 'played on deck'—but with whom or what was never recorded. We also appear to have had 'lessons with Daddy'. We went to Church, and it appears that Beak was quite sick—also that there were 'Sports', and that 'I won two times, got half a crown (whatever that is) and a luvvley hat. . . .'

Singapore, Colombo, Mount Lavinia, and the Taj Mahal Hotel, standing by chalk white sands and giant surf. Alongside the jetty at

Port Said I awakened Nanny with screams that my feet were all pins and needles. Muttering, she clambered down from her bunk, put on the light and discovered that 'two million ants (at least)' had climbed up the side of the ship and through our porthole to get at my box of Turkish Delight and, unfortunately for me, their roadway lay across my bare feet!

The dark blue Mediterranean and Marseilles, where a man sang *O Sole Mio* for hours under my porthole. I didn't find it romantic. I thought he was hungry and kept throwing pieces of bread to him.

Our parents left us at Marseilles. 'We're going to Paris, darlings, a little honeymoon. We'll meet you at Tilbury—be good.'

We watched them clattering down the gangway, pausing to wave and disappearing beyond the black Customs buildings. Then we turned back and went up on the funnel deck. It seemed as good a place as anywhere.

Through the grey fury of Biscay, where the ship lurched and shuddered, the tables were chained to the floor, and it was too rough for lessons, or playing on deck, and we were forced to sit on chairs with rugs about our knees, reading from the ship's library . . . and so I found Swinburne and Rossetti.

Finally, the docks at Tilbury, under a chill red sunset. Everything seemed grey, and people who had been lying about in white suits and big white shoes seemed to have changed their personalities, and now 'rugged up' in heavy coats and furs seemed to have no more time for us, but rushed hither and thither with their passports, calling impatiently for luggage labels and stewards.

'All stay with Mary, I have work to do,' said Nanny, and disappeared.

We clung to the rails, the five of us, our eyes eagerly searching the milling crowd below for our mother and father, while the chill sun hid itself behind a dirty cloud.

'Is this England?' asked Beak.

'Mm,' I replied.

'Glad I got shoes on after all,' said Bebe. 'Look, it's all dirty and nasty down there.'

They *must* be there somewhere, I thought, they *said* they would be. . . . Maybe an accident . . . the train turned over. . . . The sickness started rising again in my stomach—when suddenly I saw them!

'Daddy! Mummy!' I bellowed.

'Where?'

'There!'

They were standing on the quay near some rails. My father was holding his handkerchief by two corners like a flag. It was the first time that I remember seeing him do this, but forever after it became a signal between us.

They tore joyously up the gangway, carrying large cardboard boxes from Paris. Five different coloured coats, that raised five exclamations of delight.

'Peacock blue for Muggins.

'Rose for Bebe.

'Chestnut for Beak.

'Pink for Beattie.

'Green for Johnman.'

We went ashore, our bright new shoes snapping at the hard pavements. Struggling into a taxi, we drove through monochrome streets, past pallid-faced, hurrying people and black houses, here and there lit by the redness of a London bus, until at last we came to a tall, thin house called Chester Gate.

Bebe and I held hands tightly as we stood on the pavement and looked up. I glanced to my right, to the darkness of trees under the illuminated London sky.

'Put Amah's coffin in the cellar,' mother said behind her hand to my father.

'That's where the boiler is,' my father replied. 'It'll probably warp.'

*

The days in my diary after that read bleakly:

'We went to a plaice called Regents Park and fed squirels. Aunt Jessie and Cousin Clara came for tea. Went with Daddy to buy a coat for Beak . . . the one from Parris was too big. Aunt Cissie Bell came for tea. We rote to Father Christmas.'

One hundred aunts and cousins must have streamed through that gaunt house. Every day there was another group appraising the five of us above their Wellingtonian noses.

'There's no question that they're all Bells.'

We stared back, hand in hand. . . .

Though some of them were dressed in the weirdest of flowing garments, one was conscious of the fact that they all seemed to possess long, beautiful hands, thin legs like sticks and slim feet standing in an odd assortment of shoes.

'That's Bethia!' said one pointing at Bebe. 'Dennis will certainly end up by looking like Frederick, but one hopes he will have more *magnitude*—'

'Tea, Cousin Clara?' My mother's voice quavered slightly.

I found myself put in front of Auntie Cissie, a formidable lady of eighty years and no more than five feet high. Her shining white hair was wreathed about her head, her back was as straight as a pole; her bright blue eyes looked down into mine and there was a small twist to the smile about her lips. I stared back, my eyes narrowed. I hoped I looked fierce.

'Which side do you take after, Mary?' she asked.

'Half of me is Recompense Sherrill,' I replied. 'The other half is Irish. . . .'

There was a murmur of laughter.

'Well said, girl, well said. . . .'

Someone touched my hair in passing. 'She carries the old orriflamme . . . but none of us will live to see what she will do. . . .'

That night I made a great decision.

'We're in a new kind of a place and everything is going to be different. The Macao names must go. We're going to be different people from now on—so Bebe, Beak and Beattie must be changed . . . you've got to be Wyn, Den or Ned, Liz or Lozenge. I will be Maria, and Johnman will be Johnman.'

'You'll always be Baba to me,' the new Wyn said sleepily.

*

'Aunt Cissie is so kind; you must find her a little Christmas present,' said my mother.

It was another shaming day at a shop in Tottenham Court Road. Wyn and I were left alone for a moment, looking wildly around the vast second floor, full of china.

'What's that?' I asked a man, pointing at a full morning tea set in pieces on the floor.

He smiled grimly.

'An accident—my dear.'

'Can I buy it?'

'Buy it? You can *have* it for nothing. It's no good to us!'

We scooped up the crown Derby set of flowered cups and saucers, and took it away in a carrier bag.

That night, laboriously, we packed up the shattered china and sent it to Aunt Cissie with Christmas Greetings.

Her distraught letter read: 'Your lovely present, alas, owing to the clumsiness of the General Post Office, arrived in fractured and ruptured pieces.'

Wyn and I were dishonestly content. . . .

We went on the Serpentine in a boat, all staring dismally at the tame placidity of the oily water. 'I'd rather walk,' I said. 'I'd rather walk twenty miles.'

We loitered about in shops which didn't interest us, and on one occasion when Wyn hesitantly asked the price of something and was told it was twelve shillings, to the astonishment and outrage of the sales girl she replied: 'I'll give you five shillings.'

Our mother had to explain hurriedly that we had 'Come from the East, where everyone barters.'

On Christmas Eve, we went for the first time to Leicester Square. We stood in the middle of it, while a million starlings shrieked at us from the trees over our heads.

'That is Daly's Theatre,' said my father, 'and that the London Hippodrome . . . and that the Alhambra, and across the square, the Empire Music Hall. . . .'

'Oh,' I said.

'And now we have a great treat for you all. Your first theatre—*Where the Rainbow Ends*.'

I shall never forget it. The red plush and the gilt paint, the people sitting hushed and crushed in the circle, breathing heavily, laughing and talking. The orchestra playing the Intermezzo from *Cavalleria Rusticana*. Then the moment of silence, the flutter of programmes, the sudden magical silence, darkness . . . and the slow curtain rising upon an enchanted land.

We stared open-mouthed, our eyes riveted and unblinking upon this hitherto unknown world of witchery and magnetism called the theatre. . . .

'Don't speak to me!' I said as I went out. 'Don't speak to me, don't touch me or say anything.'

By the time we were back at Chester Gate, not only was I besotted by St George of England, but I could easily spout most of his lines, which I did from the bed, wielding a poker as a sword: 'Unnoticed and unsung do I lie hidden in the hearts of men. . . . Yet at my country's call, quick as in days of old, shall this same sword leap to its scabbard to defend the right. . . . God for England, Harry and Saint George!'

As I lay in bed that night, I knew that one day the theatre would be mine. I was not yet ten years old and there was a long, long way to go.

*

I had to go back to Leicester Square again and again. My father was intrigued that it meant something to me. Hand-in-hand we went to everything in Leicester Square, including the chestnut sellers. We strayed farther, to Covent Garden and the Opera.

I saw *La Bohème* fourteen times, and to hear the music today is to dissolve into tears for the lost faces, lost voices, lost years.

Cavalleria Rusticana, *Madame Butterfly*, *Aida* . . . Puccini, Tchaikovsky, the Ballet. *Peter Pan*. . . . My blunt pencil flies across the pages of my notebook. The Albert Hall where the 'violins and the myriad bows were like sleet against the window pane'.

'You like London after all, don't you, Muggins?'

'Like it? I'm *genuflecting*!'

He laughed.

'One day, Daddy, that's what I'm going to do. Something in the theatre.'

'Oh Muggins, I don't know much about it, but I've always heard that there's a lot of unhappiness behind those bright lights. People who smile and sing beyond those footlights are often hungry and lonely. When the lights fade, they're small, sad people, unless they're big stars like Henry Ainley.'

'I don't care. One day, that's where I'll be, behind the footlights. In Leicester Square.'

*

After Christmas, we went to a house called Berry's Croft at Burford Bridge, near Dorking. My parents had taken it for a year in order that we could go as weekly boarders to Burchett House, known naturally enough to its pupils as 'Birch it House'.

Berry's Croft was not a particularly pretty house. For one thing it was surrounded by laurels, which always carry an air of extreme gloom, but it was warm and cosy, or at least my mother made it so. It had flowered chintzes and big bouncy sofas. There was a gravelled drive, and a large lawn. There was a vast cedar tree for climbing-up purposes, and a high grass bank for rolling-down purposes. In the vegetable garden were raspberries which are still remembered as the biggest and best I have ever tasted, and in the summer there was no greater delight than to lie on one's back under the canes and pick the fruit, just out of view of the kitchen window where King, my father's ex-soldier servant and his wife held sway.

Mother had friends in the neighbourhood and Sir James Jeans, the astronomer, lived close by. Best of all there was a most beautiful house called Polesden Lacey. Giant hollyhocks and sunflowers leaned against its mellowed walls and the hot sun brought out the scent of rosemary and wistaria. It was the most romantic house I had ever seen. I was determined one day to have one like it.

My father bought a car. It was a high, anxious-looking Ford, like an emaciated fly, which was immediately named 'Precious', and in it we bowled along the Surrey lanes, peering at everything. My father was not one of the world's best drivers, for he had no thought for unimportant items like petrol. Once he mistook a ditch for part of the grass verge, and the whole car turned over, while Dennis's voice, rising through the din, advised 'Put the brake on, Daddy. Put the brake on!'

During that summer my father decided to take me on a walking tour. We were to walk to the New Forest. I was to take nothing but a change of stockings, a sweater, hairbrush and toothbrush, and these were to be tied up in a red-spotted handkerchief and carried on the end of a stick over my shoulder.

Occasionally, if I looked a bit weak at the knees, my father would thumb a lift from a passing truck, but mostly we walked. I wasn't impressed.

'Was it like this in Burma?' I asked a trifle disappointed.

'It was a sandy road,' he answered shortly.

We must have gone in and out of a hundred churchyards. 'Good place to get names of people for books,' he told me. At Lyndhurst after a long hot day's walk, and a sit outside a pub with a glass of shandy and a bit of cheese, he decided he was going to sleep in the churchyard rather than the pub.

'On a grave?' I asked fearfully.

'On the grass,' he said.

'How do you know there aren't graves under the grass?'

'There are, but you like churchyards, don't you?' he asked.

'S'pose it rains?'

'Then we'll go into the church.'

'There'll be too many people,' I said hesitantly.

'Not at *night*, Muggins Juggins!'

'I mean Night People.'

He laughed. 'They won't hurt us. It'll be an Adventure.'

It didn't rain, and we didn't have to go into the church—luckily, for when I tried the door the next morning, it was locked. But it was an Adventure I could have done without. I could not sleep. Shivering with cold and goose pimples I couldn't even lie down. I stared wild-eyed at the dark silhouettes of ministering angels and black crosses on the neighbouring tombstones, a trick of the light and my tired eyes making them seem to be floating towards me; and when an owl hooted derisively in the yews, I went to pieces. I leapt upon the recumbent figure of my father, whispering hoarsely that I was about to be sick.

The expedition wasn't considered to be a success, and the next day, my mother, driving 'Precious' defiantly and intrepidly into the yard of the inn, took us home.

'I got seriously ill,' I explained to the questioning faces around me.

*

I remember little of Burchett House, chiefly because I wanted to forget the array of desks, the long walks through wet woods in 'crocodile'—a chain-gang of small convicts. On one of these walks I sought to brighten my companion's ashy face by telling her about the pirates in Macao. Her eyes widened, and encouraged, I plunged on with exaggerated, gory details. To my astonishment she broke ranks and fled from me and with quivering chin tearfully told Miss Somebody-Or-Other that I had been telling her lies about pirates.

'There aren't any pirates!' the little monster blubbered.

The crocodile came to an abrupt halt and all the little identical faces turned to the hubbub.

Miss Somebody-Or-Other advanced upon me, dragging the little misery with her.

'There aren't any pirates!' shrilled Misery again.

'There are!' I shouted, backing away like a cornered rat before the sticks of his tormentors.

'Now Mary Hayley Bell, we don't want to tell lies, do we? We don't want to be called a liar, do we?'

'I'm not!'

'I'm afraid you are.' She smiled grimly.

'I'm not! I'm not!' I shrieked. 'Damn your eyes to hell! Mother of a pig!'

There was consternation.

'Oh!' said Miss Somebody-Or-Other. 'Oh!' She shut her mouth quickly as though she was afraid of her teeth dropping out. 'You *naughty*, *wicked* little girl! You shall pay for this!'

'It's true,' I wailed.

'How *dare* you!'

'But it is true. About the pirates, I mean. . . .'

'Go to the rear and walk by yourself, Mary Hayley Bell, and when we get back to House, you'll be dealt with.'

I walked past the row of little grey faces. They were practically drooling with pleasure and anticipation.

I was confined to my room. 'Solitary confinement' for three days with nothing but my exercise books and constant bowls of porridge. I pretended I was Oscar Wilde in Reading Gaol, but it didn't work. . . . I gave most of my porridge to a robin who sat on the window sill, and I killed innumerable flies and stuck them in a spider's web. Then I decided to run away.

I waited for my last dish of porridge, heard the key turn once more in the lock, and waited happily for dark to fall.

I climbed out of the window, slipped past the rhododendrons and out onto the road. It was a long way from Dorking to Burford Bridge, but I remembered the way. The journey seemed to take hours, but finally with a burst of joy, I saw the warm light in the windows of Berry's Croft as I turned the corner.

They sat staring at me from the dining-room table, astounded, their table napkins held to their mouths.

The next morning I returned to the school, accompanied by my father, who apologized to Miss Somebody-Or-Other, and then insisted on addressing the whole school on the subject of pirates in China.

After that I did everything that was required of me in every possible way—and waited eagerly for the weekends. Often, we were taken to Burwash, to see a cousin. I enjoyed the drive, and the house, Batemans, was lovely, with lawns and yew trees clipped into the shape of birds. At first I didn't take much to our cousin, though he was always delightfully courteous and understanding to talk to.

'So,' he said, putting his hand on our heads, 'you too are part of that great company of the Outcast Children of the East, eh?'

I looked up at him. He was quite small; his deep, sad eyes stared into

My mother (in her nurse's uniform) and father at about the time of their marriage.

Me and my first friend, Amah.

The Commissioner's House at Macao, on top of the four hundred years old wall.

The Tiles, with me, Bebe (Wyn), Beak (Dennis), and Beattie (Elizabeth).

Innumerable old steps led up to our mother's joyful garden of colour and scent. She is holding Johnman and Nanny Day holds Beattie. My father, Beak, Bebe, Pongo and I complete the picture.

From left to right, Beak on Hooky Walker, Bebe on Brownie, and me on Wee Willie Winkie.

Aylmar House, Sherborne School for Girls. I am fifth from the left in the back row and Elspeth Mackenzie is sixth from the left in the second row. Miss Bishop and Miss Rowe are seated and Wyn is sitting on the grass on the left of the front row.

Below left: Johnman, our father, and Dennis, at Wellington.

Below right: Johnman at Dartmouth, 1934.

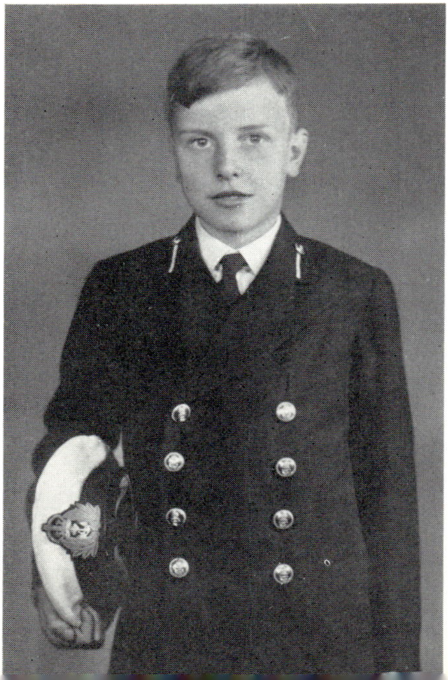

mine from behind his glasses, and when he kissed me his moustache always tickled fiercely.

'Are you one?' I asked, not quite knowing his meaning.

'Now, Baba,' started Mother.

'Baba?' He smiled. 'Baba Black sheep, eh? I wrote a story once about someone called Baba Black sheep,' he said. 'It was a sad story.'

'I *like* sad stories,' I told him.

'And you like books?'

'Oh, yes. Poetry especially.'

We went up the staircase hand-in-hand, to his library. I thought it was immense then, although I have seen it since, years later, and it is quite small. He took a slim book from the shelf, and wrote something on the flyleaf and gave it to me. It contained only one poem, and I started reading it aloud:

'If you can keep your head when all about you
Are losing theirs and blaming it on you,
If you can trust yourself when all men doubt you,
But make allowance for their doubting too;
If you can wait and not be tired by waiting,
Or being lied about, don't deal in lies,
Or being hated, don't give way to hating,
And yet don't look too good, or talk too wise:

If you can dream—and not make dreams your master,
If you can think—and not make thoughts your aim;
If you can meet with Triumph and Disaster
And treat those two imposters. . . .'

'I like this,' I said. 'I don't think I've seen it before.'

'Perhaps you haven't had to,' he said.

'Who wrote it?' I asked.

'I did.' On the flyleaf he had written: 'For Mary, with love from Rudyard Kipling. . . .'

*

The day came for my father to return to China. He'd been appointed Commissioner of the Kowloon Frontier with a residence on the Peak in Hong Kong. He and my mother were delighted.

'It's the Blue Riband of the Customs Service,' he told me jubilantly. 'Mummy will love it. There's a terraced garden looking down onto the harbour a thousand feet below, where the cruisers and destroyers look like toys on the water.'

I listened in silence.

'Beattie and Johnman will go with me, and Nanny of course—'

'And Amah and her coffin.'

He laughed.

'Mummy will stay until she's put you all in school. You and Wyn to Sherborne, and Dennis to Oakfield, where I went at Rugby.'

Panic reared up like an animal in fear.

'How long will you be away?'

'Three years, maybe four.'

'I shall be quite old when I see you again.' He looked away and kicked a stone.

'How long will Mummy stay?'

'Until you're in school. You can't expect her to leave me alone in that great house. Lot of entertaining, you know.'

'Yes, I know.'

He cleared his throat noisily.

'Time goes very quickly. She'll be back in another year or eighteen months.'

'Yes.'

'You'll like staying with Auntie Violet Campbell for the holidays. She has a bunch of kids, and a wonderful farm just outside Tenterden.'

He put his arm around me.

'You must take care of the others now, Muggins. They're your responsibility. Be a good girl. Work hard at school, learn all you can and make some friends. And watch that old temper. Sudden rage is a kind of madness, you know.'

'Wish I was coming too!'

'I know. So do I. I shall miss you awfully, particularly when I go to Macao.'

Macao! I couldn't speak, and I had the sense not to try to.

The April sun had gone down under the blossom-wrapped almond trees of Regent's Park, and the twilight that we never saw in Macao was stealing across London as we walked to the theatre.

*

Two days later, standing miserably on the quay and staring cold-eyed at the walls of the great ship, we saw him off at Tilbury.

'Wave, Baba!'

I took a small hankie out of my pocket and held it up by the corners. It was a very small flag indeed, but the holder of the opposite flag saw it, for he raised his up and down, and so did I.

The ship started downstream. The lump in my throat ached and I found it hard to swallow.

'You *do* look fierce!'

'Fierce! I'm going to be sick.'

'Not again!'

I looked at my mother. There was no smile on her face. She wasn't even waving any more. I wondered what she was thinking about.

6

A WEB OF SCHOOLS

When I first saw Aylmar, which was to be our House at Sherborne School for Girls, I said to Wyn: 'What a tall house. I wonder what the other houses think of it.'

'Looks like a prison to me,' said Wyn.

'And that's what it'll be,' I promised her.

Miss Beatrice Rowe, a short, middle-aged lady with glasses hiding bright brown eyes like marbles, rose from her desk as we were ushered in.

'*Do* sit down,' she purred.

We sat, our knees pressed nervously together, our hands twisting unseen in our laps.

'So these are your girls,' she said rather obviously to our mother.

For a moment or two our gaze was interlocked.

'She doesn't like me for a start,' I thought.

'Well now! What class shall we put you in, I wonder?'

I stared at her, making my eyes as basilisk as I could.

'What do you know?'

'Nothing,' I replied.

'Nothing? Humbly put, but we hope a little erroneous!' She smiled thinly at our mother. 'Let me put it this way, what do you know mostly about?'

'Macao?' I started hopefully.

My mother cut in:

'Mary likes reading, and writes quite well for her age. . . .'

'Ah! Miss Henry will be pleased.'

Encouraged, I pressed on: 'I know a lot about Marco Polo, Genghis Khan, Ricci—'

'Ricci?'

'He was a famous Jesuit Priest who—'

Her eyebrows disappeared into her hairline.

'Are you Catholics?'

'No, Buddhists.'

Mother cleared her throat and laughed nervously.

'We're a mixture. My husband leans towards the Buddhist philosophy but I am a Presbyterian, my father was—'

'What church do you want them to attend?'

'Church of England.'

'It's as well to know. Baptized, I suppose?'

Mother nodded.

'Well now, History. How far have you arrived in History?'

'Portuguese history, history of the East India Company, the Chinese Dynasties.'

She frowned slightly, and pushed a straying hair off her cheek.

'What about England?'

'One day England will be the poor relation of America,' I said slowly.

'Who on earth told you that?'

'My father. I know quite a lot about Bacon, Clive, Warren Hastings—'

'*That's* better!'

'They were all corruptionists.'

She sat back against her chair.

'Really?'

'So was Wilberforce.'

'You're quite a little *non-conformist* aren't you?'

'No—Buddhist. . . .'

My mother leaned forward hurriedly and pressed my knee.

'Baba, don't be foolish. You see, Miss Rowe, they've been brought up in a rather unconventional way. They had a Portuguese governess.'

'Don't worry, Mrs Hayley Bell. We understand here. There are all sorts in this school. From Africa, India, Aden. . . .'

Outcast Children of the East, I thought to myself.

'There's a girl who came here last term, such a *nice*, *pretty* girl. I'll put Mary in her dormitory.'

'Can't I be with my sister?' I asked.

'No dear, we keep the younger ones together. You'll like Elspeth Mackenzie, her father is something in India.'

'Mary's French is quite good; so is her Portuguese and Chinese—' my mother began, trying to salvage something from the interview. She failed. 'We don't carry the last two languages in our curriculum, Miss Rowe interrupted with a bleak smile, and rose to her feet.

'Now come along and I'll show you around, and you must meet the Head.'

'Whose head?' asked Wyn.

She smiled indulgently at my mother.

'The Head Mistress, Miss Mulliner!'

She put her arm round my shoulders as we left the room.

'We'll have to stop biting our nails, won't we?'

Traversing quadrangles full of netball nets, and wet green playing fields, we came eventually to the School House where, in an even colder and more impersonal study, we came face to face with Miss Mulliner. She was a woman of square perimeters, with a flabby face, rubbery lips, pale, coiled hair and icy blue eyes. We shook hands. Hers were wet and cold. I wiped mine surreptitiously on the back of my skirt. She can't be healthy, I thought.

We followed her, a ship in full sail, down long shining school passages, with glass doors flashing right and left to show cavernous rooms full of the inevitable desks.

'This is the Great Hall, where we have morning prayers, concerts and lectures,' she boomed.

I peered round, feeling miniscule.

'D'ya play cricket?'

I shook my head.

'You will.'

'Well,' said Mother hopefully at lunch at the Digby Hotel. 'What do you think?'

'I'm just wondering why you want to send us to a place like that,' I answered.

She looked down at her roast beef, and took a deep breath.

'I suppose everything goes by opposites. You see, I never went to a public school.'

'Lucky you,' said Wyn.

'I wished I had. That's why I want you to go.'

'Public lav,' I muttered.

'Baba, I will *not* have these asides. You must learn discipline, my darling. You'll love it when you are part of it. You'll look back and say that schooldays were the happiest years of your life.'

'*Will* I . . .!'

I pushed my plate away.

'Why can't we come back to China and do what you did? It was all right for you! We'd be all together. Please Mummy. I'll work so hard, you'll be proud of me!'

'It isn't possible. And it's too late.'

I looked at Wyn. She was playing with a cat under the table and laughing. I looked down at my bitten nails and vaguely pushed back the rough cuticle.

'I don't like the place,' I said. 'I don't like the one with glasses and scarey teeth, and I don't like the big fat one. And I'll tell you something else, *they don't like me*!'

The table lurched as Wyn came up.

'Oh, shut up, Baba. At least we'll be together. Think of poor old Den.'

*

The uniform was grass green. Grass green suits, gym dresses and games skirts. Straw boaters, for formal wear, berets for crossing the 'Quad' to school, and large, outsize snowboots to pull over black slippers and black stockings. . . .

The man at Harrods picked his nose thoughtfully.

'Then you'll need a lacrosse stick and a hockey stick, dear.'

'Why?'

'It's on the list, dear.'

'What do you do with this?' I asked, eyeing the lacrosse stick.

'Catch the ball, dear,' he said disinterestedly.

'Hockey sticks, lacrosse sticks,' I said to Wyn as we dragged along behind all the shopping. 'It's a wonder we didn't come out with cricket stumps and bails.'

'Don't be so piggish to Mummy, Baba. She's only doing what she thinks is right for us, and it must be beastly away from Daddy.'

I felt piggish.

Mother saw us off at Waterloo. The whole station seemed to be filled with grass green suits, straw boaters and lacrosse sticks, trunks, suitcases and girls of all shapes and sizes, talking loudly and shrieking with false laughter.

Wyn and I clung to each other.

'When does the *Nagoya* sail, Mummy?'

'I've told you, darling, next week. You will be good, and take care of Wyn?'

An attractive young woman slid towards us.

'I'm Miss MacDougall, the games mistress. I'll look after them; train's just going.'

The usual sickness rose up in my stomach. I started muttering: 'Almighty and Everlasting God who alone can work marvels. . . .'

'Goodbye, darlings. Write to me.'

We were on the train. She was hidden by a dozen green bottoms that filled the window. 'Goodbye, Mummy!' I screamed. For a moment I could see her, smearing the tears clumsily across her face. There was a jerk as the train started moving. Flat faces drifted past, and the train gathered speed.

'Thank God that's over,' said a fat girl, throwing her hat on the rack. 'Hate Ma's and Pa's at stations. They should know better.'

Not daring to speak, hand-in-hand, thin, cold, remote and alone, our feet hardly touching the floor, Wyn and I sat squashed together at the end of the carriage, our straw boaters with the red ribbon of Aylmar crammed down over our noses.

'*Tons* of new squids,' said someone laconically.

'They should all be stuffed in the same carriage.'

We sat motionless, hoping not to be noticed.

*

Nervously I placed my small suitcase on the bed. I sat down heavily and looked around. A suitcase and trunk were already on the floor by the other bed. I caught sight of the label which read: 'E. Mackenzie—Bombay.' All references to Macao had been erased from mine.

A hygienic looking woman in a stiff white uniform and cap over a well-scrubbed face stood before me, smiling:

'I'm matron.'

'Oh.'

'Have you had your periods yet?'

'My what?'

'How old are you?'

'Twelve.'

'Then you haven't? Unless you have a new-fangled name for it?'

'I'm sorry—'

'Didn't your mother tell you about the facts of life?'

A walk in the gardens of Polesden Lacey with her flashed through my mind. She had called it 'My Friend'. I felt embarrassed.

'Oh, *that*! Yes, I know about that. No, I haven't.'

'Well, when you do, you use these.'

She produced an armful of large hand towels.

'Rather thick, aren't they?'

'They go to the laundry and get thinner. You can unpack, put everything on the bed for me to check and then have a bath. Along the corridor. I'll turn it on.'

I did what she said hurriedly, longing for the privacy of the bathroom.

Matron was checking my list when I got back. Suddenly she put a thermometer in my mouth.

'I'm all right,' I said, half choking.

'We always take temperatures night and morning for two weeks,' she explained. 'In case of anything catching.'

'Oh.'

'Get into your clothes and go down to baby supper.'

'Baby supper?'

'That's what it's called for the under thirteens.'

Baby supper was presided over by Miss Bishop, the largely Jamaican Housekeeper, sitting in the middle of the floor in a high-backed chair. She had a great sense of humour and would shake with laughter at nothing at all.

There were six of us. Directly opposite to me was a tall, dark girl with a face like a Christmas rose. She grinned and gave me a big wink. Elspeth Mackenzie was the best thing that happened to me at Sherborne. Her philosophy of life was to giggle. With her I giggled my way through the short time I was there, and today, as Elspeth March, she is one of those particular friends I count on the fingers of one hand.

That first term rolled on. I was desperately shy, and I clung to my new friend more than she realized. Elspeth's gregarious ways, her gift of laughter, and her ability to take everything as an immeasurable jest, delighted me, and I certainly became less solemn.

I was in Class A with Elspeth for English, History and French, but I was in B2 for Mathematics, a completely blind spot in my brain, perhaps owing to Miss Da Silva's dismissal of it. When, eventually, I took the Cambridge School Certificate examination I distinguished myself by getting 'Nought' for Arithmetic, Algebra, *and* Geometry.

My English teacher was a bit wary of me from the start. I answered her cheekily, knowing that I could get a laugh from a beautiful girl sitting next to me—Diana Reader Harris, now the Head Mistress of Sherborne.

'What is this, Mary Hayley Bell? I asked for an essay to be written in prose. You have written a poor piece of poetry which you call "Requiem pour Recherche du temps perdu!" Why?' Miss Henry demanded.

'I wrote it for myself.'

'You'll please confine such writings to your bedroom.'

'I do, in my laundry book.'

'Stand up.'

I stood up, smirking at Elspeth.

'What have you to say?'

'An artist in writing may be known by what he omits,' I quoted haughtily. 'Schiller said "Words are like leaves and where they most abound, much fruit of sense is rarely found." '

A titter ran round the classroom. Miss Henry froze, for she was in the minority.

'Don't show off. You may leave the room and stand in the passage-way.'

I stood there for the rest of the lesson, dreading the sight of that huge vessel in full sail, Miss Mulliner, and prepared to be on the point of fainting should she appear.

I became passionately immersed in lacrosse. I could run fast and was pretty soon in the top game. 'You should be in your house First XII,' said Miss MacDougall with a smile. I was thrilled to death. I gave her my jade brooch from Granny Hogg.

'That's very sweet of you, but why?'

'I like you,' I said, 'and I've got a lot more.' Miss Rowe saw to it that I was not in the first twelve. 'Too uncontrolled and unreliable,' she said. I was in despair but I didn't show it. I became naughtier.

'Where's that Indian bearer?' I shouted, and Elspeth would go off into gales of laughter. I got the reputation of being daring for breaking rules. Elspeth followed me through forbidden windows, and stood on lavatory seats, pulling the chains of our neighbours, so that the entire toilets were in an uproar. Apple pie beds and an endless succession of booby traps were run-of-the-mill hazards for other girls and the mistresses. The final straw came as a result of a game which consisted of waiting behind a hedge until some poor wretch passed by, and then jumping upon her and pulling her green beret over her eyes.

On this occasion, I was stationed beyond Elspeth. I saw a figure advancing in snowboots and beret, a thick coat wrapped round her against the wind.

'Now!' I shouted.

The unseen Elspeth leapt upon the back of the unsuspecting creature, crammed her beret over her eyes, and brought her to the ground, while I jumped out, giggling hysterically—and found myself gazing down into the angry face of our Housemistress.

'I knew from the beginning I was going to have trouble with you,' she said icily. 'Sometimes I think you're slightly unhinged.'

Again and again I was in that study.

'You are impossible in this school,' Miss Rowe said in her staccato voice. 'You don't work. You're hopeless at everything except English, and that is depraved and polluted. You're a nuisance in class, you break every rule of the school and House. In fact you are such a bad influence that I am writing to your mother and asking her to take you away. . . .'

I was sitting alone on an iron seat on the playing fields, surveying the empty grounds.

Dead leaves, reluctant to lose their hold upon the slim black trees, drifted dismally across the grass, settling in drifts against the pavilion as the last of the yellow November light faded from the sky.

'I could have been happy here,' I said to myself. 'I could have done quite well if they had let me.' If you can trust yourself when all men doubt you. . . . It was the final despondency, and hope deferred.

That night Elspeth came to my cubicle and found me alone in the dark.

'What's up?' she whispered, the laughter gone.

'Nobody in this place likes me or understands me.'

'I do. I think you're marvellous, Paddy.'

'Well, I've been given the Order of the S.A.K.'

'My hat, how grizzly.'

'Old Rowbottom says I'm no good at anything—I don't work and I'm a bad influence.'

'Cheer up. Remember Bruce and his old spider.'

'I wish I were dead. Ma is coming back from China. Pa will be livid and Ma will be peeved.'

Pa *was* livid and Ma *was* peeved.

As I left Sherborne School for Girls forever, I paused irresolutely and glanced back again at the golden light slanting through the glass dome over my head. I stepped outside. The trees around me stood out clearly. There was sadness only in the beauty of the day.

*

We went back to rooms in Tenterden, the four of us, for my mother had removed Wyn as well as me, and Wyn's accusing eyes met mine more than once. It was a silent holiday.

I carried the black dog of guilt on my back, but I wore my resentment rakishly, like a bowler hat.

'They were, by and large, all insalubrious persons,' I said airily one day, sitting in a Kentish field.

My mother didn't answer. She was inspecting our necks, which were covered in a red rash.

'Gosh!' she said. 'I do believe we've all got measles.'

And we had.

Obeying my father's orders, my poor mother set out with some trepidation to find us another school. She feared no one would accept me, and this was my hope too, but two little ladies, the Misses Dawson of Malvern Girls College, agreed to.

They were tiny, and surveyed me up and down, looking up into the brooding, angry eyes of the basilisk with considerable amusement.

'We like to tackle difficult cases,' they whispered.

I was sent to a House called Ivydene Hall; the House Mistress was a Miss Pulham. She had clear blue, untroubled eyes, and a very gentle voice.

My behaviour was little better. I was watched carefully as if I were a wild animal that had just been caught in the African jungle. I was treated with kindness and courtesy, but as they watched me, I watched them, my eyes sullen and my manners morose and churlish. I scowled and frowned a great deal. I turned my back on would-be friends. I missed Elspeth.

One day I noticed an aeroplane landing in the adjacent field. I heard from a day girl that the owner took people up for 'Flips'. 'Of course, it's against the rules for boarders,' she reminded me, and that clinched my determination. I went up for a glorious flight round the Malvern Hills. On alighting, I noticed the mother of one of the day girls waiting to board the plane.

I went straight to the Misses Dawson and told them what I had done. As I left their study I noticed the day girl's mother waiting to go in. I paused. 'We know all about it, Mrs Robinson,' I heard the elder Miss Dawson say, 'and though we reprimanded her for breaking rules we prefer that she should have a sense of adventure than that she should tell tales. Good afternoon.' When the red-faced Mrs Robinson emerged I gave her a grin of triumph.

Some weeks later I was reprimanded by Miss Pulham for bad behaviour. She shut me in her study for two hours to 'think things over'. When she returned, everything on the mantelpiece and tables was on the floor. The room was a shambles.

She sat slowly down on a velvet chair and told me to put everything back.

'There's only one thing to do with you,' she said.

My throat tightened.

'Expel me, I suppose.'

'No, Mary,' she said quietly. 'That wouldn't help either of us. I shall make you a prefect.'

I stared at her with narrowed eyes, then I burst into tears, my head on her knee.

She pushed back the long hair from my face and went on talking in her calm, gentle voice. 'You're a born leader, but you're running in the wrong direction! I shall expect great things from you.'

From that moment I was a knight to her Queen.

The House was astounded. I was completely in control of the situation, unflinching in my work and duties. I sat in the Prefect's Room, and knew they liked me, and the house worked like an electric clock.

In a short time I was House Captain for lacrosse, and Junior Captain of the School. The Misses Dawson invited me to dinner to meet Evans of the Broke, an old friend of my father's, and I was able to allay their concern by saying he only drank milk.

One day, when I was in the sick bay with a temperature, Miss Pulham came in and sat on the bed.

'You've been selected to play in the Trials for the Midlands lacrosse team, Mary,' she said.

'When?' I asked, shooting upright in my excitement.

'Tomorrow,' she said. 'What a pity you have a temperature!' The colour drained from my face, and she laughed. 'All right, Mary, you can borrow my fur coat—and see to it that you come back with those red stockings!'

We went to Birmingham by bus. It was raining heavily, great sludges of mud splashed against the windows and the Malvern Hills had disappeared from view. I sat warm and snug in Miss Pulham's fur coat, happily eating a bun out of a paper bag. The ground at Birmingham was running in water and thick mud. The perspiration that flooded my face was, I knew, from the temperature, but it gave me a kind of heady excitement, and I was charm itself to all and sundry!

I played in eight or nine games over a period of several hours. I was drunk with excitement, I ran like an eland, and couldn't be either caught or tackled. I had never been happier. At last I was needed. I was upholding the honour of the only school that cared whether I lived or died, and of a woman who had seen fit to give me responsibility instead of punishment. I sang as I ran. I sang to the ringing, singing hills of Malvern.

Twilight had come before we finished. The gasworks of Birmingham stood out black and stark against a violet and orange sky. The ground was full of dark figures silhouetted against it and our breath hung in clouds about us as we stood waiting for the results, waiting to hear the most important thing in our lives at that moment. The Midlands Team.

The England Captain was tall and thin and elegant; she had a high and rather royal, hesitant voice. 'I am now about to read out the team for the Midlands,' and she scratched the back of her knee.

She started with the Centre and went slowly through the field. I watched the breathless faces, and only listened when she came to: 'Right Attack Wing: L. Armstrong. Left Attack Wing and reserve for England: M. Hayley Bell.'

I took my time to get off the bus. I wanted to savour the moment, big or small. Miss Pulham's light was on and she was reading. I knocked at the door.

'Come in,' she said, and looked up.

I held out the red stockings to her without a word, for I couldn't speak.

'Well done!'

'I'm glad I got them for you. I always thought I was a failure.'

'We often think ourselves a failure when the world doesn't,' she said.

Three weeks later, I played for England at the Crystal Palace where, thirty-five years later, my son played hockey for the Southern Schools.

It wasn't important really, I suppose, but it's exciting when you're young, and I was the same age as he was—fifteen.

•

A year later, our mother came back to England again and took Haygates, a house at Eversley, in Hampshire.

I loved it. It was always full of young people and a wonderful sense of security pervaded it, because our mother with her great gift for home-making was there. The scent of sweet peas and lavender, of horses and roast chestnuts invaded and soothed our souls.

Dennis was at his preparatory school, Crowthorne Towers, struggling to pass his Entrance Examination for Wellington College. The Head Master had a whole collection of very attractive and amusing children. The eldest was Midshipman George Collett, aged eighteen. He had just won the Sword of Honour at Dartmouth, and was a local hero. The first time I saw him across a dance floor, tall and fair and handsome, my heart missed a beat. The age of chivalry is not past, I thought to myself. Here, surely, is St George himself. At a party my mother gave for my birthday, having danced with him alone all evening, he tried to kiss me in the study. Unfortunately, he left it too late, and at the precise moment that I had calculated I could reasonably surrender, the Band struck up *God Save the King*—and being in uniform, he was forced to let me go and come smartly, tense faced, to attention!

My father came home for a brief spell during that winter, but when he and mother returned to China, we went back to our various schools, and a succession of holiday homes for 'Outcast Children of the East'. The lovely time was over.

Three weeks after I returned to Malvern College, I received a bleak and blurred pencil message on a card from Dennis:

Darling Maria.
I have failed.
Goodbye.
Den.

*

My father was going through a bad time in Canton, on the Pearl River. There was trouble in China. Sun Yat-sen, hitherto in most British eyes rather a theatrical figure, one day fulminating against the British, the next fleeing from his own people to the protection of a British gunboat, had died at Peking, leaving a so-called 'Will' that preached a Bolshevik jehad against the foreign Imperialist.

In the next few days, we read that the river steamers leaving Hong

Kong were crowded with Chinese, an unfailing sign of trouble within that odd triangle of cities, Hong Kong, Canton and Macao. First the rich, their women and households; then the shopkeeping classes and artisans. It was plain something was about to happen. The Englishmen put away their golf clubs. The Volunteers were called out.

'They say,' my father wrote from Canton, 'they are going to take the settlement tomorrow morning. Well, let them play the Russian's game. Let it be so. Bring it to a head. They've called off all our servants and office staff. Trade is at a standstill. Let the Home Government sit up and take notice! . . . the rattle of ice in the cocktail shakers, and "Tipperary" and "Keep the home fires burning" is taken up by everyone—decidedly there is a thrill in the air!—The women and children are to remain in their houses and in the event of a general alarm to gather at the Consulate.'

How I envied Lozenge and Johnman out there! I scoured the papers daily. I could picture my father striding in the early mornings along the creek . . . the houses and shops along the front closed and shuttered, like a back scene in some opera, shadowed and devoid of any movement. . . .

A week later, crossing the Bund on his way home, he was set about by a dozen Chinese, and beaten severely on the head. He collapsed in the street, and taking fright his attackers ran, leaving him lying in a pool of blood. He was picked up and taken home, where for weeks he lay in a dark room with bandages on his eyes, totally blind.

Alexander Cannon, a brilliant man and a close friend, spent hours at his bedside. My father did everything that was asked of him, and several weeks later when the bandages were removed, he could see dimly. But the alert dark blue eyes were never quite the same, for he had a new way of narrowing them and almost peering, as though he were in the twilight; but his spirit was unchanged and with Cannon's help, he not only managed to survive cholera, but in a comparatively short time he resumed life as he had known it.

Some of Seymour Hicks's Vintage Wine *Company from Daly's Theatre, a photograph taken at the Blackpool Pleasure Beach for sixpence (the 'stars' were above this sort of thing). From left to right in the back row: Gemma Fagan, Oliver Gordon, Sonia Somers, Hayley Bell, Marjorie Playfair, Patrick Baring and Stella Mantovani. In the front row, Sheila Scarlet, the assistant stage manager, Phyllis Thomas, Stanley Vilven, Miss Gentry (Seymour's secretary), and Kathleen Weston.*

Hayley Bell as Lady Jane in Victoria Regina, *on Fay Compton's Australian tour,* 1938.

As Johnnie saw me on 15 *May,* 1939.

Johnnie in Of Mice and Men *at the Apollo Theatre* 1939.

Janet Johnson and I joined the Ambulance Brigade.

My father with Johnnie.

Pilot Officers Francis Hayley Bell and Dennis Hayley Bell.

On 16 January 1941, Johnnie and I were married.

7

THAT BOY

Eighteen months later, our mother returned again, this time to take Wyn and me away from school and back to China. The picture was a sad one, for she brought home with her Lozenge and Johnman, who were now, with Dennis in charge, to undergo the same trail and trial of schools and holiday homes!

We had one rather heart sinking and dejected holiday together in the Colletts' house. I was kept in a spirit of 'couleur de rose' by the prospect of marriage with St George himself, who returned at weekends from H.M.S. *Rodney* at Portsmouth, but even then secretly I knew it would never be any good, and the man I was looking for I hadn't yet seen or heard of. He was to be a combination of my father, whom I adored and admired, and someone whose life would parallel my own. Someone I wouldn't have to share with a ship or a Regiment: someone who could like life as it is, its beauty and its grossness, its solemnity and its incredible funniness: someone who could soar a bit . . . and wallow a bit too.

There was a long way to go.

*

Life in Hong Kong was full of dining and dancing and parties on Royal Navy ships, of picnics and paper chases on small Chinese 'griffin' ponies and dinners at Government House. It was at one of these dinners that for the first time I sat next to Noël Coward. He was on his way round the world with Lord Amherst, and I remember one of Hong Kong's leading hostesses addressing him across the table: 'Why can't you write a *good* play, Mr Coward . . . like *Journey's End*?'

He got his own back in a song. She was, he said:

. . .
Not dulce but extremely fernienti—
A little dull at thirty-four,
A bore at forty-four,
You really are the fountain head
Of fun at Singapore.

It was never published, but it swept through Hong Kong and Singapore like a forest fire. It was bawled in clubs, harmonized in bars, warbled in drawing-rooms, whistled in barracks, hummed in nurseries, and chanted sotto voce by the Choir in church. . . .

*

At the end of 1930 my father was appointed Commissioner to Tientsin.

The house was enormous, and so were the gardens. We used to get up every morning and ride on the Race Course. We went to Peking and stayed with Daniel Vare, the Italian Ambassador, and author of several books like *The Maker of Heavenly Trousers*, rode into the Gobi Desert, and explored the Great Wall and the Forbidden City. I was happy. I was back in the land of the sun, the land of my forefathers.

I missed Dennis, and thought of him often. He had eventually crawled into Wellington College, and was at Talbot House. His spidery writing arrived periodically, but it told us nothing of his feelings. He had 'played soccer' for his house and was considered a good shot with a rifle. That was all we knew.

My father was happy. My mother longed for the babies, Johnman in particular, who was doing well at Crowthorne, and had already announced his intention to go into the Navy as a submarine officer.

From time to time I noticed a tall and elegant Chinese Mandarin who slipped quietly into the house for a couple of hours at a time. He wore the plain clothes dress of an Emperor—the long robes of the Manchu, and a lapis lazuli button on the top of his small round black cap.

'Who is he, Daddy?' I asked once.

'Mr Pu-i. He comes to learn English.'

'Mr Pu-i?'

'If times were different, he would be called the Emperor of China.'

One day I trapped Mr Pu-i as he was on the point of leaving.

'I like the button in your hat,' I said shyly.

'I have a better one for ceremonial occasions, when I wear a white peacock's feather in it—or I did,' he said sadly.

The following day I was standing among the raspberries when he left. He waved his hand to me and I joined him.

'They are both yours,' he said. 'Time makes them of no importance to me. There is a saying: "If you have but one loaf of bread, sell it and buy white hyacinths to feed your soul." ' And he handed me the two buttons; they stand on the mantelpiece in Richmond today.

He became a romantic figure to me. I read all I could about him, the last of the Ch'ing Dynasty which had started in 1644, the last of the Manchu Emperors!

I could picture him quite clearly as a boy two years old, dressed in the robes of the Son of Heaven, ascending that great and colourful throne, nephew of the childless Kuang Hsü, while his father Ch'un became Regent; could see him wandering through the glorious gardens of the Summer Palace with the great pools of multi-coloured tropical fish hiding under the lotus flowers; see him, a baby still, and unaware, forced to abdicate a few months later, when Sun Yat-sen and Yuan Shih-k'ai had power to constitute a Republic, and Royalty ended, in 1911: 'He was to retain his title for life and to receive a large pension. . . .'

I stood among the raspberries watching him as he moved silently, erect, and with great dignity, through the gates of our house. The Chinese sentries didn't even salute him.

Many years later, on a visit to Hong Kong, I asked someone at Government House:

'Do you ever hear of Pu-i? I know he was in a Siberian prison for some years. . . .'

'Oh, yes,' was the reply. 'He's one of the lucky ones.'

'Lucky ones?'

'Yes. He's the gardener at the Summer Palace, so he can grow his own vegetables. . . .'

Through him, I was inspired to study Chinese literature, art, sculpture and architecture. . . . I read and read and read, and wandered again through the Summer Palace, the Imperial Palace, the Temple of Heaven, and stood on the Great Wall looking away to Shanhaikwan.

The T'ang Dynasty, 618–906. The Golden Age of poetry. The poems of Li Ho, equal to the early French symbolists . . . Confucious, Taoism,

Buddhism. Absolute reality, 'one is all, and all is one', a family feeling I have tried to sustain, and 'The greatest understanding to be achieved, is love'.

In all this my father was the greatest of my teachers, and through his love for China, her golden years streamed away from me through the saffron, pink and jade gateways, the temples, pavilions and pagodas.

*

A curious little band of 'players' called 'The Quaints' arrived in Tientsin. They had left England over a year before, and had played in every possible State in India. They had had a considerable success in Singapore, where it was alleged that Noël Coward had stiffened in his tracks at the sight of the words 'The Quaints in Hamlet' on the marquee outside the theatre, and muttered to Lord Amherst: '*This* I have to see!'

He had also amusedly fallen in love with them, and refused to go to any party from the High Commissioner's to the lowliest Tamil haunt, unless accompanied by the whole troupe. He had even played Stanhope in *Journey's End* for them.

From Singapore they had gone to Hong Kong and Shanghai with a huge repertoire and the same success, and were feted from one end of China to the other. Tientsin's British colony awaited them with heightening excitement.

The list of entertainments that they offered was intriguing:

Mr Cinders
Hamlet
Julius Caesar
When Knights were Bold
Journey's End
Young Woodley
So This is Love
Funny Face
The Girl Friend
etc.

For some reason, we didn't attend the first night, but I remember that the following morning, having ridden furiously round the Race Course, and about to devour our breakfast—the daily routine of the colony—someone clutched my arm: 'Look, there's the leading man and the leading lady!'

We watched them mount a couple of horses, and trot confidently towards the course. Slim, dark-haired, both attired in jodhpurs and white shirts, they presented an attractive picture in the early sunlight.

Suddenly, to everyone's warm and smiling faces came a look of horror.

'My *God*!' said the bank manager, and sat down heavily in front of his scrambled eggs. . . .

'I *say*. . . . I mean . . . well!'

The couple were cantering the *wrong way* round the course!

That night we went to see *Mr Cinders*. We sat enchanted, for neither Wyn nor I had been to many theatres since our Chester Gate days. I leaned forward and stared at the boy in the centre of the stage who was dancing and singing. He was smiling, and he made me smile. There was something about him that pulled at my sleeve, and I looked at no one else; in fact, even now, I can't remember any part of the story of *Mr Cinders*, or who else was on the stage that evening. Somehow I only seemed to see him.

'Who's that boy, the one who looks like a sort of leprechaun?' I asked Wyn.

She consulted the programme.

'John Mills,' she said.

Some days later my father announced that he had asked the Quaints to lunch and tea, and to play tennis. They arrived shyly and in huddles, in the way of theatre people when faced by total strangers from another world. My father, with his enormous charm, introduced them one by one to the family and our friends: 'Mr Salisbury. Mr Grant Anderson. Mr Brentford. Mr Bruce Carfax. Mr John Mills. Miss Raymond. Miss Betty Hare. Miss Towyna Thomas. . . .'

Stripped of the warmth of the footlights, the magnetism, the magic spell of the theatre, they stood together making ordinary remarks about ordinary things, like the garden, the weather, how intrigued they were by China, how good people had been to them. . . . They all seemed to be smaller. But I was conscious of something they didn't bestow. A private comradeship, almost a private language, which I longed to share. We were the interlopers, the intruders into their world, not they into ours.

They enjoyed the Chinese food, the wine, brandies and coffee; and thus fortified they were prepared to attack the tennis court. 'Who's for tennis!' asked John Mills, and they laughed. We looked round at each other nervously, for we were not without perceptivity.

'I thought you were marvellous last night,' I said to him rather inanely. I realized, and realizing made it only worse, that for the first time in years I was feeling shy, and that my cheeks were getting hotter and hotter.

He looked at me. His dark blue eyes reminded me of my father's.

'Did you?' he said gravely. 'That's nice; actors always like to hear that.'

'Tomorrow night we're coming to see *Journey's End*. We saw it in London, at the St James's,' I blurted out, noticing that his finger was bandaged and wondering why.

'I think I enjoy playing Raleigh more than any other part,' he said. 'I *am* Raleigh, that's the point,' and he grinned. I smiled back. I had the feeling that we had known each other for years, been together before.

The tennis wasn't a success. No one was any good at it. There was a lot of laughter, and asides which none of us intruders could catch, and though there were Chinese coolies to retrieve the balls, Wyn and I sweated our way through the afternoon—running, catching, throwing tennis balls to the Quaints, eagerly snatching at every 'Thank you, love' that was thrown at *us*.

They had tea in the shade. They talked about their tour, and made us laugh at some of their experiences.

They had cocktails. It was Sunday and they could afford to. They rose in a body, thanked my mother and father, *kissed* Wyn and me, and went jogging erratically down the drive, arm-in-arm.

I envied them.

I remember we went to church for evensong that night as we had missed the morning service, being busy with our preparations, and saw, rather to my surprise, John Mills across the aisle.

The sun that bids us rest is waking
Our brethren 'neath the Western sky,
And hour by hour, fresh lips are making
Thy wondrous doings heard on high.

I glanced up at my mother. She was swallowing hard, and unable to sing. I put out my hand and touched her arm. . . .

Across the aisle, I noticed that John Mills was not singing.

*

A few weeks later another incident took all our attention. Lennox Simpson came to town. . . .

For some time I had been aware, through hearing conversations between my father and mother, and from seeing Chinese gentlemen like

T. V. Soong, Nanking's Foreign Minister, the Garrison Commander Fu Tso-i and others, in the house at various times, that there was an air of hostility—and what can convey that better than the expressionless mask of the Asiatic. Reflected from the sunlit courtyard outside, the light stared back from two ink pools that supplanted their eyes.

'What is it all about, Daddy?' I asked one evening.

'Too involved to explain, Muggins, but so far I can tell you, the Nanking Government is about to fall. Marshall Yen Hsi-shan is on the other side and he has ordered me to send the Customs monies—thousands and thousands—to the Northern Government instead of to the Ministry of Finance. In fact he has already seized revenues lodged in a Customs Collecting Bank. But the Customs Service should be kept entirely out of party politics; as the Inspector General said, it should be administered for the good of China as a whole.'

He was right. It *was* too involved. But his anxiety increased daily, and he could see visions of the Canton Incident repeating itself.

On Monday 16 June 1931 when he went to his office, his secretary said that there was a collection of gentlemen to see him.

> There was a very serious development in connection with the Tientsin Customs on the morning of June 16th. As soon as the Customs House, which is located in the French Concession, was opened, the Chinese Superintendent of Customs called upon Colonel Hayley Bell, the Commissioner, and notified him that he had received instructions from Marshall Yen Hsi-shan to take over the office and install a new Commissioner. He then ushered in Mr B. Lennox Simpson (better known as the writer Putnam Weale) who had been appointed to succeed Colonel Hayley Bell. Simultaneously the outside telephone wires were cut isolating the Commissioner from all external communications, and the premises were invaded and surrounded by a number of plain clothes men, who refused to allow anything to be removed. . . .*

For several hours my father was locked up in the Customs House, refusing to hand over control to Lennox Simpson. At the same time, the Customs Guards who stood at our gates were removed, and a more sinister couple replaced them. In retrospect they looked startlingly Japanese.

The papers were full of the Incident.

> It is no exaggeration to describe today's events as the gravest in history of the Chinese Maritime Customs. For six weeks Colonel

* From *The China Illustrated Review.*

Hayley Bell, while maintaining the friendliest relations with local Chinese Authorities, has been stoutly resisting all attempts to interfere with the integrity of the Service. If his efforts are now to prove unavailing, there is good ground for fearing that the whole Customs Administration will fall to pieces. . . .*

Lennox Simpson gave unfortunate interviews:

The seizure of the Customs House would never have taken place had it not been for the deliberate defiance of Mr Bell. . . . Mr Bell is like a small pet dog, smart and agile . . . he is no match for me who could be described as a fierce looking hound.†

and received a stinging reply:

Would anyone in their senses describe as a small pet dog a British Customs official, who had resigned from the Service to enter the Army and served through the Great War . . . wounded twice . . . mentioned in despatches . . . risen to the rank of Colonel in Command of the Queen's Regiment and received the D.S.O.? . . . If Marshall Yen ever establishes a New Government he might be glad of numerous 'small pet dogs' of the Hayley Bell type. . . .†

My father was over six feet tall.

The Customs Code was important. Telegrams and letters were unreadable without it. It was hidden in the house where we lived. My father had seen to that in the event of such a happening as this. The message which came to my mother telling her all was well with him was in their own private code, and there were other messages besides.

One afternoon, early in the troubles, my mother told me to put on my elastic bloomers. She gave me the codebook wrapped in paper to hide in them. We got into our car and drove off. At the gate we were stopped and the car searched. We smiled engagingly and were waved on and drove to the Ambassador's Residence, where we were ushered in to Sir Miles Lampson. I had removed the codebook from my bloomers and mother handed it to His Excellency.

That night my father returned. He hadn't slept all night and was grey with weariness. For the first time I saw him as a tired, ageing man. He stood silently in the room for a moment, a look of bewilderment on his face as though he had forgotten something. Then: 'We have three days to get out,' he said.

'Where to?' she asked.

* From *The China Illustrated Review.*
† *The Peking Tientsin Times.*

'Any old where . . . at first I was only given twenty-four hours, but the Consul has got them to increase it to three days.'

Out came the packing cases and trunks and suitcases once more. The marble floor was covered with straw. The servants wept in terror. In the garden the flowers bloomed on.

Wyn and I went for our last ride round the Race Course. It was a hot June afternoon. The dusty roads were thick with flies on the chewed sugar cane and watermelon peel, and crowded with a terrible collection of humanity. Beggars in rags, gunny bags and less, lounging and scratching; waiting for the daily dole of rice. . . .

'We shall never come back here in all our lives,' she said.

Four months later, three men entered the Customs office in Tientsin, and shot Lennox Simpson through the back. The papers said that should he survive, he would surely be a cripple. I never heard of him again.

*

Suddenly we were all home again in England; the whole family together, kissing and hugging, standing back, and eyeing each other shyly . . . lanky boys and girls. All strangers.

'Golly, you have *grown*!'

'Look at Johnman!'

'What about Wyn, she's nine feet tall!'

We took No. 111 Sloane Street. My father decided he was going to have the time of his life. Do the London Season. It was a riot.

We did everything and went everywhere. Lunches at the House of Commons where our cousin Dennis Herbert (afterwards Lord Hemingford) was Deputy Speaker. The Flower Show. Ascot. Goodwood. The Aldershot Tattoo. Buckingham Palace, and endless teas and lunches at No. 10 Downing Street, where another cousin, Stanley Baldwin, was Prime Minister.

My father and I sat one day on a seat beside the Serpentine.

'Enjoying yourself?' he asked.

'Madly,' I replied, 'but it can't go on forever, I mean, can it? I have to *do* something.'

'What do you want to do? Do you know?'

'Yes, I know, Daddy,' I replied. 'I still want to go on the stage. I want to be an actress. I want to go to the Royal Academy of Dramatic Art.'

So, I went to the audition. It was a frightening experience, with Sir

Kenneth Barnes and others sitting out in the front of the theatre. I did a Shakespeare speech and a comedy scene.

They laughed and I failed. I went back to Sloane Street ready to cut my throat.

'You're allowed another go,' my father said. 'Come on, I'll help you. . . .'

I scraped in, rather in the same way that Dennis had scraped into Wellington College. Anthony Quayle was at R.A.D.A. Hermione Hannen, Hamilton Dyce, Dorothy Hyson, Griffith Jones, and so many others who have made a success of their lives in the theatre. The months I spent there were heavenly. I loved everything about the place and worked like mad.

*

'You know, Muggins,' my father said one day on one of our walks through Hyde Park, 'I've been retired from the Chinese jolly Maritime Customs! Actually I've been given the sack; they don't like individualists.'

'You're joking,' I replied in horror. 'What will you do?'

'Well, the time had to come. . . . I've got a good pension—and a lump sum. I shall do something with it and make our fortunes!'

'But China!' I said. 'How can you live here, without the sun, without the Chinese . . . ?'

'Oh, I'll go back!' he laughed. 'I *can't* live without them, or without the sun. I'll get a job that takes me back there.'

In a few months, the job came. He joined a firm called Ardal, and his job, amongst others, was to return to Shanghai and try to sell to the 19th Whampoa Army, saddles and various accoutrements made of the alloy they manufactured.

I didn't want to leave R.A.D.A. and go back, but Wyn and I were considered too young to be left unsupervised in England. . . .

Once more we said goodbye to Dennis, Lozenge and Johnman, who were to be left in England. 'It's a terrible thought,' I said to Wyn, 'but I don't *know* Lozenge and Johnman at *all*! We hardly ever *see* them. . . .'

'It's hell,' she agreed, and then, surprisingly, added: 'It's been hell for years!'

*

We had a house in Kinnear Road in Shanghai. It was a nice, comfortable and attractive house with a garden. By now no house meant anything to me. It was never *our* house, it was always rented, or lent, and in every journey, something was lost: my 'things' were constantly lost, and so to a great degree were little bits of me. I wanted to be an actress and for that I had to be in London. I cared little about the social life of Shanghai; it was, after all, the same as the social life of Hong Kong or Tientsin. I was getting older, thinking more, caring less about parties and dances and cocktail conversation.

Night clubs used to stifle me . . . the dark, and the smell and the nostalgia, especially for a song remembered from London. *Bye Bye Blackbird* was all the rage. I had had a note from Johnman, saying really nothing, as schoolboys do, but it ended with the words 'Bye Bye Blackbird'—it's the only note I still have of his.

Wyn caught typhoid and days and nights full of concern held each other by the tail. In the middle of it all my mother was bitten by an Alsatian and developed erisyphilis; she was desperately ill for weeks. With Wyn in one room with typhoid, and my mother in the other, there was little time for social activities, and I spent a great deal of my time reading.

Back to Confucius again! 'Man can make truth great.' How enthralled I became with the three universal virtues of K'ung Fu-tzu: Wisdom, Love and Courage. And 'the man of perfect virtue' whom he called the 'Gentleman', not in terms of birth but of character. I looked round hopefully for my gentle man, but didn't find him. Instead, I found myself wondering what John Mills was doing, and where he was.

*

About this time, an American company appeared in Shanghai with a production of *The Barretts of Wimpole Street*, and the girl who was to play Henrietta Moulton Barrett became ill. I was asked if I would take her place for a few weeks. I accepted with alacrity, and started rehearsals with them.

The first night opened in a snowstorm: 'The cast played up wonderfully well, and the producer was fearfully bucked' is written in my diary. Also: 'Daddy sent me some gorgeous flowers and a bunch of carrots, with the words: "The first of many." '

8

THE JAPANESE

In February 1932 the Japanese Riots started in Shanghai. The Chinese were powerless militarily, but had a weapon in the boycott which they invoked to the great cost of Japanese trade. Friction became acute. Offices and banks were closed and the Shanghai Volunteer Corps marched about in uniform. Fighting broke out all over the city. I worked in the Shanghai Volunteer Corps office. I thought it splendid. It was war, and like my father, I seemed to thrive on it. I drove a car belonging to a boy friend, Douglas Smart, with a large S.V.C. sign on the front that allowed me into any sector of the city. No one knew that I could never get out of bottom gear, because I had never had a driving lesson in my life.

It was midnight when the Japanese chose to move. Packed standing, rifle in hand, forty to each open truck, the round expressionless faces distinct in the glare of the petroleum flares, they converged slowly by parallel roads from Hongkew upon the Chapeh and Paoshan districts, towards the railway through streets shuttered and empty. Snipers harassed them from windows and roofs. They retaliated with shells, fired point-blank from an armoured train standing up the line. Throughout the night the Japanese attacked, but they were unable to effect any footing in the station that was clearly held by a large force.

The dark lanes and fetid narrow alleyways that ran back from the swarming tenements were choked with a struggling, demented flood of humanity, and war had lost its splendour for me.

With morning came at least the relief of light, but many dead were strewn in the streets and houses far around the station stood deserted. With dawn came the Japanese aircraft.

There is something peculiarly hellish in bombing from the air to which no resistance has been prepared or is possible. . . . There were only five of them. Five hovering birds in perfect formation overhead . . . musing . . . no hurry. . . . Then five tiny arrow heads, quickening through the air, down, down till they disappeared below the roofs. A long time seemed to elapse, the nerves bracing with it; then the roar of explosion, the crash of tiles, glass roofs, iron . . . the thundering roll of sprawling brickwork; then silence, and the slow uprising gasp of dark yellow dust smoke. . . . That first, in retrospect comparatively mild, air-raid on Shanghai impressed and frightened me far more than anything I experienced later in the Blitz on London.

The Argyll and Sutherland Highlanders marched in full dress to C Blockhouse and the many attractive girls in Shanghai deserted the Race Course and got down to work in the Volunteer office. 'The Japanese forces have laid waste to a large portion of the city,' I wrote in my diary, and all day long and all night too, lying in bed, we were aware of sporadic gunfire.

The French missionary priest, Père Jacquinot, who had left one arm in Verdun, and became well known for his Refuge Zone for the care of the homeless from the battle areas round Shanghai, went to the British Headquarters to report that many Chinese women and children and old men were trapped in the ruins between the opposing forces and suffering horrible experiences in Chapei.

A truce was arranged for 12 February. All firing was to cease between the hours of 5 a.m. and noon, in order to evacuate wounded, refugees, old people and children. My father, who spoke the 'Wu' dialect, was put in command of a rescue party, which consisted of Père Jacquinot himself, and a party of nuns from the Sacred Heart Convent.

It was still dark when he came into my room that February morning.

'Come on, Muggins,' he said.

'What's happening?' I asked sleepily.

'I've got eleven nuns and Père Jacquinot . . . and counting me that makes thirteen! I want you. Here's a sheet.'

He held up a white sheet.

'What's that for?' I asked.

'There's a hole in the middle of it and the nuns have put a red cross on the front. Put it over your head and jump in the lorry. We leave in six minutes.'

I brushed my teeth and got the sheet over my head. Fastening it with a belt, I thought for a moment that I looked more like a ghost than a nun.

The quiet, sweet little nuns were all nodding and smiling as we drove through the deserted, silent streets of Shanghai towards Chapeh. As we crossed the bridge at Hongkew, someone handed me a tin hat.

'Not that I trust the little buggers,' said my father, 'so watch out for yourself, and if anybody shoots, get down flat on your face.'

At the railway crossing, we stopped and alighted from the lorry. I found my heart thumping. I had the impression that there were eyes everywhere, and there was certainly a pungent stench.

We walked slowly, zigzagging through the rubble and the dirt. The tranquillity and composure of the nuns was transferred to me, but I kept remembering what my father had said and prayed that if any 'little bugger' aimed at anyone it wouldn't be him.

'Don't look to your right,' he said suddenly in my ear.

I turned my head and looked to my right.

What met my eyes was something that I have never forgotten in the smallest detail, and it is as clear and terrible today as it was in 1932. A line of naked Chinese soldiers were hanging by their necks, their eyes wide and staring; their private parts had been cut off and stuffed into their mouths.

I stared in sick horror. 'Doubler ses torts d'un affront,' muttered Père Jacquinot, crossing himself.

There is a weird, almost unearthly transformation that comes over that place where unexpectedly, irrevocably, the ingenious fury of man against man has been released. To some dull spot, perhaps unmarked till then, where you have walked a hundred times, there comes an air that marks it out from other places, and fills it with something akin to awe. The very sunlight takes on a different colour and appears unreal. Silence there is, but multitudes seem to be listening. Scents, trifling and irrelevant—a whiff of dry dust? burning? or, most unforgettable, the smell of blood?—become like the separate notes in a chord which instantly take their place and will have their part in your memory forever. Life and Death stand there, shoulder to shoulder. Fear walks unseen. God's eye appears to be upon it—everything waits.

Weak-kneed, we trailed through the cobbled streets, through the filth and stench of unburied bodies which had lain there for days . . . of half-burnt children, lying, face down . . . of an old man, leaning out of a gutter against a wall. He was dead, his eyes wide open, a look of bewilderment on his waxen face. Another youth, a rag doll tossed violently into the air, had fallen in a grotesque caricature of supplication.

Chattering, terrified families crowded doorways, an early dawn light coming up behind them, so that they were carved silhouettes, outlined and shadowed.

Père Jacquinot and the nuns were soon at work, trying to hush and comfort them while I staggered behind carrying a large bucket of boiling water, which every now and then slopped over my shoes.

I heard my father explaining above the din to the Chinese that they had seven hours in which to collect themselves and any particularly valued possession, and follow him through the streets to the Sector held by the Argyll and Sutherland Highlanders.

It is a stupefying thought, to be told in the midst of terror to select your most treasured possessions and follow a sort of Pied Piper looking like Wellington in a tin helmet.

In a moment of Life and Death, what is your most treasured possession? I asked myself. No material object can be of any value. It must surely be that at such a moment, beyond the value of Life itself, the only thought can be for the loved ones . . . a mother or father, sister or brother, wife, lover or husband. . . .

I struggled on with the bucket of water, unrolling bandages, my eyes on the quiet, compassionate nuns, my ears listening for the sniper's crack from a roof top, and wondering what my instant reaction would be . . . and who would get it in the heart or the neck. . . . A cold perspiration broke out over me.

The families, chattering, some laughing hysterically, but all contriving to sound like the starlings over Leicester Square, were slowly trying to marshal themselves into some order, while my father's voice rang over their heads.

Their treasured possessions were a weird and bizarre collection. Most of them had their oiled umbrellas, one an old tea pot, but for the most part they carried only children of all sizes. One woman carried four slung in a blanket over her back . . . their little black eyes agape, their black hair on end.

One old man refused to leave at any price. He said he was a hundred years old, and he had no further use for his things or himself. . . .

The crack of the rifle came from over my head. It was very loud, and seemed to be very near. I collapsed as instructed, the remains of the bucket of water soaking me through. My first thought was for my father, and I turned my head to find him. He was still standing, in the middle of a screaming collection of Chinese women, but he had turned instantly, his revolver pointing at the roof above me. He fired. There was silence. For a few seconds he paused, and then he turned back to the group of women, whose chattering began anew as if nothing had happened. I staggered to my feet, but my knees might as well have been made of jelly, for I couldn't walk. Tears of panic streamed down my face while I stood in that eerie street as the sun came up.

Père Jacquinot was attending to someone on the ground; he turned and looked at me and smiled, making a small sign of the cross with his finger. . . .

The long, straggling cavalcade of two thousand Chinese eventually limped through the gates of the Blockhouse. There was a lump in my throat as I saw those blessed, cheerful Highlanders, in their kilts and white spats.

'Over ye come, lassie,' they said and I was standing among them. My father was busily conferring with their Commanding Officer. I saw one or two officers whom I knew—Boy Black, Freddie Graham. They winked, and I laughed. I must have been near to hysteria. My father turned and saw me.

'Oh, by the way,' he said to Boy Black, 'can a despatch rider take my daughter home?'

So I sailed through the streets of Shanghai that morning, up the Nanking Road and the Bubbling Well Road to Kinnear Road on the back of a motor bike, clinging round the comforting waist of a Highlander. . . .

PART TWO
THEATRE

9

BYE BYE BLACKBIRD

A year later, it was time for my mother to return to England, taking Wyn and me with her. Dennis was now sixteen, Lozenge fourteen, and Johnman nearly thirteen and about to take his Entrance Examination into Dartmouth. My father was to remain in Shanghai. He had several hopeful commitments and didn't want to go back to England anyway.

In London, mother rented a basement flat in Oakwood Court. The rooms were large and the furnishings pleasant enough but it was dark and we never saw the sky. Outside it was June and the sun was shining, and both Wyn and I were restless. Wyn decided to take up a course of dressmaking, which has stood her in good stead. The others were at school. I decided to attack the theatre.

I had no idea how to go about it. I tiptoed nervously and shyly into agents' offices. I stalked Shaftesbury Avenue, eyeing the theatres and afraid to approach any managers. I wrote endless letters, enclosing stamped addressed envelopes. I marched into the Playhouse one noon, when Leon M. Lion was rehearsing, and shouted in a loud voice from the circle: 'Mr Lion! What have you done with my stamped addressed envelopes?'

There was a ghastly silence.

'Throw her out,' said a high voice from the shadows.

I scuttled down the stairs and was out before anyone could lay a hand on me, though there was a young man on my heels—who years later was to be the Stage Manager in one of my plays!

On the way home to Oakwood Court, my eye was caught by a small Aberdeen terrier sitting in the window of a pet shop. We stared at each other, both in a kind of private prison. His brown eyes held mine. His shining snout was pathetic and touching.

'How much for that puppy?' I asked tentatively.

'Well, 'e's got a good pedigree, but that one ear won't stand up the way it oughter. Lots of people have turned him down because of that darned ear.'

I looked at the puppy. He wriggled towards me, tail wagging, begging, entreating, his anxious brown eyes on my face, his defective ear hanging incongruously over one eye.

'Looks like an old boot, don't 'e?' the man said affectionately.

I picked the puppy up and he smothered my face with kisses.

'How much?'

'Should be three guineas.'

'I can only afford two pounds.'

He looked at me and the squirming puppy. 'Take him for two pounds then, and I'll throw in a collar and lead.'

'Boots' never ceased to be grateful for that reprieve from prison. His hard little body and stiff black hair tickled me in bed, in the same way that Nosey Parker had comforted me years before. He was always there at the door to welcome me after a hundred unsuccessful expeditions round the agents. I was 'Home' when I had him curled up on my lap.

*

Months passed, and I had achieved nothing. Johnman had passed into Dartmouth with distinction. In his midshipman's uniform with his red hair and his dark blue eyes, he looked like one of Burne-Jones's Botticelli Angels. He had a great wit and sense of humour, and learning to know him after all the years we had been apart was wonderful. We went down to Dartmouth, met and talked to his Head Master, Captain Kempson, who was full of enthusiasm for his future as a sailor.

Wyn was at the 'Paris Academy of Dressmaking' and doing well. Dennis was at Wellington College, a tall, thin, shy boy, with little to say. Lozenge was at a school in Sussex.

I tramped aimlessly and angrily round London trying to get myself into the theatre. My trouble was that I was fundamentally as shy as Dennis, and would stand for hours outside an agent's office pretending something was wrong with my shoe, rather than enter.

An old R.A.D.A. friend suggested to me that I should try for an audition at Daly's Theatre: 'Seymour Hicks is casting a play called *It's You I Want.*'

'How do I get in there?' I asked.

'Spin the stage doorkeeper some yarn or other,' he replied.

I walked up the passageway between Daly's and the Hippodrome. I was dressed in my best, and was very nervous. A group of laughing people passed me.

One of them was John Mills.

I started towards him, my mouth open to say something, and he turned his head as he went by and grinned at me, and then went on with the others, disappearing into the stage door of the Hippodrome. He didn't remember me.

I walked back to the corner of Leicester Square for the hundredth time. It was a brisk October day and the warm sun dappled the pavements. I went into the chemist's. People were buying sticks of '5' and '9' and I knew they belonged to a theatre somewhere. I bought the same. It was stupid really, as I had no need of it, but I thought it made me look important and that it might bring me luck, give me courage.

I walked steadily back to the stage door of Daly's, and went in. The doorkeeper eyed me suspiciously over his spectacles.

I coughed slightly to give myself time:

'Can I see Mr Hicks?' I asked.

'Got an appointment?'

'Yes,' I lied unhappily. 'He told me last night at a party to be sure and—'

'He's on the stage now. Can't be disturbed. Better wait.'

I waited five hours. People came and went: 'Hullo, Ted.' 'Any mail, Ted?' A red-haired girl gave me a nasty, scrutineering look as she swept through: 'I'm late, Ted!'

On and on I sat. Ted went to his lunch and came back.

'Smoke?' He offered me his pack.

I shook my head. I didn't smoke; my father wouldn't let me, I told him.

Ted looked at his watch and sent a boy for two cups of tea. . . . He'd been in the theatre forty years, he said, born in The Elephant. Where was I born?

'Near the Elephant,' I said, hoping to please.

The October gloom settled heavily in the courtyard outside. Footsteps passed again and again. A young man came through the swing door. He was tall and had red hair, too.

'Thank God *that's* over, Ted,' he said, and swept out.

'That's Ronnie Waters,' Ted said. 'He's a character! Must mean rehearsal is over.'

I rose to my feet eagerly, stiff in the joints. . . .

Three more people came through the door. 'Finished?' asked Ted.

'Yes,' said one of them. 'The old man's going through the front of the house'—and they swung out.

Ted looked startled.

'Look,' he said. 'He's going through the front of the house . . . the only way to get him now is to meet him out front—hurry!'

I fled down the alleyway and arrived just as the great man was getting into a taxi.

'Garrick Club,' he said.

Before he had time to close the taxi door I was in it with him. He looked astonished but faintly amused.

'Who the hell are you?' he asked.

I flung myself on the floor clutching him by the knees, and proceeded to go through a whole speech from *The Barretts of Wimpole Street*, beginning: 'Papa, papa, I'm not a bad girl. Remember you and Mama. . . .'

He pulled me off the ground and pushed me onto the seat.

'What *are* you doing?' he laughed.

'An audition,' I spluttered. 'I've waited five hours to see you, and see you I will . . . and have,' I finished lamely.

'What have you done?' he asked.

'I've been through R.A.D.A.—and I did *The Barretts of Wimpole Street* with a first class American company all over the Far East,' I lied, looking him straight in the eye.

We had arrived at the Garrick Club. He paid the fare and the taxi drove off. My skirt was twisted and so were my stockings.

'I *could* go and get any old job,' I said. 'But I want to work for you.'

'Why?'

'Because you're the greatest, and I want to learn from the greatest.'

He smiled down at me and put his hand on my head.

'I like guts,' he said. 'Come to Golders Green Theatre tomorrow morning at ten. We're going on tour with *It's You I Want*.'

'Does that mean . . . that . . . ,' I asked tremulously.

'Certainly it does,' he said, and skipped up the steps into the Garrick Club.

I leaned against the walls of that dear old place, and the tears of exhaustion gushed from my eyes.

The next morning I was at Golders Green Theatre before even the stage doorkeeper had arrived. He eyed me with some suspicion as he unlocked the door.

'Mr Hicks said I should be early,' I explained.

'Hmmm,' he replied. 'Better go and get a cup of coffee. You've got an hour before anyone will arrive.'

I stared at the pictures in the front of the house: 'Seymour Hicks, Jean Colin, Viola Tree—in *It's You I Want*.'

A sense of familiarity flared up inside me! I was to be part of it all. He had said so. . . .

I returned to the stage door, charming the hell out of the stage doorkeeper with my smiles. He indicated a small dark attractive woman: 'This is Mr Hicks's secretary, Miss Gentry.'

'Mr Hicks said I was to come down here this morning.'

'Yes, he told me,' she answered. 'Go onto the stage, he'll be here soon.'

Without demeaning myself by asking anyone the way, I finally found it, after first being in the boiler room, the orchestra pit, and the men's lavatory. I stood, flattened out against the dock doors, very nervous, and very small, listening and watching as people came and went.

Suddenly he was there. 'Come over here,' he said.

I walked towards him, still smiling.

'What's your name?' he asked.

'Mary Hayley Bell,' I replied faintly.

'Too long, isn't it?' he said with a laugh. 'You'll have to be Hayley Bell.'

I laughed nervously in return.

He took me by the elbow and led me onto the stage where a group of people were standing.

'Good morning, Mr Hicks,' they said in chorus.

'This is little Bell. She is going to be Jean's understudy.'

Jean Colin approached holding out her hand.

'Hullo,' she said, and gave me a warm, welcoming smile.

'Good morning, Miss Colin,' I replied in a strangled voice.

I took the script home. I sat up all night and by the morning I was pretty well word perfect. Sweet as Jean Colin had been to me, I prayed and hoped that a thunderbolt would hit her, or that she would lose her voice or twist an ankle—but not *too* badly, I added anxiously—so that I could go on in her place. At every performance I watched her like a lynx; every move, every turn of her head, every expression was carefully recorded. I was certain that at any moment she was going to be 'Off' and that I would go on for her, and instantly be a great star!

Mr Hicks watched an understudy rehearsal. 'Well done, little Bell,' he said and walked off. I swallowed heavily.

We moved to the King's, Hammersmith, to Wimbledon. . . .

When I wasn't watching Miss Colin, I was sitting on the top of the theatre in an enormous dressing-room designed for thirty chorus girls. It was cold and dirty, and empty except for the other understudy, Sonia Somers, the girl with red hair. We became great friends, and we both luxuriated on the princely sum of four pounds a week.

Seymour Hicks seemed to have forgotten me, for he rarely addressed me, but my diary notes that he was often 'in the hell of a stew about something or other'. But one day he stopped me at the stage door. 'Why are you walking in such a funny way?' he asked.

'I've got a pain in my back,' I told him.

'Come up to my room,' he said.

I limped into his dressing-room, which by comparison with mine was Buckingham Palace. Warm, colourful, full of flowers and pictures.

'Get the doctor, Richard,' he said to his dresser.

'Doctor?' I bleated.

He sat me down and gave me a glass of Champagne.

'I'm doing *Scrooge* at the Victoria Palace,' he said. 'You can play Tiny Tim.'

'What have I got to say?' I asked.

'One line . . . "God help us every one",' he replied abstractedly, peering at his face in the mirror. He turned. 'But you'll have crutches, and you can do a hell of a lot with one line and crutches if you're canny.'

The doctor said I had lumbago and gave me an injection. . . .

*

We started a tour at Manchester, the Prince's Theatre. Sonia and I had digs in Ackers Street.

'Is this where we're living?' I asked.

'Looks worse than it is,' said Sonia cheerfully. 'It's all right when you're inside—and there's a fire in the sitting-room.'

We staggered in with our suitcases. It was warm, but there was a smell of steam laundry and onions. Mrs Lait was a small, cheerful woman with half her hair hanging down her back.

'Here's your room, then,' she said, and lit a match and jerked the gas jet over the bed.

The warm glow cheered the look of the room and ran along the brass rails of the bedstead. I looked around. It was rather exciting. I'd never been in digs! I wasn't particularly pleased to be sharing the brass bedstead with Sonia but it was a first experience, and perhaps it wouldn't be so bad when I was used to it. There was an illuminated scroll over the bed which read 'It's later than you think', and a ghastly painting of violets over the cracked mirror on the dressing-table.

Before we went down to tea, we pushed open the bathroom door for a wash. We didn't bother to light the gas jet, and left the door open. Sonia spat into the water and crossed it.

'Mustn't wash in the same basin without doing that,' she said. I did the same: I didn't want to seem too unsophisticated.

There was a movement behind us. We turned to look. An Indian gentleman was lying in the bath immersed in water.

'Christ!' said Sonia.

'It's no matter to me,' he said in the familiar Indian sing-song voice.

We ran for the stairs.

'It would have been no matter to him if either of us had been sitting on the bog,' she said angrily.

The sitting-room we had engaged was full of bric-à-brac—stuffed birds filled a whole table and religious pictures cluttered the walls, but the tablecloth was clean and tea consisted of baked beans and sausages.

'Not bad,' I said amiably.

'One huge fart,' Sonia replied. 'I'll have to dye my hair tomorrow—what a blinking bore.'

'Dye it?' I asked innocently.

'Mmmm, the roots are beginning to show.'

'Isn't your hair red?' I asked.

'Brown,' she replied. 'But I give it the old kick-up with henna now and again. You're lucky.'

'Why bother?' I asked, stuffing away the baked beans.

'Reckon you're likely to get the odd job if you've got red hair. They seem to notice you.'

I thought Manchester a dreadful city. Dark, wet, and most nights fog filled the theatre. The dressing-room I shared with Sonia was big and designed for even more chorus girls than the one in London and the mirrors were covered with lipstick messages, mostly accompanied by suggestions which I knew must be rude but in most cases didn't begin to understand.

One night when the fog was at its worst, and the only light seemed to come from the flashes on the trams which squealed down the greasy streets, Sonia bought a bottle of Emu wine to cheer up our baked beans. It was the first time that I had ever been completely intoxicated, the first time I had ever reeled up what appeared to be a moving staircase, or lain upon a bed watching the ceiling go round and round and round, while the scroll above us told me that it was later than I thought in triplicate and blurred quadruplicate.

We went on to Birmingham, to Glasgow, to Edinburgh. Wherever we went we shared a double bed. Sometimes hard, sometimes suffocating in its deep softness.

At Leeds we stayed in Chapel Street. It overlooked a dismally wet cemetery. The skyline was shrouded in smog, and the fire in the sitting-room smoked continuously. We had to share this grey, sooty room with a member of the Debroy Somers Band, and on the second day he observed in his high thin Cockney voice that we were both scratching a lot.

'Bedbugs, I reckon,' he said.

'Could be,' Sonia replied in a matter-of-fact voice. 'Though I don't see any.'

'Only one way to catch the bastards,' he said. 'Cake of soft soap . . . you can't never catch a bedbug no other way . . . *and* you got to 'ave patience.'

The three of us armed ourselves with cakes of soap and stripped the bed. Suddenly our companion made a dive at the centre of it, and jubilantly holding up his cake of soap said: 'See! What did I tell you! Bedbug!'

A small round black bug was encased in his cake of soap.

'And where there's one there's two . . . and where there's two there's bloody 'undreds!'

An hour later, with three pieces of Lux toilet soap covered in bedbugs, we packed our cases and walked haughtily and noisily down the dark stairway.

The landlady came out of her room and stood at the foot of the stairs, a cigarette hanging out of the corner of her mouth.

'Where you think you're going to, then?' she asked in a nasal voice.

'We're going to the police station to inform the officer that your beds are full of bugs,' Sonia told her. 'And we have three cakes of soap to prove it.'

'What about my bill, then?' the woman asked, vainly trying to bar our way.

'You know where you can put your bill—and you can stuff the cakes of soap in with it,' shouted Sonia, and we marched to the door.

'You each owe me twenty-five bloody shillings for the week,' the woman whined.

Sonia paused on the doorstep and turned.

'One more bloody word from you and we'll go up and set fire to every goddam mattress in your goddam house, so shut up!'

We returned to London at the end of the week. The train, I remember, was held up a considerable length of time owing to the fact that Seymour Hicks's case of Champagne had not been delivered and he stood with one foot on the platform and the other on the train until it arrived.

He crowded us all into the same compartment, and from nine in the morning, for a good five hours, we drank Champagne, played poker, and listened to endless stories about the theatre.

I staggered home. My mother opened the door.

'You smell like a brewery,' she said distastefully.

'I've been in a brewery for five hours,' I said, and went straight upstairs where I slept at last and alone in my own bed, for twenty-four hours.

*

At Christmas 1933 Seymour played Scrooge and I played Tiny Tim. It was one of the acts at the Victoria Palace, where Florrie Ford was the star of the show. Her rich, ripe, loving voice filled and thrilled the theatre, and night after night I could hear the call boy banging on her door, 'You were the best, Miss Ford.' Lily Morris was another singer, and before I had been a week in the theatre, I had told Seymour that I wanted to stick to music hall. 'You could cut off your hair and do a choir boy act,' he laughed.

In the New Year, we opened at Daly's with *Vintage Wine*. 'I'm so elated,' I wrote to my father. 'There's Seymour, Julia Neilson, A. Bromley Davenport, Clare Luce, Gemma Fagan, my old nutty friend Ronnie Waters—and Sonia and I are the two maids. . . .'

We had only been playing a few weeks when one night, in taking my exit through a door, and supposed to wink at Seymour to give the feed to his laugh, I found I couldn't move the right side of my face.

He stormed after me into the Green Room.

'You fool of a little Bell, you ruined my laugh! Instead of winking you stared. What the hell are you doing?'

'My face won't work, Seymour,' I told him. 'It won't move and it's all numb.'

'Try it now.'

I tried.

'Take her to Charing Cross Hospital after the show,' he told the stage manager, and we went.

The House Surgeon, Jimmy Whaley, had taken out my tonsils a year before. He looked at my face and laughed. 'I don't want to make a pun,' he said, 'but you've got something called Bell's Palsy!' I didn't think it funny, particularly as the right side of my face was paralysed for two months, and I was out of the show. During those two months Seymour paid me my salary each week although I never went to the theatre.

At last I could stand it no more, and one night I returned to Daly's an hour before the curtain went up.

'I'm back,' I told Seymour.

'You look very thin,' was all he said.

I dressed with Sonia in our vast dressing-room, muttering my remarkable first line: 'Ah! Signor Popinot, splashing in the fountain.' They were difficult words to say even without half one's face paralysed. What came out on the stage was a frothy, sibilant hiss, like a goose in pursuit, a high snuffling whistle, for having not raised my voice at all for two months, and having the line under some control in a quiet register, the moment I tried to project the line it became: 'Ah! phinophopino phaphin inaphounin.'

Sonia's eyes were enormous, as she turned her rigid head upstage.

Somebody laughed, out there in the auditorium, then another and another and another, until there was a great roar of laughter, egged on further by my open-mouthed blank stare.

I was destroyed. My paralysed legs full of sawdust, I could hear the angry mutterings in the wings and knew full well whose they were. 'Come *off*, you bloody little fool!'

Somehow I got off, up a rickety wooden bridge. He was waiting for me at the top, but before he could speak, I burst into tears.

'I can't go on again, ever!' I squawked.

For a moment he looked at me without speaking, then raising his right hand he hit me hard across the side of the face, and I reeled against the scenery.

'That'll help, you'll find,' he said, and pranced on to the stage, full of what he called his '*joie de vivre*', as if nothing had happened.

During the play, his dresser Richard came up to our room: ' 'ere, Miss Bell, 'is Nibs wants you to go to supper.'

'Good-oh!' shouted Sonia.

'Rules, after the show. Wait for him at the stage door. . . .'

'I've only got a skirt and sweater!' I said to Sonia in a panic.

'You can have my orange dress if you like, but keep sitting, it's got iron mould on the backside! And keep your hand on your halfpenny.'

I trotted down the alleyway beside him to the waiting taxi. He opened the door and stood back with a bow.

'This time it's an invitation.'

I had never been into Rules before and was too entranced by the red plush and gilt to remember that I was attired in a flaming orange dress with iron mould on the seat.

'How's the face?' he asked.

I had been so used to its numbness that I hadn't thought much more of it. I wriggled it about.

'Better, I think!' I said—and it was!

It was an evening remembered in detail.

Seymour never spoke particularly softly; he was always in a hurry, always alight with enthusiasm, full of plans for tomorrow, and loved nothing more than talking about the theatre.

'Little Bell. . . .' He dropped his voice slightly, thank heaven. 'I hope you are not looking for Glamour on the Stage.'

'No—' I began.

'Clamour yes, but the glamour is like Utopia and has to be discovered! Let me give you some advice . . .' and he started pouring Champagne into huge goblets. I hoped I wouldn't get too gay, say the wrong thing, or fall over my feet and show the iron mould. He put out his hand and covered mine, raising his glass. 'Here's to you, little Bell. Whatever you do, wherever you go, keep your excitement about life—and don't think it makes you a genius to forget to wash your neck.'

I could feel it going crimson against the orange. He threw back his head and laughed loudly. Catching sight of someone across the room he waved his hand. 'That's old Martin Harvey . . . go and see him in *The Bells*. And talking of old actors, don't get trapped into that belief that they're too old fashioned to bother about. Their methods are well worth studying. Use 'em like a lemon, darling, but squeeze 'em before casting them aside.

'I'll give you three axioms of mine to remember. Never forget that an audience is your enemy, and never mentally take your eye off them. If you have personality, and heaven help you if you haven't, you can always check 'em with a look or gesture. Finally let me assure you that repose is even more difficult than movement, for to listen well is to act very well indeed!'

Between the Champagne and his words, I was a small, seething anthill of excitement. I wished suddenly that my father were sitting beside us listening. I felt too small, too inadequate to interject the questions I wanted to.

'Think before you speak. . . . The value of pausing is priceless . . . you're still at the stage where you rush at your words because you're nervous. All the great actors have been heralded for their use of silence; nothing can stir an audience to its depths like pain, passion or terror which rises in silence from the heart of a great artist—and by the way, little Bell, while I was giving my all the other night I was furious to find you, Sonia and Stella playing the fool. I can tell you there's nothing an audience detests more than a private joke. . . .'

He leaned back and regarded me from the red plush, his face in the shadow. 'As a matter of fact, when all's said and done there's no such thing as good or bad art, there's only art. Charm is one of the greatest assets to possess, believe me, for it covers a multitude of sins. Go and see Noël Coward, John Gielgud, Leslie Banks: watch Laurence Olivier. Then there are the ladies—like that one over there.'

I turned my head and saw Jean Forbes Robertson.

He was still rolling out the names, no longer talking to me alone, but to the restaurant at large: 'Yvonne Arnaud, Ursula Jeans—she's coming into the play soon—Mary Jerrold, Gladys Cooper, Fay Compton. I've always been in love with Fay Compton. I wish you could have seen Mrs Kendal; she was the greatest of them all. She said to me once when I was a boy, "Never pause unless you have to, Seymour, but if you feel you must, and you are able to, pause as long as you like".'

As we walked along behind the stage door of the Vaudeville, he said suddenly: 'I think we'll have to change your name.'

'Oh!' I was startled. 'I'd rather not if you don't mind. Isn't Hayley Bell all right?' He twirled his stick as he walked: 'Mmmm . . . what about Gloria Trevelyan?'

I stopped and stared at him in disgust. He burst into gales of laughter.

*

Vintage Wine was doing well. Seymour swayed volcanically between good humour and bad temper. I was being paid five pounds a week now and very glad to get it, for things were not going well at home. My father was finding it hard to keep his head above water, as he was working on commission for what he sold to the Chinese Army, and money came through only erratically. In spite of all this his letters were full of what he hoped to do in the future.

To economize, I ate at home as little as possible. Sonia and I used to eat sausages at a little café called Billy's in St Martin's Court. One day, we sat at the next table to John Mills. He was with Evelyn Laye and Ernest Verebes.

'I know him,' I said behind my coffee cup.

'He's taking over from Ernest Verebes in *Give Me a Ring*,' Sonia said.

They seemed to be having a great deal to laugh about.

'He's nice looking, isn't he?' she said appreciatively.

I looked across at him. Memories of Tientsin floated in front of me. The dust, the heat, the Chinese. I felt intolerably sad.

'Why don't you speak to him?' she asked.

'He wouldn't remember me,' I replied. 'I just threw tennis balls for him in China.'

I walked all the way home through Regent's Park. It was one of those melancholy April days. The sun had brought out the forsythia and the almond blossom, and then abandoned them. There was an air of gloom over everything.

Down Kensington High Street, up Holland Road and back to Oakwood Court. I peered through the railings as I went, hoping that if some of the basement-dwellers looked up, for once they would see a face instead of just legs. The light was on, as usual, and Wyn and my mother were packing.

'It's Johnman,' my mother said. 'He's got measles and a double mastoid. He's been sent to the Naval Hospital in Plymouth.'

The usual sick feeling of nerves was beginning to run through my body.

'Is it serious?'

'Yes. Wyn is coming with me, Dennis is on the way and Liz is coming up from school. I think you should ask Seymour to let you off after tonight's performance.'

I took the night train to Plymouth, sitting squashed between two jolly sailors who must have had a private joke of their own, they laughed so much.

'So what are you goin' to Plymouth for?' one asked.

'My brother is very ill at the Naval Hospital. He's a cadet at Dartmouth,' I replied, trying to put them off.

Their grins faded. 'That's bad, that is. What's the matter with him?'

'He has a double mastoid and they might be going to operate.'

'Poor kid,' the elder of the two said and offered me a cigarette.

' 'ope 'e's goin' to be all right,' said the other. 'We need good officers.'

The train thundered on through the night and I sat biting my nails.

It was raining hard when I alighted from the train. The platform was long and draughty. I went through the barrier and stood uncertainly outside the station, wondering if I could afford a taxi. My two sailors came up and stood beside me.

'Where to, girl?'

'The Royal Hotel, but—'

' 'op in this taxi,' they said, and I was whirled off through Plymouth. One of them opened the door of the cab. ' 'ere you are, then. Good luck to you, and your brother.'

I watched the taxi drive off. I hadn't even said thank you.

There was a red light beside my mother's bed. She was wide awake.

'Glad you got here, darling,' she said.

'How is he? How is Johnman?'

'The news isn't good, Baba. They operated today for a brain abscess. They won't say much—but I'm not very happy.'

I lay down on the couch in the corner of the room, conscious all night of the noise of the trams. Please God, I prayed, make him all right! I had seen so little of Johnman since Macao.

The shrill ringing of the telephone brought me to my feet.

'Mrs Hayley Bell?' I handed the phone to my mother.

We watched her, wide-eyed, as she talked to the hospital, and when she slowly put down the phone, we asked nothing.

'It wasn't a success,' she said quietly. 'They think he has meningitis.'

*

The smell of ether pervaded our nostrils, and the shiny hospital corridors snapped at our heels as we walked towards his room.

Johnman lay against the pillows, his bandaged head and his face as white as they were. A waxen flower, a passion flower, with the same purple veins under his eyes. A nurse sat at his side.

'Johnman?' my mother said. There was a note of gaiety in her voice, as though she were talking quietly to a child whose dreams she didn't want to disturb, a child she didn't want to frighten.

The nurse bent over the bed, touching his forehead with her long fingers. 'Mummy's here, Johnnie,' she said softly.

He opened his eyes, darkly blue against the whiteness of the bandages and the pillows, and looked up at my mother. A tiny smile lifted the corners of his lips as he put out his hand and she shook it. A mist of sudden tears blurred him and the room, and I could see nothing.

'We're all here, Johnman—Baba, Bebe, Beak, Beattie.' I noticed she used the childhood names. She leaned over him, smiling, as she must have done a thousand times at bedtime.

Christ, she's brave, I thought.

'Daddy?' The voice was a whisper.

'Daddy will be here soon, and soon, so soon, you will be home again with us all, and have a lovely holiday. We'll go to the sea . . . you'd love that, wouldn't you? The sea. Cornwall perhaps. . . .'

He sighed deeply, a sigh of content at the thought of the sea that he loved so much, then the dark blue eyes closed, black lashes caressing the waxen face. My mother's smile faded as she stood over him. The light went out of her face, and left it grey. The very skin tightened over the bones of her cheeks and jaw, her eyes hardened into grey marbles, and suddenly she knelt beside the bed, her head on Johnman's hand.

Wyn and I clutched each other in terror. . . .

'No!' Wyn said, as if in answer to a question. 'No!'

I took a step forward. There was so much I had wanted to say to Johnman. He seemed to me to be smiling, his eyes half open, as though he were thinking of something lovely.

All that day it rained, splashing against the road and into our faces wherever we went. . . .

In the late afternoon we went to the mortuary. I didn't want to go. I dreaded it, but Wyn said I had to. 'And stop wringing your hands, it upsets Mummy,' she said.

Johnman lay on a bank of primroses. Someone, perhaps many people, must have spent hours arranging them. On his waxen face was a look almost of delight at the sight of so many. His hands were crossed on his uniformed chest, his eyes were closed and the pleasure on his face was as though he was listening to a wonderful piece of music. A ray of the last moment of sunlight, streaming through a small window, lay across his bright hair.

We had to endure as best we could without father, all the trappings of a Naval funeral. The gun carriage, the escort, with lowered heads and rifles reversed . . . the slow march from the hospital to the Naval Cemetery to the song of the muffled drums. Whispered words of sorrow no longer meant anything, and we turned away from them, refusing to look at the small flag-draped coffin.

The air was cold and fresh for April, but the wind had dropped and wreaths of smoke lay over the grey city. The long, straight, endless road glistened silvery wet in the rain, and here and there large brown puddles collected.

Outside a public house, children were playing hop-scotch. They paused as the cortège went past, staring dispassionately at the slow-marching sailors, while the muffled drums punctuated the sobbing march. . . .

'We seem to give him back to Thee Dear God who gavest him to us. Yet as Thou didst not lose him, so we have not lost him by his return. . . .'

Don't look at it . . . don't look at anything . . . hum another tune under your breath, whistle *Bye Bye Blackbird* . . . pinch your bottom until it hurts . . . till you're only aware of the pain of the pinching . . . close your brain to everything . . . don't let anything in. Close your eyes so that you can see nothing, nothing of the solemn escort in wet macintoshes, heads bent in sorrow, rifles reversed. Shut out, oh shut out your father's voice in the galleries of memory saying, 'There is no death. There is only an overcoat to be laid in the ground and remembered. . . .' Lift your eyes to the hills across the Sound . . . don't, oh *don't* look at *that*! . . .

Suddenly, fight as one would, a familiar sound cleft my brain. I hadn't heard it since we were children together in Macao . . . across the Bay, night after night, our childish lullaby. 'The most beautiful sound in the world,' I could hear myself saying with great authority.

Who would have dreamed, in those far off days, that we should stand limply in these black vestments on a lonely hill over Plymouth Sound, to hear it played so poignantly by a Naval bugler—for our fourteen-year-old brother Johnman. The Last Post, with its final questioning notes.

*

20 April 1934
Johnman
aged 14

I never see a primrose now but I
Am back again, back in a churchyard where
The mist lies low on the hill, and the high
Haunting strains of the 'March' comes faintly o'er
A field of primroses, infinitely
Sad, like that lost voice I can hear no more.
Round the surrounding hills the mist still clings,
Making them look like green blue islets in
A grey sad sea; while white seagulls wings
Flutter down the valley, gaily to the
Sea, where watchful giants, the battleships, keep
Guard o'er that green place upon the misty lea.
Down the white path, the dripping cyprus trees
Still bow their heads in sorrow and despair
When the Last Post comes stealing down the breeze;
But in the spring, new primroses will grow
Again, and seagulls in their flight down the Vale,
Will hear his laughter, where the four winds blow.

*

My father was in the Red Sea when he received the news:

'I have been very near to you in these two days of unspeakable grief for my darling little son. Yesterday the Captain sent for me and I knew what such a summons must mean. The wireless brief and official was "Regret Cadet Hayley Bell died Naval Hospital Plymouth today. Commander-in-Chief Plymouth". We were passing through the Suez Canal. . . . I have kept to my cabin alone, I could not bear to think my thoughts and attention could be anywhere when you were laying the little fellow to his rest. Were you and Winifred there? I think so. Busy though I know you must be with your world by now, I hope Wyn was with Mummy when it came. As I go through the Indian Ocean, I shall picture Mummy, you two and Dennis all together this time at the flat. Our Johnman wouldn't wish that you should be sad about him and from now on this must be only from the inner heart and sometimes. You have been through a lot, dear Baba, as each thing passes, one feels one can never be quite the same again. In all my life too I have never known such sorrow as now. You children are the world and all to Mummy and me. All that we think and do is for our happiness together as a family first and each one of your futures after that. Everything seemed to point to a successful career for Johnman. How can such awful mistakes be. Is there anything more we could have done? I feel so beastly lonely. Keep together and look after each other. . . .'

The luminous flying fish would be scurrying away from the sharp-pointed bows of the ship, and for a moment he would feel guilty; just for a moment he would feel utterly alone as the yellow moon stood staring at him, accusing him before he turned away and walked the short distance to his cabin. Did he glance up at the masthead lights furrowing through the stars . . . and sleep, pushing away, as usual, responsibility?

10

HELL'S BELLS

Towards the end of 1934 *Vintage Wine* finished at Daly's, and I was plunged into the pool of out-of-work actresses. I hung about agents' offices, fought my way into auditions, and finally landed quite a good part in a play called *Summer's Lease* at the Embassy Theatre, Swiss Cottage, with Dorice Fordred, Wyndham Goldie, John Hickson, Peter Ashmore and Patrick Barr. John Fernald directed it, and for the first time I had several good scenes, and even a notice in the *Evening News*. After a few weeks it transferred to the Vaudeville Theatre in the Strand, and we used to save up so that we could have a good blow-out once a week at Rules, which was opposite the stage door in Maiden Lane.

It was here one night that I noticed a particularly beautiful girl dining in a corner.

'I know that girl,' I said to Peter Ashmore.

'It's Elspeth March,' he said.

'Elspeth March? . . . That's Elpie Mackenzie from Sherborne School for naughty girls,' I replied, and tore across the room, flinging my arms round her neck. She was with Clem McCallion and they were working together at the Birmingham Repertory Theatre. Her laugh rang round the restaurant, and I was delighted to find her again, for there was little laughter at home. The shock and aftermath of Johnman's death had not subsided. My mother went her way, a sad, unsinging ghost, and the grey eyes that had turned to marble on that awful day were nearly always full of tears.

From the Vaudeville I went to understudy Diana Churchill in Michael Egan's *The Dominant Sex* with Richard Bird at Daly's Theatre.

Diana was a wonderful person to work with, always ready to help and recommend young actresses, and I was one of the many who owed much to her.

I wrote endless letters beseeching my father to return home, but he seemed to have little money and was always mixed up in some minor skirmish on one frontier or another.

I found myself going home less and less. On the days when I had no matinee, I spent my time in the galleries of other theatres. I have the programmes still. The Duchess was playing *Night Must Fall*: I was fascinated by Emlyn Williams and went again and again to the gallery. *The Mask of Virtue*, with the illuminatingly beautiful Vivien Leigh; *The Old Ladies*, with Edith Evans, Jean Cadell, Mary Jerrold. *Viceroy Sarah*. Owen Nares in *Lovers' Leap*: Van Druten's *Flowers of the Forest*: Robert Douglas in *Men in White*. *The Maitlands*, by Ronald Mackenzie, with John Gielgud, Stephen Haggard, Jack Hawkins and Catherine Lacey. *Reunion in Vienna*. *Sixteen*, with Alexis France, whom time and again I had tried to understudy. *Till the Day I Die*, by Clifford Odets, with Kazan. Given the chance, I thought, given the chance! I'd work till I dropped. A few months later came a letter from my father written at five in the morning when he couldn't sleep.

'I am very low. Everything seems hopeless. Tomorrow may bring light, there's always hope. I've no more pay to come. The job with the ruddy Chinese Army is over, and never was much. You all say come Home, but I ain't got the passage money! Oh, for another tiny inoffensive war somewhere! I have £500 overdraft in the bank . . . not a sou can I get for that £1,200 "worth" of Ardal they are holding against it. . . . Big hopes if I can sell the car, I could get back on that if the Bank will let me go! The world seems to be strewn with our "*things*" that I can't afford to own, store or even send home. Things one loves. Whatever happens the small white box of my best "things" will never be left behind. If I can only get back to you all, I'll sit in any old gutter and write!'

Three months later, late at night, the white box under his arm, bearded and thin, with no luggage, he opened the door and sat down among us.

'I've sold everything, and got here by the skin of my teeth. In fact I walked from the station!'

'What's in the white box?' I asked anxiously.

'Books,' he said with a guilty grin. 'Everything will be all right . . . we still have a few pennies here, and my dear old friend Johnnie Dodge is going to lend us his house in Connaught Square till I can get on my feet.'

'But, Hayley, there's no furniture in it!' my mother said.

'We have one or two little bits . . . we can buy necessaries like beds and blankets. . . .'

My diary records these words.

'Hell's Bells! . . . no money, an empty house, with one chair, a bath and lavatory which are mercifully stuck to the wall. A bed each, some knives and forks, and the romantic possibility of eating, sitting on newspapers upon the hard uncarpeted floor. Poor old Daddy who deserves so much! and though his sense of humour is as good as ever, their agony of mind must be awful.'

The picture that will remain with me always, is the sight of him pushing a barrow across Hyde Park with our remaining belongings. Incongruously, a top hat and a chamber pot registered strongly, and when we met him again at Connaught Square, the chamber pot contained a bunch of anemones.

The night before we left, on my return from the theatre, Boots, with his usual rush of welcome, was run over in front of my eyes by a taxi which turned the corner too fast.

We rushed him to a vet, but he had a fractured pelvis and ruptured bladder. On 16 February Boots, a small Aberdeen terrier of no real importance, except to me, died.

'Today, Boots died. It is also Johnman's birthday. He is dead too. One must not be sentimental, like old ladies are about their cats and dogs, but he was my best friend since that dear old black and white Rat. I shall always expect to find him on the rug. See his lovely old brown eyes, bark of greeting, black furry body in bed after a bad day with the agents. None of it will ever happen again. I hope he wasn't afraid. I hope people dying aren't afraid. I've seen a few dead things now. They don't seem to be anything. My faith is beginning to doubt. The wind howls mournfully. . . . Brownie? Johnman? Little coats laid away. I wish I was sure of anything.'

I stood about wringing my hands.

'For God's sake, Muggins!' said father.

'It's not the house, or even what you and Mummy must be going through, or that it's cold, or that we're often hungry. It's none of that. All *that* is rather exciting to me, and if we're short of food I'll steal it. It's none of this, don't you see. It's Boots. Did he wake up through the morphia and think I'd deserted him?'

'For God Almighty's sake don't start being neurotic about a *dog*!'

I faced him as I had done before.

'He was my friend. My *thing*! *You've* destroyed *all* our things! . . . None of us has *anything*! It was all right for you and your bloody wars, and Adventures all over the bloody globe. We have *nothing*! And if I weep inside for the death of a dog you should bloody well be ashamed. That's all you've given me, bar some ribald education which I never asked for. You've indulged yourself in Adventures, and you'll go on indulging yourself. Look at us! Look at Den! Where's your son at this moment? Standing guard on some sodding barrack gate in *your* Regiment. But not with a commission! Oh no! As a potential Lance Corporal! And coming from a public school possibly even being hated by the men he has to live with!'

His hands kept wiping the small table, as though there were hundreds of crumbs.

'Cruel words, Muggins. . . .'

'Something always triggers things off. I'm sorry for you. I think fate has treated you harshly but there must be some blame at your feet. Ever since Macao, what has life been? Here, there and everywhere.'

'Our life made it that way—'

He was fiddling for his glasses.

I thought of him in Canton. Could see the shadowy figures, the sticks that hit him on the head, could see him fall to the ground, could see him fighting for his sight and never somehow regaining it.

I put out my hand to him.

'I'm sorry. Forgive me for hitting you when you're down.'

'I'm never down, Muggins. Any day now, things will change. I may sell a story.'

'Yes. Any day now.'

'You must remember, if you will, that times have changed. I wasn't all that well educated. My life was China. I worked hard at the languages. The Customs didn't want me any more. I was never any good about money. I made a mess of my investments. I was taken for a ride. I'm a total failure, but I'm not sorry for you who are young. I'm sorry only for Mummy. But I have a Micawberesque hope that something will turn up along the road.'

Next day he had a haemorrhage, caused by a stomach ulcer. 'He'll be all right,' said mother. 'He'll always be all right.'

*

I was now playing in *Summer's Lease*, working for the Repertory Players in *Nights in Vienna* with Max Adrian on Sunday nights, *and* making the film of *Vintage Wine* at Twickenham (for three pounds a day!) I was rich, and able to buy Dennis a mac.

Jimmy Whaley wrote to my father:

'She is overstrung. Don't underrate the death of her dog, or her brother, or the situation as it is now. She is well under weight—six stone. She should have a holiday, and stop wringing her hands.'

'Shades of Auntie Alice,' said my mother.

My father had sat up days and nights writing a story, *Captain Andrade*, for Blackwood's Magazine. They accepted it, and paid him moderately well. He bought a carpet and endless flowers, daffodils and hyacinths.

'Victory!' he shouted. 'Where that came from will come more! It just means work and work never hurt me. I could sit up all night forever if someone wanted me to.'

He did.

Getting off the bus at the top of Edgware Road, Jimmy Whaley and I would walk across Connaught Square. All the other houses in the Square had neat curtains but ours was different. Ours was curtainless, and where one would expect to see an elegant drawing-room one saw only the gaunt figure of a man sitting on a packing case, with another packing case before him as a desk, and on this packing case a very old typewriter.

'He's writing a story for Blackwood's Magazine,' I told Jimmy with some pride. 'There are a lot of writers in our family. Way back, starting with William Hayley, whom Byron hated! Rudyard Kipling's a cousin. Major Evans Bell, who wrote about the Indian Mutiny, my grandfather John Macgowan, who wrote about China, and my father. . . .'

I stood in the cold night, helplessly wringing my hands. . . .

'Any Ovaltine in your kitchen?' he asked.

'Maybe,' I said, my mind far away.

'That's what you need, Ovaltine,' he said.

*

Summer's Lease finished and I was out of work again. I sent Robert Donat a telegram saying: 'Would you like to interview talented young actress?'

He replied that he would. I was delirious with joy and arrived at

His Majesty's Theatre just before the curtain went up on *Mary Read.*

More promises—as hollow as they sounded, I thought. But after he had seen me he sent me into the pit to see the play and I was utterly enchanted by it and captivated by him. I remember that evening very well, for Peter Ashmore was to take me out to supper in Soho in his M.G. But he had a puncture, so instead we took a hearse belonging to his father—an undertaker. There was considerable trouble as he parked it on a bus stop, but no one dared remove it or complain, as they were expecting to see a coffin come out of the house opposite.

That July the heat in London was intense, the pavements hard and dusty, and my diary records a succession of worn out shoes. My father finished his story *The Canton Incident*, and Blackwood's accepted it. He bought a bottle of Champagne in anticipation of payment.

We all sat drinking it and enjoying the cool evening after the heat of the day.

'And now what?' asked my mother hopefully.

'I'm going back to China,' he answered quietly.

We stared in dismay.

'I want to go to Nanking. I'll go across Russia. I may join Chiang Kai-shek . . . but anyway I have something I want to write, and I want to write it there.'

The bank wouldn't advance him any money, so he converted his Life Insurance Policy to get a ticket.

'How much money have I got, darling?' he asked my mother.

'Seven pounds, I think,' she said bleakly.

The day before he went, we spent together in the City. I lost my gloves and he bought me another pair. He also bought me a Woolworth's small round red beanie hat with green lacing.

'Wear it at auditions and stand with your back to the audience; see if they don't pick you out in that.'

We drank orange juice through straws and ate marshmallows.

I didn't see him off. I stood at the door waving, watching him and my mother cross the square, till the tears blinded me so that I couldn't even see him turn the corner.

I went up to the drawing-room and closed the windows. His battered typewriter was open and I noticed some writing on a scrap of paper. It was in Chinese: 'Che huar tei ch'ang chio shui te.'

I remembered it from years before, a message from my mother to the gardener: 'This flower must be watered.'

A few weeks later we heard that owing to passport difficulties, he had been shut up in a Russian gaol in Harbin with another man, that they had both grown beards, had escaped, and that he was on his way to Shanghai.

He wandered to Nanking, to Hankow. He wrote that he had been finding it a struggle to write, that he was trying to escape himself, that it was his 'hour of test'. Then suddenly he began writing *The Wall*, and was full of hope again that something would turn up—and then we heard that he was now playing the organ in Shanghai Cathedral, as his father had done before him!

*

Christmas came and went. It was a cold relentless winter, and the rain never seemed to cease. I was making no progress. I could get no work, and the situation was not helped when, one day, running into Gemma Fagan in Leicester Square, she told me she had seen a 'rough cut' of *Vintage Wine*, and that Sonia and Stella Mantovani looked beautiful. 'How do I come out?' I asked excitedly. 'Well . . . your face is too long to be beautiful . . .' she replied. 'But your eyes are good!'

I walked dejectedly across Trafalgar Square, turning left towards the Playhouse. I leaned against the Embankment wall and considered jumping in. The brown water swirled by, while overhead the white gulls wheeled. I thought of Johnman, of Boots, of Brownie and my Rat. Of my father somewhere in the sun, pretending to be having a wretched time and enjoying every moment of it. Running away, that's what he's doing! I told myself, just running away. Tears of self-pity poured down my cheeks. I must get away. I must. I'm no good to anyone. I was never going to be any good as an actress. I was never going to be any good at anything. I hadn't even got a proper boy friend, let alone a lover, like most of the others. Why? Because I was forever looking for someone I would never find, and when I did find him, he'd either hate the sight of me or belong to someone else. The only thing to do was to drown myself, here and now. I meant it, and I was in such a good place for the purpose.

A voice spoke behind me: 'Keep the light burning.' I swung round. Two men were standing quite close to me. One held a match in his hand, the other was fumbling for his cigarettes. He put one in his mouth and bent towards the match. 'Thanks,' he said to the other. 'You saved my life!' And with a nod the two went in opposite directions.

I turned away from the wall. It was getting colder, and a little mist hung on the water. I could feel the smile on my lips, and on the way home I bought a pot of white hyacinths for my mother. White hyacinths to feed your soul. . . .

'Seymour Hicks phoned,' said my mother. 'He's doing a short tour of *Vintage Wine*, and wants you to go.'

'*Vintage Wine!*' I turned away in disgust, but two days later I was rehearsing it again at the Victoria Palace.

A valuable and lasting friendship I made in the next few weeks was with Patrick White, the Australian poet. A tall, lanky, shy man with pale blue eyes, his attic—and it could only be called an attic—in Ebury Street was always full of painters and writers, actors and ballet dancers, and it was here one night I saw Augustus John expertly cooking sausages over a primus stove. Eric Portman with his endless fund of stories was often there; Bernard Lee, Robert Donat, Diana Gould, all lying about on the floor drinking beer and eating sausages.

*

In August I was offered the juvenile lead at the Manchester Repertory Theatre. I remembered Manchester grimly. I talked it over with Seymour. 'I can teach you much more than you'll learn there,' he said primly, but in the end he agreed, with some resentment, to release me from *Vintage Wine*.

I bumped my old suitcase down the stairs of Connaught Street, and went to Manchester on the morning train. I had arranged to go back to Ackers Street, at least confident this time of getting the bed to myself. I was to be paid £4.10.0d. a week, and Mrs Lait only charged 25/– a week for the bedroom, sitting-room, breakfast and dinner.

She was pleased to see me back. She asked after Sonia, filled me with tea, and told me she'd put some anemones in the sitting-room.

'People do say unnygnomes is for tears,' she told me, 'but I don't know as that's right.'

Everything was the same. The same brass bedstead, same gas lighting, same chamber pot with a view on it of Brighton Pier under the bed. I felt miserable and lonely as I hung my things in the narrow wooden cupboard and wished I hadn't come. I missed my family and my friends already, and I went to the Rusholme Theatre full of doubts and misgivings.

The Rusholme, on the main Oxford Road, had once been a tram shed, and somehow intended to remain a tram shed forever. My heart fell with a crash when I first saw it.

The new company was standing on the stage facing the photographers. Director Dominic Roche. Leading lady Enid Hewitt, leading gentleman John Citroen. And Maurice Jones, Fred Essex, Eileen Draycott, Yvonne Le Dain, Charles Lamb, Peter German, Brian Melland and a young man who was so nervous that when he was introduced to me, he burst into guffaws of laughter which he couldn't stop. His name was Thorley Walters, but for some unremembered reason I was soon calling him 'Swizzlestick'.

During the afternoon we had a coffee break. Thorley, Peter German and I sat down at a glass-topped table and stared at each other.

'Isn't it hell!' said Peter.

'Well we can only go *up* from here,' Thorley remarked. 'We can't get any lower, for this is the ultimate bottom.'

'The theatre!' I groaned.

'*The Silver Tassie* for the first play!'

'You're all right, you've got a decent part. I'm the Ward sister all got up in a white habit and falling over a bloody great crucifix,' I reminded him.

'Never mind, you'll *look* lovely,' Peter said with a grin.

Thorley and I have remained friends from the moment he laughed in my face. His great charm was that he literally could not refrain from laughing, and anything would send his shoulders heaving, on or off the stage. He was the liveliest of companions, and on many occasions turned a foul day into a hilarious one.

Ackers Street was too far away from the Rusholme Theatre, and I told the tearful Mrs Lait that I would have to move. I needed somewhere near to be able to rush home between the twice nightly shows and learn my lines for the following week while I ate my supper.

The search was a spiritless affair until I found Miss McClure. I liked the neat tidy little Scot the moment I saw her, and her house in Roberts Avenue was shining bright and clean. I remained in Roberts Avenue for the rest of my time in Manchester.

The Silver Tassie passed off with no problems beyond the fact that I was forever getting the large crucifix caught between my knees! *Sally's Husband* was the next play, and then came *Abraham Lincoln* and *The Trojan Women.*

My mother came up to stay with me at Roberts Avenue. She adored Manchester and Miss McClure, and the pair of them sat for hours in the kitchen talking about Scotland!

Living Dangerously, *Two Gentlemen of Verona*, *The Voysey Inheritance*,

Strife, *Pygmalion*, and so the weeks went by. Wyn came up to see me, so did Jimmy Whaley. The local Mancunians were very hospitable, but mostly it was hard work, with little time to want any other relaxation than bed and a book. During those nights I read all Synge's plays, Shaw and Shakespeare. I had great hopes of a small success in our production of *Strife*—I considered myself 'rather good' as Madge Thomas—and was bitterly disappointed when I received no mention in the paper at all.

The Streets of London by Dion Boucicault was one of the highlights of the season, for in front of a packed audience, revelling in every moment of the slightly bizarre melodrama, one member of the cast, who had been out during the interval to liven up his hangover, rushed onto the stage at a breathless speed, undid his flies and commenced to urinate into the fireplace. Amid shrieks of laughter and catcalls, the curtain came down abruptly, and didn't go up again that night.

Green Grow the Lilacs, a musical comedy, *The Mocking Bird*, and so the weeks went by. Sometimes a yellow moon gleamed through the soot that hung across the city, or a sudden wind showed the mackerel skies overhead, but in my memories it is nearly always raining on the greasy, shining tramlines.

One night during the run of *The Professor's Love Story*, a note was brought round to my dressing-room. It read: 'I am in front. You are very good. Will you have supper afterwards. I want to discuss something. Robert Donat.'

At first I thought it must be a joke, but when he appeared at the stage door after the show I knew it wasn't.

At supper, he told me that he was about to do *Red Night*, a new play by a Manchester journalist, James Hodson. There was a small part of a French girl in an estaminet. Would I like it?

'*Like* it!'

'Can you do a French accent?'

'*Can* I!'

I couldn't believe it! I was sitting in the Midland Hotel with Robert Donat, talking about a part in his new play! I stared at him, open-mouthed at my good fortune.

'Who else is in it . . . besides you, I mean?' I asked.

'Meriel Forbes, John Mills, Bernard Lee.'

'John Mills! I know him. How funny to be in a play with him.'

The next morning I was up early and round at Thorley's digs, sitting on his bed, sharing his breakfast, telling him about it. 'I shall give my notice in at the end of the week,' I said. 'I shall come too,' he answered. 'I couldn't stand this place without you.'

'Mother McClure' burst into loud sobs when I told her I was giving in my notice, and wept inconsolably for hours. It was awful. As I walked to the theatre, I was aware suddenly that the grey skies, the cobbles, and the black houses had of a sudden become dear to me. Perhaps I wouldn't give in my notice. Perhaps I should wait until I was sure of the part in *Red Night*.

A newspaper man was waiting for me when I reached the stage door. 'Thorley Walters has told everyone, and everyone is so pleased. You deserve it, Miss Bell. Can I have your photo?'

The Manchester evening papers were full of it: 'Robert Donat chooses girl from Rep.' I had some misgivings. Maybe I shouldn't have spoken so soon. I tried to telephone Robert Donat at his hotel only to find he'd gone. Dominic Roche was very nice. 'But I wish you'd stay for the next two plays, *Cyrano* and *The Fugitive*. You've got good parts and I'd hate to lose you so suddenly.'

I agreed to stay. I wanted to stay. I hated making sudden decisions. I went to bed incredibly tired and in the middle of the night was very sick. I remember calling to Miss McClure and then I passed out completely. I lay in that small bed in the narrow room for a week and even suggested to Thorley that he should get a priest, for I was certain I was about to die.

I longed to see a rose madder sunset over a long river, with the dark quiet trees and reeds standing out sharply against the luminous water, see vinegar-coloured fields, with figures walking slowly and softly across them as they do at evening. It had been too long since I had seen green fields or heard a blackbird. I was glad I was leaving. I was glad of Robert Donat.

Miss McClure came in with two letters. One was from Sonia to tell me she had at long last married Jack Raine. The other was from Robert Donat: 'It has finally, after much talk, been decided that as the part is that of a French girl, it would be better perhaps after all to get a French girl to play it. I'm sorry. I do know what disappointments mean.'

I closed my eyes and turned my face to the wall. . . .

*

My mother, unable to stand the house in Connaught Square any more, took a small furnished house at Camberley with Wyn, and I spent Christmas there with the family. It was as warm and friendly as she said, and holly and the tree made it a sentimental occasion, for I was pretty sure it would be the last one we would spend together for some time. I walked for miles through pine trees and dying bracken in the pouring rain, sniffing with pleasure the moist moss and wet earth, realizing how stifled I had been in Manchester. The house was constantly full of people, Thorley, Ronnie, and Patrick White. The Collets at Crowthorne gave a dance, and St George himself appeared! I hadn't seen him for years. He told me that I was 'the only girl in the world'—and then I caught him kissing a stranger under the mistletoe in the conservatory!

I went out into the garden and looked at the moon. Wherever we are, my father had said, we can look at the same moon. Where was he, I wondered.

> You that keep
> In a land asleep
> One Light Burning till break of day

There was a letter from him when I got home, sent on from Manchester in Miss McClure's shaky writing. It was from Peking.

'Let everything that happens to you,' he wrote, 'disappointment or sadness, be part of your steps to knowledge, for it all helps as Life which you wish to portray. Read aloud; you will find it has a curious effect upon you, bringing often to your brain meanings which the eye alone has not comprehended.'

In the New Year the lease of the house at Camberley ran out and Wyn and I went up to London to look for a cheap flat. For a week we searched from Bloomsbury to Battersea with no success and every night spent hours crammed in a single bed in a friend's flat, until at last I could bear no more and slept on the floor. Then one day we found it, in Chelsea. King's Mansions was a lugubrious enough looking edifice, but the flat was on the top floor, looking over the trees with a view of the Thames, and though our legs used to get tired walking four floors, I loved it, and with the unexpected arrival of a cheque from an uncle, which enabled us to furnish it, we were happy there for a short time.

I was able to resume my search for work. I saw Bronson Albery at Wyndham's Theatre. I fought my way through a multitude of people for an Ivor Novello audition and through another for the Lunts' audition of *Tovarich*: I walked boldly in on Nancy Price at the Little Theatre and told her I was a personal friend of Mazo de La Roche—

only to find that it *was* Mazo de La Roche sitting in the opposite chair. In the Strand I bumped into Thorley Walters, who told me he'd been sacked from Bill Walker's *Revue*, and that he was seeking a quiet place in which to cut his throat. As we walked down the Strand he bought a paper. The headline read: 'Rudyard Kipling dead'. My friend, the Outcast Child of the East, was buried in Westminster Abbey on my birthday.

*

Seymour Hicks asked me to go and see him at his home in Cheyne Walk. He received me in his drawing-room.

'Little Bell,' he said. 'We're taking out a short tour of *Vintage Wine*.' I couldn't believe it. Not again! Was my life to be one long revival of one of the silliest plays in living memory?

'Can't I play the granddaughter this time? I've been understudying it since the year dot.'

'No, I want you and Sonia to play your own parts.'

'What about the salary?'

'What did you get last time?'

'Four pounds ten.'

'I'll give you five pounds.'

The tour started at Bristol. Oxford, Golders Green, Norwich, Yarmouth, Leeds, Birmingham. In Birmingham Sonia and I lived in a bed sitting-room in the attic. The roof was so low that when we got out of bed we always bumped our heads. 'Let's do a moonlight flit,' said Sonia. 'Look. Through the window, there's a flat roof and a staircase.' We turned towards it hopefully. The window was nailed down!

*

Someday when I am old and far away from here
I'll make you laugh with tales of our abode,
'Mongst lice and filth and crying dark despair
In Belgrave Road!

I wrote for Sonia's autograph book.

*

Back in London there was a letter waiting from my father to say he would be home in a couple of weeks. But the letter had been held up in Siberia and we barely had time to rush to Liverpool Street Station.

I saw him long before the others did. His familiar walk, the constant smile addressed to no one in particular. A smile of pleasure.

'You *are* thin,' my mother started.

'Nothing to eat for nearly two weeks,' he said, 'and only ten shillings in my pocket! But great news . . . I *think* I have a Government job which will take me to Singapore at the end of the year!'

'Oh, Hayley!'

'Interviews next week and a salary of nine hundred a year! If I get it.'

'I'm not going to get excited,' she said. 'Things don't seem to come too easily to the Bells.'

'A job! A place in the sun again . . . money in the old pocket . . . able to look blokes in the face.'

'Able to pay bills,' I added bitterly. 'Buy new shoes. Throw away Mummy's old dresses and coats, her broken down shoes, laddered stockings, cheap clothes.'

'Baba!' said my mother.

He bit his lip.

'She'll have servants, a car, a house with a garden in Singapore. Tell you something else, Muggins. I've finished *The Wall*, and Blackwood's have bought it.'

It was a great day. He took us out to lunch, but he was cautious. We went to a pub in the King's Road and had Cornish pasties and a bottle of wine.

The following week in Torquay with *Vintage Wine* I woke up shivering. At the matinee I discovered that I was covered in a rash. 'For God's sake don't tell Seymour until after the show,' Sonia said and called my mother on the telephone. 'The doctor says it's measles.'

Measles! And in the spring, like Johnman! Mother was in a panic. Jimmy Whaley came down to Torquay at her request and insisted on taking me back to London.

'She has measles, a touch of pneumonia and one infected ear,' he told Seymour who found the whole situation tiresome.

We travelled on the night train after the show, arriving in London at three in the morning. During the journey he proposed to me. I had a temperature of 103°, I was feverish, and I accepted.

By the time I recovered, *Vintage Wine* had finished forever!

*

My father got the job. My mother, Wyn, and Liz, who had now left school, were to follow him out later.

He came to see me playing the lead with Richard Bird at Daly's in *The Composite Man* when Diana Churchill, whom I was understudying, was 'off' for two weeks. The next afternoon I found myself once again walking round Regent's Park with him. Once again it was April and the almond blossom was out. It seemed to me to be almost a repetition of that earlier conversation.

'Mummy will love Singapore, except that the weather is worse than Hong Kong.'

'What exactly does the job mean?'

'D.S.O.I.—Defence Security Officer. I shall have to learn Tamil. . . .'

He was digging at the water's edge with his stick. I noticed his shoes had split at the seams, that his cuffs were frayed. Tears stung the back of my eyes and I looked away.

'How long will you be away this time?' I asked.

'Four years.'

'Four years!'

'By that time you will be a big success,' he grinned, 'and you can buy me a pair of new shoes!'

I shrugged my shoulders. 'I don't seem to be getting on very fast, do I?'

'Just be ready when the opportunity comes, that's the point. But look here, why don't you give it up. Come to Singapore. You know how you love the East!'

I shook my head. 'I have to go on trying. I would be a failure if I gave up trying. I want to go on.'

'I'll be able to send you a little here and there, but not much. Maybe a friend could share the flat and pay her whack.'

'Maybe—'

We walked back through the trees. The sun was setting, just as it had last time. 'What about Jimmy Whaley? Are you going to marry him?' he asked suddenly.

I shook my head again. 'I don't seem to be able to find the one hundred percent right person do I?' I laughed. 'The trouble is, I suppose, I'm really looking for you.'

'He'll turn up,' he said. 'But do wait for him, won't you.'

Two months later he had gone, leaving me with a cheque for thirty pounds and a ticket to Singapore. I locked them up in my Chinese box with my other 'things', and went to the theatre on a 19 bus.

II

THESE FLOWERS NEED WATERING

Dennis and I went with my mother, Wyn and Liz, to Paris. We stayed the night in a cheap hotel in Montmartre and spent the evening at the Folies Bergère. My mother didn't enjoy it. She held onto my hand as though she couldn't bear to let it go. Early next morning they left from the Gare de Lyon to catch the ship at Marseilles.

The flat in King's Mansions was grimly cold and silent when Dennis and I returned to London. The peace and security that always surrounded my mother had departed with her. The next day Dennis went back to Guildford and I was left alone. I shall become the sort of person who talks to herself, I thought. I shall bang my knife and fork on the table to stop myself from being frightened of being alone!

Coming back from the theatre that night I found myself peering into other people's windows, staring at the warm friendly light. I went up the stone stairs to the deserted flat that stood in darkness, then I turned on all the lights and started cleaning out the flat. It took me until two in the morning.

There was something there of my mother after all. I could almost feel her grey eyes upon me, smiling: 'This is your responsibility now, Baba, keep it nice and learn to make a home.'

One torch lights another. Everything that I had ever admired about her homes, now became my obsession. Any pennies I had over were spent on flowers, towels, soaps, smells for the bathroom, while I spent hours learning to improve my cooking. This grey little flat became my home, my nest. I learned to embroider cushions. I painted walls, and painted little pictures. When Dennis came home for weekends there was always a small roast ready for him. I bought a small tree and some coloured lights for Christmas, but the butcher forgot to deliver the meat, and we had practically nothing to eat. The gas bill was our only Christmas present, except for a rather nasty bead bag from one of the aunts. On Christmas Eve Dennis bought half a bottle of Champagne, which we drank, and we walked along the Embankment and went into a couple of pubs. Beer on Champagne was never a good mixture.

Christmas Day we spent with Diana Churchill's family, stoking up because we were so dreadfully hungry, and on Boxing Day we bought a packet of ham, and had a coffee in Lyons Corner House.

'Listen,' I said. 'Reggie Tate is in *Jane Eyre* at the Queen's. Let's go and see him.'

We ended up in the stage box where Reggie put us, our packet of ham on the floor. The theatre was full of white fur and tiaras watching him play Rochester, and every now and again Dennis and I dived down to our packet of ham and ate ravenously, clapping enrapturedly between times, not only for Reggie who had given us the box, but because it was so wonderful to be warm, and to gulp down the bottle of white wine he had sent us through his stage manager.

The New Year I saw in from my bed. I had 'flu and a high temperature. I wrote to my father:

'The "Light" often wavers and nearly goes out, but we shade it from the wind with our frozen fingers. Already, curiously enough, they are selling daffodils and tulips in the street and spring must be somewhere along the line. It has been a dreary and unhappy winter of fog and rain, and one's spirits have almost been crushed by the ceaseless dripping against the window panes. Everyone we have loved has disappeared and the streets are full of wet dogs, forlorn umbrellas and the splashings from passing cars.'

*

The second week of January found me still in bed and full of aches and pains. Dennis had gone back to Aldershot and I was quite alone, living on a diet of Bovril and toast.

Bills were pouring in, some of them large ones that my mother had forgotten to pay. I had to go to my private box and take out my father's cheque. In no time there was nothing left of it, so his field glasses went to the pawnshop where so many of my 'things' had gone. I stared at my Blue Buddha but thought I would sell him last of all. He went two weeks later, with the Siberian amethysts.

Letters came from my father:

'I seem to be living in a kind of trance of late. The day's a long rush, in anxiety to make good and get an extraordinary nebulous job done fairly decently.'

He was a failure. He loved life and pursued it, but whenever he came up against reality, he turned his face away.

He went on: 'All you say is quite true about writing and how I ought to have done more for all our sakes. It is too true. But it's almost impossible. I have written a lot, but *it is no good*, I know and I won't let bad stuff go out. It is a reputation that one has to make, more than money.' I leaned my head against the wall and sobbed.

*

Peter Dearing rang me to go to an audition for the tour of *Call it a Day* with Fay Compton and Owen Nares.

I stood among a crowd of other people on the stage at the Globe Theatre, reading the part of Vera, a kitchen maid.

'Very good, Miss Bell, but unfortunately you have red hair and Miss Compton doesn't like anyone with red hair.'

I smiled bleakly towards the stalls, biting my lower lip.

Suddenly, a most beautiful voice spoke from the circle: 'Who says Miss Compton doesn't like anyone with red hair?'

'Oh, Faydie. I'm sorry. I thought—'

The pure voice flowed from the circle, 'Give her the part, she's very good.'

I shaded my eyes against the footlights, peering up into the circle.

'Thank you, Miss Compton.'

There was no reply. She had already left the theatre. . . .

I danced my way to the 19 bus, singing *Bye Bye Blackbird*, bought myself a Cornish pasty, washed my hair and went to bed early.

The next day I came face to face with Miss Fay Compton, and I thought she was the loveliest person I had ever seen. I wasn't to know then that she was to be responsible for changing my life by her extreme goodness and kindness.

Back to all the old familiar places. Manchester, Oxford, Leeds. Only this time I had enough money to go to cheap hotels. My name was in black lettering outside the theatre. Blackpool and Liverpool. Aberdeen, Edinburgh, Bristol, York.

Fay asked me to her house at West Peckham in Kent for a weekend.

From the moment we stepped out of the car I loved Hazel Hall. A house always full of flowers and bright colours: of the acrid smell of paraffin lamps and the scent of Floris carnation emanating from bathrooms: a garden redolent with the perfume of roses and night-scented stock: an orchard aflame with cherry and apple blossom, where lazy goldfish lay on the top of their pool in the late afternoon sunlight. It was England at her best.

It was the most haunted house I have ever been in. Night after night we would hear footsteps, pictures would fall from the wall, and a bull terrier and an Irish setter would suddenly 'point' at the fireplace, their hackles rising. Wherever I stood in the long, low dining-room, I would feel the gooseflesh rising all over me.

Elspeth and Stewart Granger spent the first night of their honeymoon at Hazel Hall. As the house was full I slept with Fay. In the early hours of the morning we were awakened by complete pandemonium. People seemed to be running up and down stairs and banging doors.

The next morning Fay asked what had been happening.

'We thought it was *you*,' said Jimmy Granger in astonishment.

'We thought it was *you* playing tricks,' Elspeth said. 'In the night someone tore the bedclothes off us.'

Fay asked Bishop James to come down and exorcise the place. 'You'll probably smell a curious fungus-like rank smell, almost putrid,' he said. Sure enough, towards the end of dinner we were aware of it. It seemed to be coming from the cellar.

On our knees in the cellar we watched the ceremony of Bell, Book and Candle; the flickering candlelight threw strange shapes and shadows across the Bishop's scarlet vestments: 'Go to the Book, quench the Candle, Ring the Bell.'

For the first time that night, as the house lay in darkness, there was silence, and during the weeks and months ahead, we never heard another sound.

Those weekends at Hazel Hall were some of the happiest of my life. I sat at the feet of Fay's guests listening to every word. Noël Coward, Ivor Novello, Bobby Andrews and Michael Wilding. People from Hollywood, people from New York. Fields of buttercups, black calves and white dog roses. Contentment and peace encompassed me, and after a long day in the fields I sank to sleep on a feather pillow.

*

The lease of the flat in King's Mansions was up. Once again I packed everything. The flat, with its memories, was tidy and quiet. I went out, closing the door with a bang.

Someone told me that there were some cheap digs in Paddington, opposite the station. Mrs Dacres, the landlady, was a grim-faced woman. 'You can have this room for five bob a week, but there's no bedclothes,' she said, leaning against the window and blocking most of the light. I tried to smile at her but she wasn't looking. She was fixing the curtain rail which had fallen down on her head.

'The girls usually get their breakfast in the station if they wants any,' she said through her cigarette. 'I don't mind an electric kettle, but I won't have no crumbs. Brings out the mice.'

'I see. Five bob a week, it's quite cheap really.' I smiled at her hopefully. 'Where's the bathroom, Mrs Dacres?'

'There's a lav upstairs. If you want a bath there's the public baths up in Porchester Road.'

I took the room and paid five bob in advance. The bed was not uncomfortable, though the street was noisy. But it was cheap, and that enabled me to have a good breakfast in the station every day, which kept me going till the evening, when I often had dinner or supper with Fay and Anthony and the others. I didn't tell anyone where I was living. I was rather ashamed of Praed Street.

A week or so after I moved in, Max Adrian told me that auditions were being held for *Midsummer Night's Dream* in Regent's Park. Why didn't I go along and audition for one of the fairies.

'But I can't dance!' I wailed.

'You can pick up *that* sort of hopping and sidling,' he said.

I went along to Regent's Park. Robert Atkins was standing in the middle of the grassy stage waving his hands about, selecting 'Titania fairies' and 'Oberon fairies'. I climbed up and stood beside him. I wore my red beanie hat with the green stitching that my father had bought me, and hoped it would catch his eye. It did.

'Over there, dear, among the Oberons,' he said, and gave me a push. Apprehension flooded over me. Most of the other 'fairies' were in leotards, and here was I dressed in a cotton dress and a red beanie hat. But there was no going back, no saying that I had never done this type of dancing in my life. I stood my ground and hummed reassuringly to keep my spirits up.

'Ten o'clock tomorrow morning,' he said. 'Give your names to the stage manager'—and he was gone.

The rehearsals were very painful. There was no doubt that I was not intended to be a ballet dancer. I worked unceasingly off stage with a girl called Peachy Hunt, and another called June, but to the end I never got it absolutely right: 'One, step, hop, hop, slide, cross over, jump . . . on your *toes*, Hayley Bell! What are you, an elephant?'

Mendelssohn's music made me weep. I was happy in my wig and white tights and being a nameless dancer among so many. The Oberon fairies wore a string of battery operated coloured lights on their arms and legs. It was a pretty sight in the dark summer evenings, but uncomfortable when it rained and we slipped and slithered about in the mud.

'One, step, hop, hop, slide, cross over, jump . . . *arms*, Hayley Bell!'

'It's no use,' I told Peachy. 'It's like maths to me. My feet don't seem to be connected with my brain.'

At weekends I flopped down in Fay's apple orchard. At lunch one Sunday she said to me: 'Would you like to come to Australia? I'm taking a tour, for about a year. You can be the Juvenile. It's not settled yet but I think it's going to be all right.'

All day I wandered about in a state of rapture. To go to sea again, through the Suez Canal. Ceylon, Australia—even Singapore!

The following week in the Park I hit upon an ingenious idea to solve the problem of my dancing difficulties. For two nights it succeeded.

The next morning Robert Atkins called a rehearsal.

'Look here,' he said angrily. 'There's a nasty gap down there by June. Spoils the whole effect. What's going on?'

Nobody spoke. One or two people cast a glance in my direction.

'Come on, come on, what's wrong up that end. It looks as if no one's there. As if you're lop-sided, one short. June?'

After a moment she spoke: 'It'th Hayley Bell,' she said in her lisping voice.

'Hayley Bell?' he looked at me quickly.

'Yeth,' June went on. 'It'th Hayley Bell, she alwayth turnth off her lightth.'

*

I saw few people either entering or coming out from Mrs Dacres's house, but there was one girl who used to nod in a friendly way. Two days before I left Paddington, I saw her having breakfast in the station buffet. I joined her, and we started talking.

'Where d'you work, then?'

'Regent's Park.'

'Bit chilly, ain't it?'

'All right when it's not raining. Where do you work?'

'Oh, all of us does the trains—'

'The trains?'

'You know, Paddington, Euston, get a platform ticket, get stuck on the train when the whistle goes, start a bit of yowling. There's always some chap ready to get you into his cabin, and you get a good weekend up North, or Birmingham way. That's nice, Birmingham.'

It was years before I saw her again. She was standing in the pouring rain on the corner of Bond Street with a dog. I took her into Stewart's and gave her a good blowout of boiled eggs and sausages.

*

At the Theatrical Garden Party in aid of the Actor's Orphanage that year, Ivor Novello asked me to be in a sketch in his big tent. I was hobbling along in my uncomfortable and unbecoming dress to get a glass of orange squash when I bumped into John Mills.

'Hullo!' I said, smiling.

'Hullo.' He smiled back warily.

'You don't remember me, in China, you were with the Quaints.'

'Of course I do. How are you? How are your three brothers?' My heart dropped. I knew it was pointless to go on.

'Can I have your autograph?' I asked.

'Yes, but I'll have to charge for it, as it's Charity.'

'How much?'

'Oh, sixpence to you.' His eyes, I noticed, were very blue. I took the sixpence out of my purse and gave it to him. Just at that moment Leslie Henson came up. 'Johnnie, I want to talk to you,' he said, and putting his arm round his shoulder led John Mills away.

'Hey, my sixpence!' I whispered, but he had gone. I hung around hopefully, biting my finger nails, and suddenly realized I was due back in the tent for the next performance. Although I searched for him during the afternoon, I didn't see him again.

'That's *stealing*,' said Sonia when I told her.

*

A few weeks later Fay's company sailed in the *Oronsay* for Australia. We were to do *Victoria Regina*, *George and Margaret*, *Red Peppers* and

Fumed Oak, and the company consisted of Bruno Barnabe, Michael Wilding, Jack Macnaughton, Stafford Hilliard and his wife Ann Codrington, Yvette Anning, Fay's secretary, myself, and Peter Dearing as director.

It was a long voyage and we rehearsed every day. We saw Gibraltar, like a rocky piece of onyx rising from a sapphire sea, with the fires glowing in the sky above Algeciras where the oil tanks had been bombed. Toulon was a haze of mist and palm trees at sunset. In the Red Sea, Michael Wilding and I sat gloomily in our cabins with ice packs on our heads, as a result of sunstroke from bathing at noon. In Colombo I saw my mother for a few brief hours, and finally we came to Australia, Portsea, and giant rollers on a chalk white beach, with Christmas turkey and plum pudding in the blazing heat.

In Auckland, the lavatory over Yvette's and my dressing-room broke, so that my wig was drenched and the smell made Fay reel backwards; in Wellington I washed my hair and went to bed with it wet, suffering for two weeks with rheumatism.

There were always new sounds, new faces. We poured out of trains, following in a long echelon behind Fay and her mountain of baggage. Christchurch . . . Timaru . . . Oamaru . . . Stewart Island, where oysters as big as plates were sold by the sack. Sometimes a big theatre, sometimes a hall, even a tent. The dusty, musty haunting smell of the theatre, wherever it was.

I had some minor success, but, when the curtain falls, what then? I asked myself wryly. I was an Aquarian, I needed no one. I was the Cat that Walked Alone . . . but I knew it wasn't true any more for me than it is for anyone else. Even the animals went in two by two! . . . No, I was a leaf before the wind, scurrying in a purposeless way, changing direction, at the mercy of a wind I couldn't even see! Throughout that long, exciting tour, I kept recalling Grankapa's words from long ago: 'A small boy a few years older, perhaps running across an English field with a butterfly net. . . .' Where was he? Had I missed him? Had I passed him through some distant swing doors somewhere, or in a London street? And, dear God, had I seen him somewhere without knowing?

*

The company were to go back to England by ship. I took a flying-boat to Singapore, where finally the plane landed like a great and elegant swan upon the waters of the harbour at sunset.

I could see them all on the jetty. My mother peering anxiously, Wyn, Elizabeth, newly gawky and tall, and my father holding out the flag of his handkerchief in our special way.

I was there for two weeks. I luxuriated in their home, with its rooms full of wild orchids, with Chinese food, and people constantly coming and going through the house.

This is it, I told myself. No more London and cold and search for work, no more moneyless days and nights of worry . . . just to be able to put out my hand to my mother, to walk through the jungle, talk with my father about his work.

'I have a long way to go, Muggins,' he said, 'before I can be a hundredth part of the importance that it all sounded in little old Chelsea. It's difficult to get one's toes into solid holding ground. It's a queer job. I'm off to Formosa in a week or so. I have to know everything, everybody and everywhere, from the Governor downwards, and what a hotchpotch of people, colours and religions, every shade from ebony black through chocolate, butterscotch and banana colours! And smells! You, who are a disciple of smells, you'd appreciate it all. I wish you'd stay here. Here is the whole of the Far East in the nostrils, and Adventures waiting just round every corner!'

His eyes lit up. 'After forty years of this sort of life I never lose the excitement of the test, exactly as I did when I first set foot in China as a boy of fifteen!'

He scuffed the grass on the lawn.

'I suppose I should start to grow up while there's still time.'

'How's the job going?' I asked him, sitting on a frangipane tree and swinging my legs.

'I know most of the place, everything and everybody including the police. I've been a thousand miles in the car, and walked too. I can tackle anybody and do. I can speak Tamil well enough. I arranged to meet a fascinating man the other day, in the Botanical Gardens, half Japanese, half Swiss. He said that if the British Government would pay him for his information on the Japanese, he could be a valuable asset.'

'And so?' I asked.

'He confirmed—amongst other things—what I've been trying to tell them, that the Japs intend to take Singapore. So I went straight to Shenton Thomas, the Governor and told him.'

'What did he say?'

My father laughed uncomfortably.

'His actual words were "No one but a fool, Hayley Bell, would suggest that the Japs want to attack Singapore".' Suddenly he became excited, the tears started, as they always did when he was emotional.

'Look, I promise you we'll be at war with Germany in England by the end of the year. Munich hasn't solved a thing, and sooner or later these little bastards are going to jump in here and take it. I *know* it. I'm on to their espionage network here, Muggins, and it's *big*. I've seen them training in Formosa, lying up to their necks in snake-infested waters in their new uniforms, living in the jungle for months on end. Goddammit, we're so bloody slow in England. I reckon that God must love us very much to have saved us again and again from so many stupid mistakes.

'It's a ridiculous position here,' he went on. 'There's no Fleet. No land protection, no adequate air-power. Half-built airfields and no one to protect them. The troops are too long out here and stale, or too lately in the East and unused to the conditions.'

He struck angrily at the tree where I was sitting.

'Their fatuous "jungle will protect us" theory and their complete ignorance of what the jungle really is! The civilians live in Cloud Cuckoo Land; they haven't even been warned to guard against sabotage and espionage, and they can't be bothered to prepare an adequate civil defence. It sickens me.'

I looked at him. His hair was thinning, his back stooped a little. I found myself wringing my hands.

'Once the Japs have taken Singapore, and they will, we shall never again know peace or security in the Far East.'

He stopped and suddenly smiled at me. His eyes were bright as I remembered them, though the little lines round them were unfamiliar.

'How about a pink gin?' he asked.

*

A week later I went with a party of people to see a film called *The Drum* with Roger Livesey. There was nothing special about the film, but it struck a chord in my mind, a bleak little wind through me, calling me back to England.

'I have to go back,' I told him. 'I could never be part of this any more than I could in Shanghai. I don't suppose I shall ever be a success in the theatre, or anywhere else for that matter. But I have to keep moving on. Maybe there's more of Auntie Alice in me than I thought! I'm always so bloody restless. I'm looking for something and I don't know what it is.'

He looked grim. I knew he was bitterly disappointed, knew that he had hoped that the relationship we had once had together when I was a child in Macao would somehow be picked up again from here. He turned to me with one of his old familiar grins. 'The fault, dear Brutus, is not in our stars. . . .'

Some few days later he put me onto a Japanese ship. I travelled steerage and during the first night I woke to find a Japanese coolie going through my belongings. I was robbed of all my money and though I ran screaming among the bunks in my diaphanous nightgown, piercing the night with my deafening howls of rage, the culprit was never discovered, and I arrived at Colombo practically penniless. There I persuaded a small sampan to transport me across the water and to the astonishment of Fay and the rest of the company who were hanging over the rails, rejoined the ship as she weighed anchor and prepared to sail.

PART THREE
JOHNNIE

12

A SUDDEN SPRING

We went back to Hazel Hall in an English twilight, whooping with joy at the sight of the cherry blossom in the Kent countryside. The dogs yelped and howled with delight, hurling themselves at Fay.

We were Home! And what, I thought, and where, is Home to me now but England! I looked out of my casement windows to the distant willows at the water's edge, to the feathery beginnings of the hops on the vines; and I knew with conviction that this, in the end, was to be my country. Despite Irish and Scottish ancestry, Chinese influences, this was where my happiness would be found. Though tropical suns might beckon, I would always have to return again to the winding lanes, hedges of hazel nuts, and the glistening white dew of the early mornings, up the valley and across the stream.

Strangely content, I started writing seriously my first play, *The Two Harlequins*. I found myself completely engrossed and happy the livelong day, striding about the countryside with notebook and pencil, stroked by the sun and refreshed by April rains.

One day, a mile or two away from Hazel Hall, I came upon an ancient collection of deserted cottages. With a stab of excitement, I climbed through a window into one of the kitchens. Exquisite old Delft tiles surrounded the wash basin. The beams were low, the rooms crooked and slanting. There was a burst of purple lilac at the broken gate, and the garden was full of buttercups and tangled weeds, with an heroic Montana Rubens rose straining to rise above the confusion. Here, sitting on an old box at a half table, I worked, alone, untroubled and undisturbed, except for a strange feeling that someone, some immortal, shared Dukes Place with me.

There was a suggestion, a flash of memory, that jerked my sleeve and carried me back to Bom Jesus, laying the same restraining hand of gentleness upon my spirit, filling my nostrils with the same warm scent of earth and moss. A sense of Holiness, of the shadows of Monks walking; not in the saffron robes of the Buddhists, but in the white of the Dominican, or the brown of the Benedictine; their chanting voices forever embedded in the now silent grey stone walls. As I looked up at the butterflies in the old buddleia tree, an awareness came over me, a consciousness that somehow a part of my life was to be woven into this background of fields and woods.

It couldn't go on, of course. I had to find work. Fay said I could live with her at Dolphin Square during the week and pay her one pound for my board and lodging.

I found myself in *Tony Draws a Horse* by Lesley Storm at the Criterion Theatre, with Lilian Braithwaite, and Diana Churchill, who had asked for me. It was an amusing company with Nigel Patrick, Henry Hewitt, and an attractive Australian girl called Janet Johnson, who became a great friend and with whom I took a bachelor-girl flat in Basil Street. She shared my obsession with the Lyons Corner House in Coventry Street, the sharp excitement of the band on the second floor, the desert of white table cloths, and the anonymity.

Dennis, now commissioned in the Royal Air Force, came to see me before he went off to Iraq. We went to Hampstead Heath Fair, and spent the day on the roundabouts and swings. As we left the Heath, the posters read: 'Trouble in Albania.'

'Here we go,' he said. 'I give it two months. Hang on to life as you know it. It's like golden water.'

In the middle of April I received a letter from my father in Singapore:

'The present world, and it has been a pleasant one as far as my home and family—is falling about my ears once more. Again the end of a phase; uncertainty ahead and much anxiety now regarding debts and how to get out of the place honourably, yet apart from the uprooting and the feeling that the girls are being robbed of their easy life in the East, I am glad it is over and I can go from here. . . . The War Office have been decent enough to cable that we *all* go home as official passengers on the *Lancashire*. . . . I shall have a lot to say when I get home. I have been, in an official capacity, through hell on earth in the last 2½ years. I truly am afraid for the British Empire in some of the things I have learned.'

A few weeks later they arrived.

I tore up the platform, straining my eyes for the familiar figures.

How pathetic they looked, standing in the clothes they had left in! Long trailing skirts and coats, sunburnt faces and mad windblown hair.

'Oh, how thin you are!' my mother cried, but I noticed that her lovely hair was white.

I gulped, clutching at them, their faces wet with tears of welcome. My father sniffed at the station air.

'It's spring!' he said. 'I can even smell it in here.'

'Liz is engaged!' Wyn told me happily. 'To Martin Weedon of the Middlesex Regiment.'

'What about you?' I asked. She smiled. 'I keep on looking. What about *you*? Perhaps we are going to be known as the Bell girls, those two old maids!'

*

Two days later Diana Churchill left the cast of *Tony Draws a Horse* and I took over the leading part.

I remember my first night as if it were yesterday. It was 15 May 1939. Anthony Pelissier had rung me earlier in the day and told me that he and Penelope Dudley Ward were having an engagement celebration lunch at Fay's flat in Dolphin Square and that he wanted me to be there.

'I can't, Ant. I'm opening tonight and I'm kind of nervous! I shall go to the Serpentine and spout at the swans,' I said.

'Noël Coward is coming, Joyce Carey, and a host of people you know; but I especially want you to come. I have a present for you.'

'A present? I should be giving you a present!'

'Please come. I know it's the most important day of your life—and I don't mean tonight's opening.'

'What are you talking about?' I asked.

'Please come. *Please!*'

'I look so awful. I haven't any clothes.'

'Wear that ghastly striped thing you made yourself,' he said. 'It's perfect.'

All morning I spouted to the swans on the Serpentine, but at three o'clock I made my way back to Dolphin Square to tidy up for the run through with Lilian Braithwaite and Nigel Patrick and to prepare for the evening ahead of me.

I went up to the second floor in the lift. I had quite forgotten Ant's lunch party, my mind was so full of my lines. The lift door opened, and I found myself face to face with John Mills.

'Hullo,' I said. 'You owe me sixpence.'

He laughed shyly, like a small boy who has been reprimanded for something he couldn't remember being guilty of.

'You're late for lunch,' he replied. 'It's nearly half-past three.'

We went back into the sitting-room together. It seemed to be full of people and smoke and empty glasses.

'Here you are,' cried Ant. 'Have a glass of Champagne! Toast our health and then we'll drink to tonight.'

'Tonight?' asked John Mills.

'Diana Churchill has left *Tony Draws a Horse* and she's playing,' Ant told him.

'I'll come and see you,' he said.

'What are you doing now?'

'*Mice and Men* at the Apollo. It's a wonderful play.'

'I'll come and see it,' I said shyly, and suddenly we were both grinning familiarly at each other, as if we were old friends. 'Here,' he said, diving his hand into his pocket and bringing out a sixpence.

I laughed, as my hand closed over it. . . . I have it still.

I wandered over to Ant. 'What was all that about a present?' I asked him.

'You've seen it,' he said solemnly. 'It's within your own two hands, but there's a long way to go. . . .'

I looked down at the sixpence.

'You can't mean this,' I said.

He laughed. 'That's only the beginning,' he said. 'My present to you is John Mills, and my present to him is Mary Hayley Bell.'

'You must be potty!'

'Not as potty as you think,' he said, and turned away.

*

The next few days were spent helping find a flat for the family, and it was nearly a week before I crept into the gallery at the Apollo to see John Mills in a matinee of *Of Mice and Men*.

I was enchanted, just as I had been years ago in Tientsin by 'that boy'. I sat on long after everyone else had gone, and then somehow found myself standing outside the stage door. He passed without noticing me.

The following week I was up in the gallery again, and again at the stage door. This time I made some pretence of seeing someone in the play.

'Oh, hullo,' I said coolly. 'I adored the play, you're wonderful in it.'

His dark blue eyes were warm in the May sunshine.

'Thank you! I love the part. It's the best I've had for years. . . . How is your play doing?'

'All right. . . . Lilian is frightfully funny.'

'I'll come to your next matinee.'

I nodded and started to move away. He stopped me.

'Would you like to have supper one night after the show?' he asked suddenly.

'Rather. What about tonight?' I asked, over-eagerly.

He shook his head.

'Next week. I'll call you next week. I'll get the number from Ant.'

I found myself out in Shaftesbury Avenue smiling happily at his pictures in the front of the house, disturbed, excited. . . . I took to my heels and ran for Carnaby Street where my family were having tea in their two roomed flat.

*

Tony Draws a Horse moved to the Comedy. I waited and waited, but John Mills never came to see it.

The family were settled happily now into Carnaby Street, as usual taking everything in their stride. Wyn had a job, but as there was no sleeping room for anyone but Wyn and mother, my father had taken a room in Beak Street, bare except for a small bed, a rickety table and chair propped up by a copy of the Bible.

'It's great, isn't it, Muggins?' he asked enthusiastically. 'It's like De Quincey's room near Soho Square, where he lost his Anne! I can write here all hours of the night and day, and no one will ever bother me by making the bed or clearing up!'

'I *hate* it for you!' I cried suddenly. '*Hate* it! Look, what *happened* in Singapore?'

'My work came to an end. Shenton Thomas didn't like me or my suggestions. I got the order of the S.A.K. again! Don't worry, I'm off to the War Office tomorrow. There must be a War somewhere . . . there'll be one here in a few months, and I shall be ready.'

Liz was marrying her Martin Weedon, and we all scraped together for wedding presents and got tight on a couple of bottles of Champagne that Fay gave us. Dennis was there in his dress uniform and there was a great deal of clanking of swords up and down the aisle at a village church. Nanny Day was there, crying a little. Mother was smiling serenely. Liz was engulfed by white lilies, the choir sang *The King of Love* and suddenly the brown slip of a child from Macao days was a married woman, who disappeared into the shadows of an English twilight on the arm of a stranger.

A week later, on my way from the theatre to Carnaby Street, I saw John Mills standing outside Ford's, staring at the cars. I stood watching him for a moment, and then touched his arm.

He swung round.

'You *never* came to the show, and you *never* asked me out to supper!' I said accusingly.

He laughed. 'Oh dear, I am sorry. What about tonight, then?'

'Don't know if I'm free,' I replied stiffly. 'I'll look in my book.'

I opened my diary and tried to stop him from peering over my shoulder. But it was no good; he had already seen the blank pages.

He threw back his head and laughed.

It's like a child's laughter, I thought to myself. Delighted laughter, like a little boy's. . . .

We went to the Moulin d'or. His close friends Laurence Olivier and Vivien Leigh were with him. I was shy and said very little, silenced by Vivien's beauty.

He thought I'd be too boring to be alone with, I told myself miserably when I was in bed. My clothes were wrong, and I'm spotty and I'm dull, and I'll never see him again. . . .

The next night we were back at the Moulin D'or. This time we were alone.

'Why do you always sit with your right hand stretched out against the side of your head?' he asked.

'Because, if you want to know, I have five beastly nerve spots I'm trying to hide from you,' I replied with some heat.

Again the delighted laughter, and 'bare winter was suddenly changed to spring'.

I went to every one of his matinees, slowly descending from the gallery to the circle, and finally, to two tickets in the stalls! I'd never been in the stalls in any theatre! I took my father—who watched with rapt attention and was completely absorbed.

'Do you like him? Oh do you like him?' I asked anxiously on the way back to Carnaby Street.

'Marvellous actor. I'd like to see the play again.'

At the next matinee we were in the front row.

Timidly we went to his dressing-room, and sat there in silence while he took off his make-up. He sent his dresser for tea.

'It's different for you,' my father said. 'We are the audience. We are so much in the play . . . it's like listening to an orchestra really.' He sipped at his tea and went on. 'One is . . . well . . . quieted. We will walk up the road, full of the story and caring about the people . . . it means so much to us what you have done . . . and I suppose *you* can go out and have a cup of tea and a sausage!'

John Mills turned and looked at him.

'It's things like you've said that make it all worth while,' he said seriously. 'That's what the theatre is about, really. The theatre, or an orchestra, is to take people out of themselves—for an hour or two.'

We walked home slowly, through Dean Street, and had a coffee. My father didn't speak for a long time, but just sat drinking his black coffee. Then: 'Yes, I like him . . .' he said. 'I like him.'

*

My father haunted the War Office, but without success. I used to writhe with discomfiture and embarrassment for him, a man who had been such a personage in the Far East and could be such a valuable asset to his country in the days that were to come. He always kept a sense of humour about the situation, but alone, in the streets of London, he must have died a thousand times.

Sitting in our favourite spot in Fleet Street, El Vino, I attacked him. 'Write it!' I commanded him. 'Write the story of Singapore and all its bloody muddles, how everyone always waited too long to do anything, always have, and always will. . . . Put it all down on paper. One day someone will, why not you?'

He wrinkled his nose slightly as though he were trying to avoid any emotion: 'Something will turn up, Muggins,' he said quietly.

He put on his spectacles and made a great show of reading an old theatrical print above my head, but I could see the tears running down the side of his face and getting lost somewhere in his collar, while I sat wringing my hands out of sight under the table.

In a cowardly way I found myself rushing away to Hazel Hall at the weekends. The country lanes were full of bluebells, cuckoos and chestnut trees in blossom, and the bitter scent of new cut grass.

Typically of the young, I ran away from my parents' troubles, not because I wanted to desert them, but because I couldn't bear to be a bystander. There was laughter at Hazel.

The night we reopened at the Comedy, I bought some sandwiches and took them to my father's black cave. I could hear the tapping of the typewriter long before I had reached his door. I put the sandwiches down on his table, and noticed, with a shock of horror, his Service revolver lying there.

'It's loaded, isn't it?' I asked in as careless a voice as I could muster. He nodded. 'Oh, why?' my voice faltered.

'I just keep it there,' he said.

There was nothing I could say. I sat down uneasily on the edge of his bed. What a long way we seemed to have come. It was my turn to help him now, just as he had helped us as children over our own childish tragedies, but I found it hard to put into words how much I loved and admired him, how much I wanted to help, but could not. . . .

'It's all right, Muggins. Uncle Bones sent me sixty pounds today,' he said.

'Good!' I said. 'I bet that's a good indication. All good or bad things come in threes. It's going to be all right, I know it is. You'll get a job that you like in a day or so, my Irish sixth sense tells me that.'

He grinned. 'Oh, Muggins.'

'Can I unload that thing now?' I asked. He nodded, and I took the bullets out and put them in my pocket. I could hear them chinking together as I went down the creaky stairs.

A few days later the War Office sent for him and gave him a job for eighteen months, and even better, Blackwood's accepted his story, *The Third Hood.*

For the first time in weeks I slept without nightmares, all night through.

*

Every spring Fay held a concert at Tonbridge Theatre in aid of the R.S.P.C.A., and actors, who are inherently generous about charities, swarmed down for an occasion which was followed by a good dinner at Hazel. Alfred Drayton and Bunny Hare brought John down, and in the evening, he and I walked together in the garden.

The new moon was hanging over the house like a silver dagger, giving the last of the apple blossom in the orchard a strange radiance, and away somewhere in the direction of Dukes Place, an owl hooted.

I sat on the gate looking down at Johnnie. In the shadowed moonlight, his face stood out palely against the antiquity of the yews. It was a solemn moment, a moment of profound recognition, a question set at rest forever. This was the boy Grankapa had spoken of all those years ago. 'A boy a few years older perhaps, running across an English field with a butterfly net.' Grankapa's face rose up before me, his white hair blown by the wind, and I heard him say again: 'John and Mary, that's a good old-fashioned combination!'

I knew without a shadow of doubt that my life was to be bound inseparably with Johnnie's. A shock of excitement ran through me, almost taking my breath away. Without realizing what I was doing, I held out my hand and his fastened to it.

We were exalted creatures who met every day at the Park Gate at Hyde Park Corner, and every evening at ten-fifteen at the stage door of the Apollo Theatre.

Every characteristic, every movement, were as familiar to me as though I had known Johnnie all my life. In the long galleries of memory, I tried again and again to place his familiarity. A queer thing, a dream really, half-memories of former days, a dim background of past years, of action and experiences entirely incidental to the romantic present in which I moved.

Everything we did was magical. Walking hand-in-hand across the grass towards the Serpentine; arm-in-arm through the darkening woods, across a field of buttercups and up a cobbled street; through leafy Richmond Park and crowded, grimy, living, haunted London. How terrible first love is!

'I've been looking for you all my life,' he said. 'What shall we do tomorrow?'

He was married, but it wasn't a happy situation any more. 'It's my fault it hasn't worked out. I don't think I *should* be married. The theatre is my love and my life. I don't like hurting anyone. I don't want to do anything I should be ashamed of.'

'You're the most intriguing child I've ever met,' he laughed at my woebegone face. 'So precise in your movements, so pedantic in your manner, and yet so exquisitely earnest I hardly know whether to be grave or gay!'

His tremendous, bubbling vivacity would dim suddenly, and such sadness stream from him that I could hardly bear it.

*

Lee Shubert came to see *Tony Draws a Horse* and said he wanted to take the play and some of the cast to America. A few months earlier I should have been ecstatic, but now there was Johnnie. We had dinner together at the Moulin D'or and I told him about it.

'There may be a war and then I shall probably never see you again,' he said.

'I won't go,' I said. 'It's not all that important to me now.'

'I'm going away for a few nights, to the country with Cecil Tennant,' he told me. 'I've got to sort things out in my mind.' I saw him off at Baker Street Station, standing in the cold draughts of the Underground, clinging to his hand, watching him step into the train.

'Wave to me,' I shouted, waving frantically. 'Nobody ever waves to me.'

The brown train started to move. 'Stop it!' he laughed. 'I don't need to go! I *know* . . . I love you!' his voice was carried away down the platform. 'I *love* you!'

A porter turned and looked at me with a grin. 'He said he loves you!' he said.

I stood watching the flashes under the train disappear out of sight. 'I love you,' I muttered under my breath, my hands clenched together. The wind blew my skirts up and my hair all over my face. 'I love you. I'll love you always.'

I was standing in a vast church making a vow, but it was the platform of the Bakerloo Line at Baker Street. . . .

*

On 23 August Dennis passed through London suddenly from Iraq where he had been stationed. He arrived at the theatre as the curtain came down. 'I've been posted to Scotland. Unless a miracle happens, we can't escape a war,' he said. 'All the fellows think so now.'

Johnnie, Ant, Janet and I had supper together, and then went back to the flat in Basil Street.

Ant produced a bottle of Champagne and we sat on the beds and drank it out of tooth mugs. The talk was all about joining up, and which regiment to join; they were keen on the Rifle Brigade, but Janet and I were sunk in gloom, and long after they had both gone, we hung out of the window looking at the lights, knowing that they would soon go out for a very long time. . . .

Will you ever let us, Fate,
Sit quietly again upon the gate
In the evenings, and say, 'What
shall we do tomorrow?'—
And then go slowly up
The lane again, and through
A wooden gate that's painted blue
To where a garden lies in starlight,
And apple blossom, painted white
Can touch our face with gentle fingers
As we pass
Across the grass?—
Bright days and evenings, softer than sleep
Lay gentle hands
Upon that garden, and keep
The dusty moonlight in your arms,
Till faint joyous laughter
Finds our ghosts hereafter.

Two days later Germany invaded Poland. All day everything seemed unreal. We played the two shows, but there were so few people in the theatre that it all seemed senseless; by evening London was under blackout.

The dressing-room was full of young men who were going to join up. Lilian brought in a bottle of Champagne, but the hilarity was a little forced, and the jokes strained. Johnnie, Stephen Watts and Ant were off that night to Royston. They had tried to join every regiment they could find, but they were all full, so they were attached to the Sappers.

'We're going down in Johnnie's Lancia,' Ant said. 'Perhaps we can sell it to the Colonel!'

Johnnie and I stood under the lamp by the stage door.

'We don't know what it's all going to be about, do we?' he said. 'It could last for years like the other one. We could all be obliterated. It's a pity. What a pity. But what has been has been good. A time to be remembered. I shall love you always.'

The only person I could find who was elated was my father, who needless to say was making every effort to go on active service, putting back his age and talking of dyeing his hair to look younger. Of Dennis there was no word.

Janet and I joined the Ambulance Brigade in a back street in Chelsea. Wyn was now working for the Ministry of Intelligence and my mother had joined a hospital. Life as we had known it ended. The Apollo Theatre closed, the Comedy Theatre closed, for most of the actors and male staff had gone to war. The face of London had changed too. By day and night great barrage balloons hung low over the city like incongruous silver hippos, wallowing with flapping ears. Gummed paper crosses appeared on the windows of buildings, and as soon as the light failed, every window was curtained with its blackout material, as though in mourning for days of peace.

My father was utterly gloomy in a happy kind of way.

'Germany will go Communist in the end,' he said. 'Which is what Russia wants, and Hitler's raids on London will probably kill fifty thousand people. War is usually fifteen months of boredom and two hours of terror.'

I talked to Johnnie on the telephone. He and Ant were in camp at Royston. 'We stand in long queues in the rain with empty plates, waiting for a cold, congealed hunk of uneatable bacon,' he told me. 'I'm growing a big red moustache to alleviate the boredom.'

The early mornings when Janet and I went to our Ambulance Station were beautiful. On the empty Embankment, the bridges stood out black against the opal and pink sky of morning. We leaned against the sandbags and stared at the small ships puffing up the river. There was no noise now, for the children had gone to the country, and the streets were empty save for an occasional cat stalking the pavements and the sad clip-clop of a milkman's horse.

Dennis, now in bombers dropping leaflets over Germany, wrote: 'The more I think of it all, the more amazed I am. Just to think that a handful of men have said the Word, and now millions of damn good fellows are taking every opportunity of throwing at each other foul things that bust and make a filthy noise. You all seem in a different world and I'm so tired I feel due for my hundredth birthday. The old matchsticks are becoming quite familiar round here, and it seems a long time since any of us had a good night's sleep.'

I thought of Johnnie, and how hard he, among many, had worked to achieve something in the theatre, and who now, because that Word had been said, stood in a muddy field near Cambridge guarding a searchlight! What would be the end of it all?

*

There was talk of the theatres opening again. I walked up Shaftesbury Avenue and stared at the closed Apollo. The notice outside read: 'John Mills in *Mice and Men*. Tonight at 8.30. . . .'

'When the theatres are open,' I wrote to him, 'I shall go back and try to make lots of money so that when the war is over and you come back I can help you to start again. I feel a sense of responsibility, as though I am one of the few who is free from the imprisoning khaki uniform.'

One sunny afternoon when it was my day off from the Ambulance Corps, I decided to go up to Royston and see Johnnie. My ambulance seemed as good a vehicle as any other, so without asking, I took it. I came upon the camp suddenly from the top of a little hill. I wriggled under the barbed wire and strolled up the lane between the huts. A corporal ran shouting after me but I was not to be balked, having broken every rule and got this far. Suddenly Johnnie appeared, looking like a convict in denims and a forage cap; his hands were covered with green paint and he had ugly heavy boots on his feet. His sergeant, Sergeant White, gave him the afternoon off and we sat holding hands in Banyers Hotel. I gave him a shilling to have a bath.

'I shall get the sack from the Ambulance Corps,' I said. 'I don't care. It's all so inefficient and none of the stretchers fits the ruddy vehicle.'

I was right on all counts!

When Johnnie came home on leave we spent a day on Hampstead Heath, with a shandy at Jack Straw's Castle. The sun was shining and we sat out on a bench under an elm tree. The wind blew Johnnie's hair around his forehead. He didn't look like a private in the Army, only a good looking little boy. 'If we get through all this, one way or another, will you marry me?' he asked, his mouth full of cheese roll. We went to his sister Annette's house in Robert Adam Street, and had tea in front of the fire while she played the piano. . . .

October ran into November. 'You're a terrible comet!' he said once. 'Sudden and swirling, one moment full of melancholy and despair, and the next moment, the gayest person I have ever met—'

'In a funny way I have never been part of anything worthwhile since I was a child,' I told him. 'I've been searching and waiting all my life until now.'

We ate our sandwiches by a stream watching daisies floating away with upturned faces. 'A lot of life seems to be waiting doesn't it?' I asked him.

He took my hand and we walked back along the path. It was green and covered with dandelions. There was no sign of war except for the signposts at the crossroads which had been half-heartedly painted over, and a few sandbags.

'The theatre seems beyond sight,' said Johnnie, 'but just for now, it's still quiet, and overhead the sky is blue and the sun warm. This moment is all that matters. . . .'

*

In the middle of November the offer from Shubert to go to New York to join the American company of *Tony Draws a Horse* was confirmed. It was a moment I had waited for. The offer was for a three-year contract, and I could sub-contract to make films. The salary was to be $45,000 a year!

We were standing on the bridge at Cambridge in the moonlight, throwing pennies into the Cam.

'You'll have to go in convoy,' Johnnie said. 'Ships are being sunk all the time. Is it so much worth it?'

'I think I have to go,' I told him. 'Not for the money or possible glory, but just so that you can be sure about me.'

I agreed to go for the run of the play, but refused the three-year contract. How could I possibly leave England now for such a long time!

I left for America three weeks later. Wyn had bought me a white lambskin coat for ten pounds and Janet had given me a pair of fur-lined boots. One of my father's battered suitcases held my belongings, and I had one last weekend with Johnnie at Ely, where he and Annette sang her song *My Heart has Wings* on the stage at the theatre.

The inkiness of Euston station, full of troops, and with the family standing together in a huddle as they always had at other partings, giggling, to stop themselves from showing any emotion. My father was unable to speak, but he was constantly grinning and blinking. He gave me a pair of gloves and a letter. Mother held out a chamois leather belt. 'Put all your money and belongings into it, darling, and wear it round your waist all the time.' Only as the train drew slowly out of the station and I caught a last glimpse of my mother's face, did it ever occur to me that *my* ship might be sunk. I hung as far as I could out of the window to see the last of them, standing in a small, tight group, growing smaller and smaller and farther away, until they disappeared into the darkness. And I thought of Johnnie. Having taken so long to find him, was I to lose him now in this senseless war?

13

SHIPS THAT PASS

The *Britannic* was a huge, squat ship, painted grey, with a gun mounted at her bows and another at her stern. The passengers boarded her in silence. Some were crying. There were children with labels attached to their jackets who looked scared and bewildered. There was no gaiety, such as I had remembered boarding other ships. I wandered round the decks. There were no deckchairs and all the shutters to the public rooms were closed and barred. I noticed the lifeboats were already full of provisions, and a thrill, half excitement, half fear, ran down my spine.

We sailed from Liverpool on the evening tide. When the passengers were allowed on deck we stood silently by the rails looking back to the coastline. Overhead the sky deepened into the richer blue of twilight, and the last of England stood out luminous and green against the afterglow.

I went down to my small cabin and thought of the family; and thought of Johnnie fighting the mud, cold and food of his camp at Royston. I put my things away methodically in my cupboards, fastened the chamois belt with my few belongings and money round my waist, turned on the portable gramophone that Johnnie had given me, and fell asleep. . . .

Heavy seas caused the ship to plunge and stagger for the next two days. Away to the port and starboard of us I could see a line of destroyers, the froth from their bows streaming away like lengths of lace. The ship was half empty. I sat at a table with a gentleman called Mr White, whose face looked as if it hurt him; a strange, shaggy man of few words, with black gums to his false teeth, and a cyst on the end of his nose.

'There's a bad English movie going on in the saloon,' Mr White said. 'You better come and see it.'

I followed him, thinking idly that he always looked as if he were sitting, even when he was standing. He was a strange man. He never told me anything about himself, nor did he ever ask anything about me. His eyes had a faraway look as though he were trying to hang on to a picture in his mind. There was a little frown between his brows and he sniffed continually. At Halifax we went ashore together, and Mr White bought me a cherry brandy to 'keep out the cold'. 'I'm getting off here,' he said suddenly.

'Oh! I shall miss you,' I said truthfully.

'If there's any kind of warning you get straight into that lifeboat and don't waste any time,' he told me fiercely.

At my last sight of him on the quayside, he was looking more like an infuriated terrier than ever, standing crouched and alone, cleaning his fountain pen. As I went up the gangway, I thought of the bridge over the Cam, and dropped two pennies into the water. . . .

*

The company assembled at the Playhouse on 47th Street. The play, directed by Harry Gribble, was put on by George Brady, a fat man who never ceased to shout 'My Gard' at everyone from the circle, while Grace George, his wife and our leading lady, took an instant dislike to me. She wore an enormous charm bracelet, and on every one of my lines that might have got a laugh, she shook her arm so that the line was lost beneath a peal of jangling brass bells.

I had a very small room at the American Women's Club on West 57th Street. The subway trains shook my room ninety times a day and ninety times a night. I developed a nervous itch which Grace George referred to as 'hives'. I argued constantly with Harry Gribble who said I was playing the part too 'English casual'—and with Brady who said I was too serious. The final indignity came when Grace George asked indulgently what colours I had worn in the play in London. 'Blue in the first act. Primrose yellow in the last,' I told her.

'You shall do the same here, *deeer*,' she said graciously.

At the dress rehearsal I saw that the set of the first act was painted blue, and of the last act primrose yellow. 'All we can see of you, ducky,' said my friend Michael Dyne, 'is your eyes. You completely *melt* into the scenery.'

I moved to the New Weston Hotel. I prayed in St Patrick's Cathedral that the play would fail. I dined with John Van Druton, danced to

Louis Armstrong's Band, whirled through the shops, and wrote endless letters and sent endless cables to Johnnie, who had now been promoted to Sergeant. Larry and Vivien came to New York from Hollywood for the opening of *Gone With the Wind.* Their presence made a great difference to me, for suddenly there was someone to laugh with, whom I could understand, and while they were there I was happy.

Our first night was a near disaster. Part of the scenery collapsed and Miss George's bracelet fell into the footlights, which brought the only laugh she managed to achieve. There was a slow handclap at the fall of the curtain in the first act, and Gribble and George Brady were both running about bleating 'My Gard!'. At the Stork Club after the show the critic Lucius Bebe's voice rang out over the radio, 'Wal folks, I've just seen *Tony Draws a Horse.* S'far as I'm concerned Tony draws a blank.'

The play staggered on through Christmas, but I was a shadow of my former self. Itching away with hives, and a stone lighter, Michael Dyne and I stared gloomily into the gaily lit shops and drank a great deal of gin.

On New Year's Day I had a summons to Metro-Goldwyn Mayer. They wanted me to go to Hollywood to do a test for *Pride and Prejudice.* 'You got good eyes and a good kisser, and maybe we can take a bit off your nose,' they said kindly.

I sat in St Patrick's Cathedral and thought about it. I fell on my knees. 'God,' I said. 'If you will let me go home safely to Johnnie I'll give all this up and just look after him and have a whole troop of kids and bring 'em up properly. Maybe one or all of them will do what I once set out to do, but now I know what's more important to me.'

A few weeks later I sailed again for England in the *Georgic.* Michael Dyne stood beside me on the quay. 'Wish I was coming,' he said absently. 'One day I'll write a play for you and Johnnie to do together.'

People on the jetty were sobbing and calling out and waving flags and balloons. There were more people on that jetty than I ever saw aboard the ship! I was so happy to think I was on my way home that I had almost forgotten those tearing seas and what might lie beneath. Who wanted to go to England now, I thought! Only me! And I heard myself singing, for in two weeks I would be back at Cambridge!

The wireless officer handed me a message. I took it away to my cabin. I knew it was from Johnnie, but I didn't want to open it; I was so afraid it was to tell me that he had been sent to France. I turned on my little bedside light and opened the telegram.

'This love of mine my darling,' it read, 'is stronger than the black sea that divides us.'

How queer, I thought, as I walked the deck, that he should send me such a message. The black sea raged around me, boisterous and turbulent, with the waves exploding in a paroxysm of surf against the bows.

The conversation was all about submarines and mines. On our bunks, everything was laid out ready for the alarm. Death seemed very near all the time, nearer somehow than it had been on the way out; for one thing, the Purser told us breezily, there were more submarines. I shared a cabin with a girl whom I called Big Ears. I can't remember her real name. I wish I could, for we had many a laugh in some of the cruellest seas.

We had put the clocks on, so it was the same time as England. We were passing Iceland, soon it would be Scotland and Ireland and then, not very far ahead now, under the moonlight, England! London and Carnaby Street, Robert Adam Street where Johnnie might be with Annette, waiting and wondering. London in the dark. . . .

Suddenly the alarm!

'Christ!' said Big Ears. 'I was nearly asleep.'

'Come on, don't be a slouch,' I said, and I was off, through the door, down the passage and onto the deck in front of the lifeboat. I didn't want to die. Not *now*!

'Have we been hit?' The words ran up and down the line.

'Someone has. It could be us next. God knows what's under the sodding water.'

There was no panic. People stood quietly, hands clasped over their bulky lifebelts, watching the boats being lowered to the level of the decks.

'We should have been home tomorrow,' somebody said.

'We're only sixty miles out of the Mersey.'

'It's full moon! The buggers must see us!'

'No one knows—'

'The crew knows!'

'I wonder what they're doing at home. . . .'

I stood swallowing, my hands clenched together. My mouth was dry. I wished I could have a drink of water. I looked across at Big Ears; her face was ill and strained.

Silently, without fuss, we climbed into the lifeboat. There wasn't much room because of the provisions and other things in it. All along the side of the ship, we could see in the half-light people sitting in other boats. It was the most eerie time that I can remember. Below us the mourning sea churned against the side of the ship. No one spoke any more. They just sat limply, side by side in silence, shoulder to shoulder, staring at the water below. There was no sign of the escort which we knew must be there. We sat, hearts beating loudly in our throats, hands folded tightly in our laps, each thinking his own private thoughts:

Could I come to Cambridge
If I died?
And find you on the same bridge
Just beside
Our moonlit water? Hear the pennies drop
And your delighted laughter at the plop
That both our wishes made,
Near the ducks, in the jade
Green water?
Could we walk there together
And not grow old?
And kick the skipping leaves no longer gold,
And hold our arms
About the Blue Boar's neck,
And chase away alarms
That haunt us, of a wreck
In grey, sad waters?—
Oh moonlight, gently kiss the square,
And powder frost, faint, everywhere
These lovers danced
That sunlit day—
Ere Death passed their way.

I closed my eyes and thought of Macao. In summer on the South China coast, the mist will lie at morning as though the very sky had come to rest upon the sea. Cirrus and cumulus fleck the still water with white feathery floes, or wreath the dark fern shade of some floating island, leaving, between pallid reflections, blue pools of space. And on this opal screen, faithfully shadowed in water-blended colour, the junks, heavy sailed, wait for the morning breeze. . . .

'I only hope,' said the man next to me, 'that I'm not taken short!' A ripple of laughter ran round the boat.

For what seemed hours we sat in the half-lowered boats, while the ship rolled onwards, the speed of the engines constantly changing. As the early light of dawn broke on the horizon, so we made the mouth of the Mersey.

From the end of the gangway, I turned, and took one last look at the *Georgic*. Squat and grey like her sister ship, which had taken me to America, secured by steel hawsers, she leaned heavily, like some old girl relaxing with her corsets off, taking a deep breath before she had to turn round and run the gauntlet of those hazardous and sullen seas once more. . . .

*

The whole country lay under a pall of snow and it was bitterly cold. I decided to go straight to Cambridge without announcing my arrival.

Once there, I told myself, I'll book a small room, and then ring him up. Maybe he'll get a couple of hours leave and we can have dinner together at a table in the corner, under the window, with a bottle of Volnay by candlelight!

Unreal, the train rolled on, the lights were green, a smell of musk clung to the seats and the weird light made the other people swaying in the carriage look like stiff corpses with decaying faces.

The streets of Cambridge were full of slush, and after the brilliance of New York the darkness was staggering, but the Blue Boar was warm and friendly and smelled of onion soup, and to my delight the familiar figure of Sergeant White was standing by the desk.

'Hullo!' I said breathlessly. 'How's Johnnie?'

'Mary!' he said. 'Look, he's not well at all, I'm afraid.'

My heart stopped. 'Not well? What do you mean, not well?' I croaked.

'He's down with pneumonia,' he said.

'In hospital. . . ?' I was almost in tears.

A slow grin spread over his friendly red face. 'As a matter of fact he's here. We were all in the bar last night, Jock and Johnnie and the others, when he seemed to be taken groggy. I got him into a bed upstairs and then told Sergeant-Major when I got back to camp. I just dropped in to see how he was. He's got a pretty high temperature.'

I hesitated, staring at him.

'Room 14,' he said. 'Go on, girl, 'op it. Key's in the door!'

I was up the stairs two at a time, along the passage, and standing outside the door. My heart was pounding.

I took a deep breath, opened the door and went in.

14

JOHNNIE COMES MARCHING HOME

Johnnie had been given a few hours leave one Saturday, and we were driving through the bare Cambridgeshire lanes and ivied grey stone walls in his little green Ford, when I noticed a sign hanging over a small wooden gate: 'Cocker spaniel puppies for sale.'

I clutched Johnnie's arm. 'Oh, do let's look!' I urged.

The puppies were playing in a yard, but one stood looking towards the gate. At the sight of us, his whole body started quivering with excitement. I picked him up, a warm, agitated mass of wet tongue and golden fur.

'Oh, Johnnie—' I began.

'Would you like him? He can look after you when you're away from me.'

'What shall we call him?' I asked as we drove back through the haggard winter trees to the warmth of the Blue Boar.

'Hamlet,' he said, without a moment's hesitation, and Hamlet thumped his stumpy tail against me in appreciation.

*

Wyn, tall, great, elegant thing, shy and grinning, was married to Owen Steel. Johnnie came up for the wedding, and we all had a lively, sparkling party in Regent's Street which even the now all too familiar drone overhead was unable to eclipse. They went up to Aberdeen where he was second-in-command of a battalion of the Gordon Highlanders. When I stayed with them I was amused to open the door one night to his corporal. It was Stewart Granger!

In November, Dennis was transferred to a night fighter squadron. 'Dangerous drivers', they called themselves: I remembered him as a little boy afraid of the dark, and now he was a man, up there somewhere between the earth and the stars, alone in his Hurricane. One morning my father called me from the R.A.F. station at Hemswell where he was commanding a unit of the R.A.F. Regiment.

'I have news of Beak,' he said.

My heart stopped at the use of the nursery name, and in memory I was whirled back to the sound of my mother's voice at Johnman's bedside years ago.

'What?' I asked, steeling myself.

I could hear the pride in my father's voice. 'He phoned about flying me down at the weekend, and ended up saying quite casually: "Oh, by the way, I've been given a Gong"—I rushed to the *Times* and saw it was the D.F.C.'

A few months earlier, Johnnie had been sent to the Officer Cadet Training Unit at Shrivenham. I took a room in the quiet little village in the house of the village schoolmaster, and in this house, when Johnnie had a night off, he used to sleep, exhausted with trying to master the mathematics of gunnery.

In due course he got his commission and was fitted out with an officer's uniform, full of excitement as he bought his first Sam Browne which he spent hours polishing to the colour of a horse chestnut.

Typically, having been earmarked for the Royal Artillery, he was posted to a Rifle Regiment, stationed in Trowbridge. We set off one stormy day to Bath in the Ford, with Hamlet in the back seat. For some weeks Johnnie lived in a wet tent, but it didn't last very long. He was taken ill with a duodenal ulcer and transferred to the Bath Hospital, where, he said, he gained the prize for swallowing 'Two and a half yards of rubber tubing'.

Soon after Christmas 1940 his divorce was through and we decided to get married on 16 January 1941.

I had taken a flat in St James's for all the family to gather in the day before. It was a sunny day and the guns were silent. I walked arm-in-arm with my father through Hyde Park to a bench by the Serpentine.

'It hurts me terribly to realize that I have done nothing for you in terms of a wedding present, Muggins, but you know something of the unending nag of old debts.'

'Please—' I started.

'Very few pounds for a pilot officer, and though I shall soon be a flight lieutenant, the pay comes at the end of the month!'

Flight lieutenant, I thought. In the last war you commanded a Regiment!

'I think you're wonderful, darling,' I said evenly.

'What worries me is that I can't buy your dress and hat and things.'

He sat down suddenly on a hard seat and stared at the ducks on the Serpentine.

'It seems only yesterday that you were a little toddler stumping so bravely round the Chefoo hills, and such a dear sportsman riding beside me on Shanghai mornings.' He cleared his throat noisily and pinched my cheek. 'So much of pain, failure and disappointment. All I was going to do for you all, the home I was going to give you. It's too late now, anyway, you've all gone. The old life *has* really been a failure you know!'

'Oh, no.'

'Oh, yes! I have treated myself to Adventure, and left you all without what any man ought to do for his family first.' He turned his head away so that I shouldn't see his tears. 'But what am I to do about it now? You don't belong to me any more. . . .'

'I do. I always will.' The ducks blurred before me. A couple passing by looked with some concern at the elderly pilot officer and the young woman in tears on a park bench.

'I don't want to bring you tears for any maudlin memories or regrets of mine. I only wish—and it's the truest of wishes—that Heaven may send you children, and with them, the happiness that you brought to us. There is no happiness to take its place.' He blew his nose sharply. 'I hope in being happily married that you are not going to let go of other things . . . your own self expression . . . ambitions . . . the dreams. . . .'

He put his hand on my knee; that large, warm, comforting dry hand I had known so long.

'Bless you, darling. Great happiness and success to you and Johnnie boy. Keep the old sense of humour. It's a sense of proportion—you want it more, not less, when you're sharing lives together! It's a safeguard against stuffiness, pomposity, even selfishness. They say that a sign of a truly happy married life is that a man and woman can, after many years, laugh with and at each other. . . .'

'Remember everything, won't you? Keep the old light burning. Remember even the worst of me, rather than forget. . . .'

I couldn't speak as we made our way back to St James's.

'Tea!' he said jubilantly to the waiter. 'Tea for two!'

The waiter paused. 'Honey, sir?' he asked. 'I know Mrs Mills likes honey!'

My eyes, wide with dismay, met my father's. He threw back his head and roared with laughter.

*

The next day Johnnie and I were married!

There wasn't a cloud in the sky. Everyone was there. My mother, father, Wyn and Owen, Dennis, Johnnie's family, Annette—his lovable, boisterous father, slapping everyone on the back with wild enthusiasm. Janet, now married to Charlie Birkin, Noël Coward and Fay Compton; Larry Olivier in the uniform of the Fleet Air Arm, Vivien, Ursula Jeans, Roger Livesey, Ant, Stephen Watts and many others, in uniforms and heavy boots. . . .

15

THE SUGAR PLUM FAIRY

How lucky I was! I had opened the door of my private world to someone who from the first gave me radiant silver-bright days where the only remembered shadows were cast by enemy aircraft.

Diana Churchill rented us our first home for twenty-five shillings a week; enchanting No. 16 Old Barrack Yard. An eighteenth-century stable mews in a courtyard, at the top of a rickety wooden staircase tucked away behind St George's Hospital at Hyde Park Corner and hard by the Grenadier public house.

Johnnie had been waiting for an Army Medical Board to decide on his future. He was told that he was permanently unfit for the Service, and that he was to await the War Office's orders. He returned gloomily to London, but a few weeks later he was asked to play the leading part in *Cottage to Let* for Gaumont-British. He accepted with alacrity—not only because it gave him something to do, but also because we needed the money, and every day he rode out to Shepherd's Bush and back on a bicycle.

I had passed through my V.A.D. training and was told to report to St George's Hospital. From the beginning it was clear that I was in no way going to follow in my mother's footsteps as a nurse. My first visit to the operating theatre was not a success, for at the sight of a spurt of blood from under the surgeon's knife, I had shamefully and sheepishly to be assisted out into the passage.

There were temperatures to take, beds to make, sewing to do, floors to wash; and at the end of the day, wrapping my scarlet-lined cloak around me, I fled as fast as my legs would carry me to Old Barrack Yard, to take Hamlet for a walk and then cook Johnnie's supper, doing the best I could with our rations.

Air-raids were a nightly routine now, and Johnnie had a great desire to find a cottage in the country where we could go for weekends. Suddenly I thought of Duke's Place! We drove down to lunch with Fay, and walked through the remembered fields to that oasis of the past, but alas it was too decrepit to consider. It was a clear cold day of high scudding clouds and we walked on up the road to the top of the hill. There, under the brow of the hill, stood a converted oast-house, its wide eyes peering anxiously down the valley from under its pointed hat. A man, clearly a sculptor by the finished and half-finished pieces around him, was working in the garden. He grinned at us.

'What a heavenly place,' I began. He looked up the grassy bank to the house with a smile of affection, and nodded.

'Unfortunately I'm going up North on a job, so I can't live in it,' he said. I dug Johnnie hard in the ribs.

'I suppose you wouldn't consider letting it to us?' Johnnie asked.

'Why not?'

'How much?'

'Twenty-five shillings a week too much?'

We went into the house with him, had a cup of tea, looked about, and fell head over heels in love with it. It wasn't exactly modernized. Cooking was on a primus stove, and there was no electricity, only oil lamps.

'There's a well outside for water,' the sculptor said. 'But in the summer it's inclined to dry up, so I have an extra tank down by my studio. What you do is to put a long length of hosepipe into it, seal one end with your hand, drag it up the bank, lie on your back, suck through and drop the hose into the well; once it gets going it's easy. The boiler works, but it's a bit temperamental!'

We followed him through the small tower rooms upstairs, the long room with the fireplace on the ground floor, and into the three acres of garden, with hedges of cob nuts, roses, herbaceous beds, a neglected kitchen garden, and back past a giant walnut tree which Hamlet eyed with every possible pleasure. We moved in a week later, and in the months that followed, living almost entirely from that wonderful vegetable garden, Johnnie's ulcer was completely cured.

In March, when lifting a heavy patient in the hospital, I had a sudden stabbing pain through my lower abdomen, and promptly fainted. I found myself in another hospital under the care of a gynaecologist, Cedric Lane Roberts, who told me that I had lost my baby! As I didn't even know that I had had one, I was thoroughly depressed, but Lane Roberts sent me to the Oast for two heaven-sent weeks, where Johnnie refused to let me do anything but cook, while he gardened, cleaned the house, shot rabbits to eat, and fought with the boiler. When I went back to see Lane Roberts, he told me with delight that, 'There's still one there!'

I rushed out and told Johnnie. 'One of the Bunch is still there! Arriving in November!'

All through April and into May we lived at the Oast. Gardening, often enough, in tin hats because of the falling shrapnel from the dog-fights going on overhead. The house was always full of people on leave. Dennis; my father, lying in an old deck chair sketching; my mother gardening with Wyn, who was also to have a baby in October. Vivien and Larry came, Rex Harrison and his wife Lilli Palmer, Janet and Charlie Birkin, Ant and Pempie, David Niven and his wife Prim. Every girl, I recorded meticulously in my diary, 'in the "Pudding Club"!'

On 10 May 1941 we went back to Old Barrack Yard for a few nights. Johnnie thought it would be fun to see Rex and Lilli in *No Time for Comedy* and then go on to the Café de Paris; we started dressing just as the sirens squealed out over London.

'I don't think I want to go after all,' he said, suddenly. 'Let's eat here, and I'll take Hamlet out for a walk later.'

The raid started and we ate our steak and kidney pie lying on our stomachs under the table.

It was a bad night and our local Warden called through the door: 'Better come down to the shelter, you two, it's getting hot.'

'What about Hamlet?' I wasn't going to leave him.

'Bring him with you.'

As we went down the rickety steps of Old Barrack Yard, clutching Hamlet and our gas masks, we could see the skies bright with flares and pencils of searchlight attempting to pierce the scudding clouds. For several hours we sat in the shelter while the city was crucified from the air. Johnnie held my hands. The worst seemed to be over when we heard the scream of one of Krupps's biggest. It seemed to be coming straight towards us. My eyes met the steady blue flame of John's. The next instant there was a crushing detonation, which flung us on the floor in all directions, covered in dust and rubble. Wordlessly, white-faced, we dragged ourselves shakily to our feet.

'You all right in there, Eddie?'

The head of a man under a tin hat was silhouetted through the shattered door of the shelter, against the black and orange sky.

'Johnnie, I can't stand this,' I said. 'I don't want to die like a rat in a trap. . . . Let's go home.'

'If it's still there!' a voice said.

We struggled out into the cobbled mews, through the stifling dust that filled our eyes and mouths.

'Where did that one land?' Johnnie asked a hurrying Warden.

'Smack bang through the middle of the Alexandra Hotel, poor sods,' he answered grimly. The Alexandra Hotel was only fifty feet away.

Some of our stairs were broken, the front door sagged backwards on broken hinges, all the windows were smashed and the flat was full of broken glass and smoky dust. We stood gazing around in despair.

'Better clean up,' Johnnie said, but he didn't move, and I noticed he had his head on one side, like a bird, listening. 'Oh *no*!' he muttered under his breath.

'What?'

'Listen!'

He flung himself on top of me, dragging us both under the table with the remains of the steak and kidney pie. The flat seemed to stagger as the bomb burst in a nearby building, and brickwork clattered down in the kitchen. Grimy and tear-stained we grinned at each other. At least we were still alive!

That second bomb, we were to discover, hit the Alexandra Hotel again, and nearly everyone who had escaped the first was killed. A group of women was found sitting bolt upright together in one room, their knitting in their laps, their eyes open and staring with an expression of disbelief. It was only when the ambulance men tried to help them out, touched them gently, and they fell over, that they realized they were dead.

*

The hot summer days slipped by. We ate our own strawberries by moonlight at the Oast House, our legs swinging out of the window of our bedroom, which looked out onto the garden.

'I don't ever remember being so happy,' Johnnie said, with his mouth full. 'Far away into the future I shall remember tonight.'

We're so lucky, I thought; I hope not too lucky. But I didn't voice the thought, I didn't dare to tempt Providence.

My father, expecting to be made a squadron leader, found himself instead in Halton Hospital. 'My great fear,' he wrote, 'is that I may be invalided out altogether.' He wasn't invalided out until the early part of the following year, but he no longer commanded his R.A.F. Regiment unit. He was sent on a course to a 'Beastly place called Elgere Wolds, "Elfire Wolds in the Slough of Duckspond", while the Air Ministry try to fit me in somewhere.'

He sat forlornly under the walnut tree, slashing at a few nettles with a stick, like a boy with dashed hopes.

'This is a young man's war, Muggins,' he said. 'It always has been. It was a young man's war in South Africa and again in 1914. I was young then so I was part of it. But this is Dennis's war, yours, Wyn's and Liz's. . . . I have to stand back and wait and watch. I can only applaud or throw myself in dust. I ain't young any more. I'm stiff and deaf and tired, have to face it. . . .'

He stayed at 'Elfire Wolds'; Johnnie went to London to play Wilberforce in *Mr Pitt*, I turned to writing again, and Wyn had a baby girl, Shirley, with a head bright with red curls! The Blitz-pummelled country still stood on its feet, and the ripening year meandered on through autumn and the gold of fallen leaves to the darkness of holly and November, with its mossy smell of dead leaves and rainy shadows, the orange glow of oil lamps, and sweet-smelling log fires in the Oast House.

Conscious, as we all were, of the nearness of Death, I found myself turning over in my mind the profound question of Birth. Who, and What, was that kicking, revolving being inside me? Was it to be a boy, or a girl? Who would it resemble, and what of his or her future?

Grankapa had said that 'if your spiritual twin is not yet born, you are separated by Time'. It had made a great impression on me, the thought that one twin would be ever searching for someone, or something, that it could never achieve or find, so that its life could fail to be perfect. The thought that such a thing could happen to this unknowing baby saddened me. Were determinations contingent upon circumstances after all? Had I not lifted that heavy old gentleman in the hospital, would that other twin not have lost its grip on life? Perplexing thoughts.

'Was it a boy or a girl, the one that went, d'you think?' I asked Cedric Lane Roberts.

He smiled gravely. 'Could have been a boy. Boys don't hang on so easily to life. I have the feeling that boys, rather than girls, have in their deep subconsciousness a lifelong wish to go back into the safety of the womb!' He laughed. 'But you mustn't take that as anything but hypothetical!'

On 20 November, Johnnie and I left the Oast at 7.30 in the morning and drove to the Royal Northern Hospital in Holloway Road, where the Bunch was to arrive. But it seemed there were no signs of immediate appearance, so we returned to Park Place, saw a film, and retired to an early bed.

At five o'clock the following morning, I was seized with tummy ache. . . . The hall porter brought us tea and described, dramatically, his wife's many experiences of childbirth. As soon as it was light we were back at the hospital, only to be told, 'There's hours yet, go and have a good day!' But by teatime I could stand no more and we went back to the hospital. Seeing me safely tucked up in bed, Johnnie left, and the battle began.

At 10.30 p.m. on 21 November 1941, 'the Bunch', Juliet Mills, finally arrived, to the discordant, unharmonious fanfare of bombs, aircraft and gunfire, under a London sky seared by the heat of the night's fires.

She, like hundreds of other babies born that night, was totally unconcerned. Her reflexes were perfect, she weighed 6 pounds 6 ounces, what hair she possessed was palely frosted, the eyes were fiercely blue, and now and again a little wind of a smile lifted the corners of her mouth, as if she knew more than she would ever tell. Outside, the snow started to fall lightly.

Johnnie was awed, delighted, and couldn't stop grinning. Sheafs of telegrams started arriving:

'I know your father. Carol Reed.'

'I'm a fan of your father's, expect to be a fan of yours in 1966. Wynyard.'

'Ah, Juliet, if the measure of thy joy be heap'd like mine and that thy skill be more to blazon it, then sweeten with thy breath this neighbour air, and let rich music's tongue unfold the imagined happiness that both receive in either by this dear encounter. Dearest love to you and your superb Mama. Aunt Puss and Uncle Sub Lieut Olivier.'

'Go easy on those milk shakes. Robert Donat.'

'Hurrah. When do I start religious instruction. Noël.'

*

My father wrote:

'I am so glad it is a daughter. I believe implicitly in the *luck* of a family headed by an elder sister, and a girl child is the sweetest thing on earth, I believe a man always wants a daughter first. She has come at a tremendous hour in history, perhaps to see the dawn of a world that will never be able to imagine or understand the world that we knew. How wonderful it is, this Renewing and Renewing. Now, perhaps, only now, do you come to know really married life—and from now you will begin, I think, to realizingly understand that there is really no growing old. So long as you keep well you are young and everything around you is young. You have had a mother who is so wonderful with us all, you will realize daily what she has been to you girls and boys, and you will pass on the lovely unselfish devotion, for, don't you think, as I do, that in that, you have the greatest foundation for a happy country.'

We took the Sugar Plum Fairy, and her Nanny, Daisy Evans, back to the Oast. There were smiling faces all around; my mother was full of practical advice, her small birdlike hands on my arm, her grey eyes sometimes bright with quick tears. Wyn with her baby Shirley and I with Bunch, two babies rolled up tightly in prams against the winter winds, jollied up the lanes full of holly berries—catching each other's eye and going off into gales of laughter. 'The Bell girls have now become doting, dotty mothers!'

The only discordant, jarring sounds came from Johnnie's endless battle with the boiler, which on Christmas morning culminated in the immortal line: 'Oh! you, you—Purple Pisser!'

*

We heard from Liz's mother-in-law, Mrs Weedon, that Martin was a prisoner in Japanese hands. Of Liz there was no word since a cable saying that she was to be evacuated from Singapore with her baby. 'We'll hear something soon,' said my father hopefully. 'She's probably being sent home by Australia or South Africa.'

Poor father. His prophecies were coming true, but he sat gloomily in front of the fire, for once not his usual buoyant self. 'There's one thing to be grateful for,' said Wyn. 'If they'd listened to you, we would all probably still be in Singapore!'

'And who would be happier than Hayley!' My mother's low laugh had something in it of relief. My father didn't answer. He went towards the stairs, and a moment later we heard him singing to the Bunch.

16

THE MEN IN THE SHADOWS

Noël Coward rang Johnnie and asked him to play in his film *In Which We Serve*, which was based on the adventures of H.M.S. *Kelly*, Lord Mountbatten's destroyer. It meant leaving the Oast for a while and the packing was a doleful affair, but Johnnie had found a small cottage to rent near the studio at Denham, and one very cold morning, we crammed everything up to the roof of the car and set off.

I looked back over my shoulder at the empty windows. More than ever before they seemed to be staring in bewildered dismay down the valley.

Mopes Farm cottage was a small fourteenth-century house in Gerrard's Cross. From the beginning the walls were running with moisture and if Johnnie left his coat hanging on a chair near them, it was wringing wet in no time. We missed the Oast miserably, but we soon settled down. There was a lamp beside our bed that had the word 'Maryon' written on it, so we decided to give it to Bunch as a second name, being a mixture of Mary and John.

Bunch was christened at the Brompton Parish Church with Larry and Vivien, Margot Oxford and Noël as her godparents. That night she slept under the stairs in the blitz which started as the Last Post blew in nearby Knightsbridge Barracks, and went on till morning.

Down at Denham Studios the cast was assembled for the film. Noël himself, Michael Wilding, Kay Walsh, Bernard Miles and Joyce Carey.

'My God! We need a baby!' Noël said. 'Johnnie and Kay's baby and we haven't got one.'

'*I've* got a baby,' I reminded him.

'Go and get it, darling, at once.'

The Oast House, which peered anxiously down the valley from under its pointed hat.

With Bunch at the Oast House.

Fernacres.

The Mills family with Hayley's pony in Richmond Park.

ohnnie as Scott
f the Antarctic.

Elmhurst school
Camberly
Surrey
July 9th

TO Darling sweet-heart mummy and daddy, I love you both so much I am dieing for the HOLS aren't you. daddy and I have a little tiny bit more work to do.

Kisses hugs again and again to you I miss you so much. Love

Juliet

XXXXOOOO XXXOOO

Dear mummy

Mummy has been beastly.

Mummy you did s
we could eat
Sausages in ou
fingers. well
said in a
sneary Voise th

wee could not w
(HER.) I tride t
let it slide o
my back but it
is Diffecult
She got in a
ofel temper a
Said she was
to give you her
money and go
The very minut

I wish you had
been there it wou
never ever have
happend it allw
has to happen
when you are
out

Love

Hayl

Letters from the children.

Sunday

Fonthill
Sussex
E.G.

Darling Mummy and Daddy
On sunday we had rasberys and Ice cream.
We fond out the scorer was not scoring proply and we realy wone wen the 1st 11 came back they had wone and in stead of me geet getting 4 I got 5.
today it isterably hot.
it said in the book you gave me that you cane get a badge on paramay
and do remember to send me that tape.

Love Jonney XXX OOO

So it was that at the age of eleven weeks, Juliet Mills appeared in her first film. It was a moment of supreme emotion for me when I carried her onto the set. In the middle of the scene, however, she forgot herself enough to allow a loud pyrotechnic to explode from the regions of her cot. Heads turned in her direction, and the camera crew laughed. Mortified, I looked at Noël.

'Hereditary, I fear,' he muttered.

*

Liz and her little boy arrived home on the day my father was invalided out of the Air Force. We all sat around staring at each other with eyes of gloom, watching him take off his uniform for the last time, fold it carefully, and put it away in the white box with his 'things'. On the same day Johnnie and I hit on the idea for a play about the French Underground Movement, prompted by my listening to a radio speech by Stafford Cripps to the V Army, while I was sitting in the bath.

For two weeks I never stopped writing all day, only getting up from my table to cook the lunch for Nanny and the Bunch, and then going back to work until Johnnie came home from the studio. I had never been so enthusiastic or excited by anything I had written. Bernard Miles used to come home with Johnnie and they read it together. They decided to try to find a management to produce it after *In Which We Serve* was finished. Noël read it and was equally enthusiastic, but he didn't like the title. I was calling it *To Stall the Grey Rat*, from the quotation 'Nothing but a man's heart can stall the grey rat and carrion worm.' Noel suggested *Men in Shadow*.

We moved up to Fairholt Street in Knightsbridge, and Johnnie took the play to Binkie Beaumont. To my excitement he said he would do it. Johnnie and I went hand-in-hand to the Globe Theatre together to see him. He was sitting at his desk, a good looking young man with an amused smile. 'Are *you* the author?' he asked. 'I didn't expect anyone quite so young.'

Johnnie was now making the film of *We Dive at Dawn* and I spent a great deal of time with the family. My father was plunged into a despair that made him snap at everyone, like the wounded animal that he was. He refused point-blank to let me use the name Hayley Bell as the author of *Men in Shadow*, and insisted on the Mary being added.

'I'm a writer too, dammit, Muggins,' he said. 'Makes me look like a poor relation.'

'I've used Hayley Bell for years on the stage,' I reminded him. 'And using *three* names is always difficult.'

'What about George Bernard Shaw? Robert Louis Stevenson? Some of the public might even think H.B. was me.'

I looked up at him standing beside me in the Park. His shoulders stooped more than I had noticed before, and his hair was very grey.

'Of course I'll do anything you want, darling. It doesn't matter to me one bit. I just thought it better to have a man's name, that's all. What will happen when we write something together!'

He smiled gravely. 'My head is as empty as a drum and only fit to beat upon.' He wheeled away abruptly, going off into his own shadows, leaving me to watch him through my tears. I thought of him all those years ago, walking high in the bamboo woods at Mokanshan amid the native scents and the passionate flowers, and standing in the moon's bright silver on the Tiles. I shivered, and turned for home.

*

The summer weekends back at the Oast slowly turned Bunch from a baby to a blue-eyed, cherry-cheeked crawler. Johnnie came and went while he was making *We Dive at Dawn*—fascinating with his red beard. Ringing, singing days of sunshine, of creepers tumbling up the house, rose briars running wild, lupins and hollyhocks—and the scent of new mown hay from the fields beyond. Sometimes I thought with nostalgia of China, of plumbago and oleander and hibiscus, and the stooping blue figures in the paddy fields lifting out the kaoliang, but I had never been happier in my life, watching Johnnie wrestling with the vegetable garden, the Bunch's small fair head somewhere near his ankles as she poked about in the warm brown earth, heedless of the waves of bombers and fighters on their way to France.

Plans were going ahead for the production of *Men in Shadow*. Frank Bauer, a young Frenchman who escaped after Dunkirk, was to do the set, the top of an old mill in France. Then the blow fell. The censors refused to pass it. It was too dangerous. It gave away too many secrets. 'Who,' they asked, 'is this author who knows so much about the escape route through the caves at San Sebastian? What Service does he or she work in that knows about the compass in the top button of the pilots' uniforms?'

The Army officer on the other side of the desk regarded me with grave surprise.

'The story is too near the truth, Miss Bell, and might endanger men escaping from Occupied Territory. How do you know about these things?'

'Well, I know there are caves on the beach in San Sebastian, and I thought it would be a good place,' I said hopefully.

'And what about the compass in the button?'

'I made that up.'

'But you have a brother in the R.A.F? Perhaps a little careless talk?'

'Oh, no! In the first place I haven't seen him for weeks, months; and in the second, he would never be guilty of that!' I replied hotly.

'And the names: André . . . Pierre . . . Robert?' he looked up at me quickly from the script.

'They're just obvious French names.'

He shook his head, his lips pressed together.

'I'm sorry. We can't pass it. At least, not in this form. Perhaps you could change it. Get an element of sabotage, rather than escape, what?' He smiled suddenly and held out his hand and I was out in the passage sunk in deep gloom. I felt as though someone had died.

Noël phoned to tell me he had seen Someone High Up, and that there was a chance, a small one.

'When you get a sock in the puss like this,' he said, 'it's all part of a plan, it must be for some good. Don't worry. The play won't date. They'll lap it up after the war!' Bleak comfort, I thought. I decided to start another play about the Black Market, but I found it difficult to concentrate. My head, too, was now a drum only fit to be beaten upon.

Then David Lean asked me to write the script of *Log Book*, a film version of the story of Frank Laskier. Frank was a merchant seaman who had lost a leg when his ship was sunk in the North Sea. He gave a broadcast talk which stirred the whole nation, beginning with words which became famous: 'I am a man and my name is Frank. . . .' Immediately I went up to Liverpool to the Seamen's Club, where I met Frank and listened for hours to his fascinating account of his life in the Merchant Navy. I finished the script in a few days and sent it to Del Giudice of Two Cities films.

He wrote that he would definitely buy it for a later production, but that it was considered by the authorities to be too outspoken, and Two Cities were afraid that the conditions demanded by my script might put men off joining the Merchant Navy!

Then, just as I despaired of ever writing a play that didn't anticipate the truth, I heard that the censor would certainly pass *Men in Shadow* if I changed the theme to sabotage. I set about doing just that. Unfortunately Binkie Beaumont was then unable to do it, so Johnnie raced round London from one management to another, until Bill Linnit agreed to put the play on.

The cast was:

Mordan	*Ralph Michael*
Kenny	*Robb Wilton*
Polly	*Hubert Gregg*
Moy	*Paul Boniface*
Lew	*John Mills*
Cherie	*Alice Gachet*

Bernard Miles directed it and we opened in Edinburgh. It was two days after Ralph Michael and Fay Compton had been married, so there was a double celebration.

We opened in September 1942 at London's Vaudeville Theatre in the Strand. I remember standing at the stage door and looking across at Rules. It seemed to me I could see myself, a coltish girl in Sonia's orange dress with the iron mould on the backside, and Seymour's voice as he said 'Never forget the audience is your enemy.'

The first night was one of the most exciting I shall ever remember. The boys in the play were magnificent, Johnnie superb. Everyone I wanted to be there was there, and I watched the play from the top of the gallery, for luck.

John's dressing-room was a seething mass of congratulations and excitement. Frenchmen bellowing in French because John's French had been so good in the play they thought he was bi-lingual; Noël, Larry, Vivien, and standing a little apart, shy, but nodding happily, my father and the others. There was another man framed in the doorway. He advanced with outstretched hand, and smiling eyes: 'I wish I'd written it,' Emlyn Williams said simply, and my cup was full.

We sat up at the Savoy with the cast until the morning papers came out. Johnnie put his arms around me. 'Oh, Baba, we've pulled off something we talked about years ago on the top of a hill in the country. Thank you, Ernest.'

Ernest has never left us. Minutely small, almost invisible, he wears a green pointed hat, and holds the Future in the centre of his tiny hand . . . in all our lives together, we reckon that any luck that has come our way has come through Ernest's intervention.

Dennis suddenly announced that he was to be married to Jane King, a slim, fair-haired girl from Cheshire, at the Savoy Chapel on 3 December, a date that was to mean something to me in the future. It was a crisp, cold day, and Dennis was dressed in full uniform, the sunlight falling across his familiar wing of white hair. I looked across at my mother and wondered what she was thinking. For my part, I had a little pricking of jealousy to think that I was no longer to be Dennis's closest confidant. I prayed that he would be as happy as I was, and knew that no one could take away our childhood together, our early tears and laughter. As the organ announced Jane's arrival, he looked back and his eyes met mine; a veiled half-grin, half-smile spread across his face, which was intercepted and caught by my mother, who smiled back with a gaiety I hadn't seen on her face for a long time. She turned to me and passed it on, and in turn I passed it to the others, and an intangible 'something' was flashed between all of us in that second, which brought tears to all our eyes, and for a second hid the best man from my view.

The best man was Johnnie, and it had occurred to me that he was looking on the puffy side. I was right, he had mumps. For two weeks I nursed him, and at the end of it looked at myself in the mirror to find that I had it too!

*

The following February, 1943, Johnnie started work in *This Happy Breed* for Noël, and once again we packed up and moved back to the studios. We took Misbourne Cottage, a tiny, timbered cottage on the edge of Denham Village, with a small trout stream running through the garden. This time, we thought, it really is to be Home! We painted it, knocked walls out and started collecting sticks of furniture, like birds building a nest.

In London *Men in Shadow* was still playing to packed houses, and Michael Wilding had taken over Johnnie's part. Dennis, now a Wing Commander, and Jane had a cottage at Bursledon, on the Hamble near Southampton. Wyn and Liz and their children shared a flat in London, and my father was lecturing around the country.

He wrote from the Red Lion in Colchester:

'. . . You must stop helping us as you have done so long and generously. I am bringing in quite a little now, and paid regularly, so long as this lecturing lasts (and I last lecturing!) Mummy is a breadwinner too! . . . I hear from Wyn that you were up in town writing hard—I hope that means you are well on your way with a new play. The Desert Places between Inspiration and action are very painful and trying, aren't they? One wonders if one will ever write again, or ever wrote before! Yet some day again the Oasis appears ahead and one knows some contentment . . . wish I had more chance of seeing you. . . .'

The sand was running out of his hour glass and I had no idea.

In September of that year, Johnnie was asked to go to Cambridge to direct a production of *Men in Shadow* for the Arts Theatre. The cast were mostly men in the R.A.F., one of whom was Ronnie Waters, playing Mordan. I was anxious to see who would play Johnnie's part.

'It's a boy called Richard Attenborough. He's far too young really, but he's keen as mustard and a good actor.'

A slight, fair boy, scarcely twenty, stood before us in uniform with the badges of a rear-gunner.

'Richard Attenborough?' asked Johnnie.

'Sir!' the boy replied. I remember thinking that he looked at Johnnie with the breathless eagerness of a boy who had been told he had won a golden apple. And so he has many times since.

Bunch, now two years old, was full of her own kind of chatter; she called a hospital a 'hopipple', and was for ever smearing her face and the wall of her nursery with 'likstip'. A dominant personality, passionate and rebellious, an inflexible leader among the other children and always obeyed by them, she was very affectionate, and with her piping voice, oval face and beautiful mouth, it was difficult not to over-indulge her. I knew it would be wrong ever to be harsh with her, for her volatile nature clearly needed sympathy and understanding. She had a grave little way of standing with her head on one side watching me work.

'Are you writin' a secret?' And when I nodded, wildly trying not to lose the thread of what I was writing, more than once she would say, 'I wish you had time for me.' It was a phrase I was to remember in the future, when she was married and had gone away, for in looking back I often curse myself for the time I spent on my writing, that maggot which got inside my head and drove me when perhaps, like so many other mothers, I should have been playing in the nursery. In a curious way perhaps our 'stars' were incompatible, but in her baby days, there often seemed to me to be an imperceptible mist between us that I could not quite see through, which persisted until she went away to her first school, and was cleared away for ever by letters of such loving affection as to make me weep.

17

KING OF THE OPEN SKY

There were cold winds and drizzling rains in March 1944. But there were occasional starlit nights, when we took our bicycles and pedalled through the Buckinghamshire lanes; Johnnie still ached to be back in uniform, but no Medical Board would take him—and I was glad to have him with me.

It was on one of these starlit nights that I heard that my father had been taken to hospital in Hampstead.

'There's nothing to worry about, darling.' My mother's sweet, child-like voice came across the wires. 'Just a little trouble with a prostate gland. As soon as he's operated on he'll be all right. It's a good hospital, darling. Don't worry, it's not a difficult operation.'

But it wasn't as easy as that. He was in considerable pain and when I went up to see him he told me that he had complained several times, only to be told not to make 'such a fuss'. Eventually, the doctor examined him, and found a huge abscess under the dressing, but try as he might, he couldn't prevent a great deal of the poison seeping into the system. Finally, after two weeks, it found its way down to his feet, which had suffered severe frostbite in the First World War.

He was desperately pale and thin, so we removed him to a nursing home in Chelsea, on the corner of St Leonard's Terrace. Here they were kind and considerate, and when the pain wasn't lacerating his body he was restful and content. But we were in continual anxiety about him, for his room was at the top of the house and he hated being carried down and jolted during the air-raids.

There was no time now to read or write, nor the inclination. I took all the family down to Misbourne, but my mother wasn't happy away from the nursing home, and she went back to London. Then Wyn's daughter Shirley suddenly developed a type of tuberculosis and we seemed all at once to be encompassed by doctors and nurses, whom I dreaded.

On Wyn's birthday, Bill Linnit told me that he would produce my other play, *Journey North*—which took place in a train going to Liverpool to meet a hospital ship; but it seemed so unimportant that I forgot to tell Johnnie for weeks after.

The days revolved round our visits to the nursing home, rushing along the street with armfuls of magazines and grapes . . . my mother sitting beside his bed, April sun filling the room.

'The doctors want to take my leg off at the knee, Muggins.' He chuckled. 'But Mummy won't let them, will you, Mummy?'

'Certainly not. Your constitution couldn't stand it; anyway, not now,' she said firmly.

'What a funny old thing I'd look with one leg. . . .'

He was full of his plans for tomorrow. He was going to write the best story he'd ever written. He had an idea for a musical play for me, a ghost story, and he would write the music.

April, I thought, was certainly *our* cruellest month. In April we had left Johnman on a hill looking out over Plymouth Sound. Ten years later, on the day that Johnman died, we stood around my father. It was a dark night pricked by the moving fingers of the searchlights and the sound of exploding bombs and gunfire. I glanced at Dennis, sensing his restlessness as he continually looked through the open windows, a fish out of water here, tied to the ground, estranged from his place in the sky. My mother and Wyn were silent shapes against the firelight in the room where my father was leaving us for the last time. Hayley, wandering Hayley. . . . I held his dry, listless hands. His long, thin, elegant feet protruding from the bedclothes, bringing the Tiles back sharply into focus. Where was he now, I wondered, what made him smile? A deeper knowledge of something? Recognition of someone? Was he able now to see through that Veil, that chance permitted only to the dying? Was he smiling at loved faces not seen for a while? Johnman?

He looked up at me with wide open eyes. 'Muggins . . .,' he said. The Light flickered in his eyes for a moment and then went out altogether, leaving me in his darkness.

Somewhere miles away beyond the Barrier in Macao, I could see him throwing his hat in the air and laughing, as three small children cantered away on their ponies. . . .

'I'm King of the Open Sky!' he shouted.

'To the Islands of the Blessed! To the Land of the Hereafter!' the children yelled back at him, and sprang away through the sandy scrub to the sea.

*

It was Dennis's idea that he should be buried there in the sea that he had crossed so many times. In a letter to my mother he wrote:

'My aircraft was waiting for me as arranged, so having unwrapped the casket and put it down beside me with your flowers on top I left London at 3.30. I dropped off the other pilot and then Daddy and I flew off on our last trip together. It was a heavenly day with a few clouds, like cotton wool. The sea was brilliant blue with white caps and the sky, friendly and warm. I called up for my Escort, but was informed there was ground fog, and in many ways I was thankful as I wanted this particular journey to be done quietly. So we flew on together, and I felt so strongly that Daddy was with me and approving. We flew on and on out of sight of land or ships, of the world itself, just Daddy and I out into the deep Atlantic, where he would be free forever in an element that he loved. I dropped the casket with your flowers on it from a height of 5000 feet. I saw it pass through a lovely big white cloud and fall into the sea. As it touched the water the casket burst open and the ashes were scattered over the ocean by the wind. I saluted him by 'dipping' and roaring my engines three times. It was the most lovely end to the life of a man we all loved so dearly, and I felt he knew he was really free forever now, out on the Atlantic Ocean, with only the wind, sky and sea all around. . . .'

*

The Admiralty had asked Johnnie and Bernard Miles to take a concert party to Scapa Flow. I was reluctant to leave Bunch and my mother, but Johnnie wisely insisted and a few days after the funeral I went north to join him. I was weary and saddened by the events of the past week, and as I watched the spring twilight creeping across the English countryside, I knew that something of me was lost forever, for in giving me my life, my father had in some way taken a fragment of it with him. Once, years before, when we had been walking among the star-studded sea pinks high on a cliff above the sea, he had said suddenly, 'If there *is* a way of coming back when my days are done, I shall find it.'

Are we, I wondered, really any more than the rose that blooms, leaving its perfume on the air? Is immortality any more than a garland of unfolding flowers living on in the memory? And yet, can the spirit of man suffer annihilation because he can no longer cast a shadow? 'Death is only an horizon,' the padre had said at Johnman's funeral, 'and horizon is only the limit of our sight.'

Scapa reminded me of all the other Naval Bases I had ever been to. The same clean blue smell of tar, and distant hills of purple and green wash with huts dotted about them. I was piloted up to the Ensa hut, boarded another drifter smelling strongly of diesel oil, and sitting on my suitcase in the warm afternoon sun, my father's rug wrapped about me, I saw Johnnie standing on the jetty at Kirkwall, familiar in his brown tweed amid the Service uniforms. I am home, I said to myself, and my heart was suddenly calm.

For the next six weeks, the eight of us took our concert party round the bases of the Home Fleet, through choppy seas in drifters, wrapped in Naval duffle coats against the freezing spray and winds.

My own contribution was insignificant. With Johnnie I sang Annette's *My Heart has Wings*, and my second appearance was in a very nasty pink, shot-silk taffeta shift. I had two cymbals attached below my knees under the dress, and a penny whistle upon which I blew fiercely, punctuating a martial march by banging the cymbals furiously together. It was so ridiculous that it couldn't fail to, nor did it ever not, get a good laugh. Johnnie did a splendid rendering of the Crispian speech from *Henry V* to cheers which resounded across the Bay: 'We few, we happy few, we band of brothers. . . .'

They were remarkable days, worthy of memory, stirring and impressive, for in a few weeks we knew that the Invasion of Europe must start, and many of the men laughing and clapping us would not come back.

The King came up to the Orkneys, and Johnnie and Bernard put on a racy stag evening for him. The next evening, as the lilac twilight crept across the water, we watched the 'Musical sunset' from one of the drifters below the flagship. Massed Marine bands echoed round the neighbouring hills, so magnificent that one felt the Germans themselves must hear the triumph of that music. Admiral Fraser brought the King to the rail of the ship. He stood there, quite still for a moment, then he took off his cap and held it high in salute, and a great wave of cheering broke out from the thousands and thousands of men around him. There were tears on many faces besides my own.

*

There is a strange beach outside Kirkwall, the Bay of Scaile, a crescent of silver sand, a haunted and haunting beach, for it was here during the first war that the only boat from Kitchener's *Hampshire* was found, a lifeboat, discovered in the early hours of dawn, full of dead soldiers. It is an eerie, ghostly beach, silent except for the shush of the waves breaking along it and the high cries of the terns. Behind it, standing alone on high ground, was a deserted house. I was walking alone across the sands when a voice said quite distinctly: 'You should write a story about this place.' I swung round, thinking it was Johnnie. But he was at least a quarter of a mile away, throwing stones into the sea and making ducks and drakes. I was quite alone, and I felt myself going cold all over, a feeling I have often experienced in places that I afterwards discover to be haunted. 'A ghost story,' the voice said, 'and use the Chinese Boat Song.' The Chinese Boat Song had been written down by my father years ago in Macao, and though I no longer had it, I remembered it quite easily. I looked around again, but there was no one anywhere near me, only a little wind that touched my face, a sudden pattering of leaves running across the sand, rising suddenly into the pink tinged sky beyond the waves, as though perhaps a boot had kicked them.

*

All through the next two months I worked on the play which had been inspired by the Bay of Scaile. There were only four characters in it. Sarclet, a retired surgeon, his sister Herda and daughter Abigail, who lived in an old castle in the Shetlands. To the castle comes a well-known poet, Cass, upon whose hands Sarclet had performed an operation. It was a ghost story, a melodrama about the sutering on of hands. I set it back in 1900, and wrote it for Johnnie. The Chinese Boat Song was an integral part of it, part of the haunting. 'Chinese Boat Song by Francis Hayley Bell,' I wrote. A ghost story, he had said, and he would write the music for me—we'd done it together, after all!

As Johnnie was up at Catterick making *The Way to the Stars*, I chose the nights to work, so that I need not feel guilty about Bunch.

She was three now, and climbed the old willow tree that hung over the trout stream as nimbly as a cat. It wasn't an easy play to write, and without Johnnie's encouragement I sometimes thought it would never be finished, that it lacked fire. I had the feeling that my father was often beside me, but couldn't always get through to my block head. Then one weekend Garson Kanin, the American playwright, came to stay. The play was finished now and I gave it to him to read. He sat in the garden all through the afternoon, his hands wreathed about his head, and I watched him anxiously from the kitchen window. In the early evening he came to look for me.

'Well?' I asked hopelessly.

'I don't like prologues and epilogues much,' he said. 'Cut those out and I think you have a very good play.'

I went up to Catterick to see Johnnie, and one night after dinner, walking round the perimeter of the airfield with Michael Redgrave, we discussed the play, which Michael had read.

'I simply cannot find the right title,' I told him. I never have been any good at titles.

'I'll think of something,' he said. Two hours later, he threw a stone up at my window.

'Hey! I think I've got it!' he called out. 'What about *Duet for Two Hands*?'

PART FOUR

JULIET, HAYLEY, AND JONATHAN

18

HAYLEY

In February 1945 Jack Hylton agreed to do *Duet for Two Hands.* Ant Pelissier was to direct it, Elspeth was to play Herda Sarclet, Mary Morris was Abigail, Elwyn Brook Jones was Edward Sarclet, and Johnnie played Cass, the part I had written for him. We opened in Blackpool, and the play was so well received that in a fit of exhilaration Ant threw his hat in the sea.

On the night that the play opened at the Lyric Theatre, we celebrated by staying at the Savoy, in a suite looking out across the Thames, and there, the following morning, we learned that the 'house' had been sold out for three weeks.

Just before we left for the theatre, Johnnie put his arm round me and led me to the window. 'Look out there and remember this moment,' he said. 'It doesn't happen every time.'

'Take care of yourself, won't you?' I said. 'There are so many lovely things to do together, we're so lucky, that sometimes I feel a little afraid.'

*

On 7 May the war with Germany was over. We kept saying it to each other, over and over again, but somehow we couldn't believe it. Then three months later Japan surrendered. 'The war is over, Bunchie,' I said, as I tucked her up in bed.

'What's that mean?' she asked.

'It means we're safe,' I replied. 'There's nothing to be afraid of anymore.'

That same month I found that I was going to have another baby. It was to arrive the following April, and I knew it was to be called Hayley.

It will be a son, I told myself, with the red hair of the Bells and Recompense Sherrill. He would be a reincarnation of my father, the wheel that would come full circle, as he had once said.

With the thought of Hayley arriving, we knew that Misbourne Cottage was too small. Rex and Lilli Harrison were moving out of their house adjoining the golf course at Denham, so we bought it. The Little House was not my kind of house at all, for it was a white stucco, modern edifice, and though the rooms were big and the atmosphere cheerful, there was no age in it. There were a few flower beds and small shavers of cherry trees, but no maturity of any kind, either in the house or the garden. It was our sixth move! It seemed somehow that I was following the pattern of my childhood as the itinerant traveller, the Hadji; but I was no longer the Outcast Child, for there was Johnnie, who was quite happy to be anywhere, so long as we were all together, for he has always been a man whose home is literally where he hangs his hat or kicks off his shoes.

For me it was different. I always had my head on one side with sadness at the end of anything, for so often it had been the end of everything. At the back of my mind I suppose that I was always searching for Polesden Lacey, for a mature garden of cobwebbed antiquity, with old gnarled trunks of wistaria, and mellowed walls where hollyhocks and sunflowers could lean for rest in a hot, sunny English summer, and where one could catch the sudden aromatic scent of Bom Jesus from herbs growing out of the cracks of flags on an old terrace.

I was convinced that Hayley would be a boy. He was to be born almost if not exactly on the day that my father had died. He would be a boy with red hair, and his life would surely be as successful as my father had hoped his would be.

On 17 April I retired to 27 Welbeck Street to await my son's arrival.

This,' said Roy Saunders, my gynaecologist, 'is Dr Lewis. He's going to give you the "minutes".'

He was a small, round man with a smooth face and white hair, and he smiled sympathetically, perhaps because he saw the trembling pulse in my throat. I remember thinking vaguely that he reminded me of a Confucian monk. He arranged his assorted apparatus. I thought suddenly of the child within me, moving towards the start of life . . . a boy, *my* boy! I set my teeth and grinned at Dr Lewis.

'Have you any children?' I asked him, to get on terms.

'No,' he said.

Juliet married Russell in our village of Cowden.

Sussex House Farm.

Jonathan, Hamlet II, and Hayley, on the staircase at the Wick.

Jonathan and me.

Laughter and Hayley.

The Wick.

The garden by the water.

Johnnie and me. Jamaica, 1967.

Across the room Roy had taken off his coat and rolled up his sleeves. Dimly I was aware of this strange committee that awaited my baby in their shirtsleeves, so different from Bunch's arrival in the middle of the Blitz. Then the pain had me by the bowels again, and I groaned aloud. Dr Lewis put out the mask and held it over my face.

I had the most curious dream.

I was standing in the doorway of an enormous building. Dr Lewis sat at the entrance, and nodded to me as I went in. The vast room was full of very small children, standing in a row as if they were at an identification parade. I found myself walking towards them, and in my mind ran an idiotic jingle: 'It isn't you, it isn't you . . . it's *you.*'

I stared at the children and they stared solemnly back. I looked down the long line, and hesitated. I thought for a moment that a small girl had lifted her hand towards me, but I paid no attention to her, so intent I was upon finding *him*. Then I saw him standing a little apart; there was no question that he was the one I was looking for, for he had red hair and was straight and slim. I pointed my finger.

'That's him!' I cried. 'That's the one!' and I looked over my shoulder to where Dr Lewis was sitting.

'Outside,' he said without looking up.

I found myself on the side of a hill looking down at a great rushing river. Roy was standing with his feet athwart it, helping a long line of children across the water.

'Coo-ee!' I called. 'I can see you!'

He looked up and laughed loudly.

'It's all a figment of your imagination,' he called. . . .

I found myself back in bed looking up into Dr Lewis's face. He was grinning. 'Show her, Roy,' he said.

Roy held a small baby in his two hands. For a second it looked exactly like the Bunch, but there was no sign of red hair.

'That's not the one I chose,' I said indignantly. Both men laughed, and as I looked down at the small morsel of humanity in Roy's two hands, I thought I saw a trickle of tears down the alabaster face.

'What is it?' I asked.

'A girl,' he said. 'A most beautiful little girl.'

'But it's crying!' I said.

'I don't think so, not really. It would be most unusual for a baby a few moments old to be crying! The tear ducts aren't working yet.'

I lay back on the pillows and watched Roy at the basin. He had his back to me and I started telling him of my dream, but I had got no farther than the fact that I had called to him, when he turned from the basin and looked at me with a smile.

'It's all a figment of your imagination,' he said.

Hayley—7 pounds 9 ounces, with a mouth like a cabbage rose. Johnnie loved her. From the start she held out her small, weaving hands to his face, and I was reminded again of my dream, of that little girl who had lifted her hand towards me. She never cried, she smiled considerably earlier than most babies, and her fat little hands were always held out to the sun.

She was called Hayley—she had to be—and she was also called Catherine after Johnnie's mother. She was called Rose, because to me it meant England, and she was called Vivien, because of my beautiful friend. Elspeth and Lilli Palmer were her godmothers, Charles B. Cochran and John Drummond her godfathers.

Two weeks later we took her back to the Little House. It was one of those cloudless May days when England is at her best and most beautiful. The house was full of flowers and smiling faces, and Bunch, now a little girl of four with brown bare legs and flying white hair, was standing by the gate waiting.

I lay back against the pillows, with sensuous pleasure as a little warm wind fanned my face through the open window. I could see Bunch playing in the garden among the daffodils—their petals touching her cheeks; she looked exactly like them only a little bigger, a daffodil of a child, slim and bending, her long hair brushing the blossoms.

'Coo-ee!' I whistled. She turned, looked up, and started running towards the house. A moment later she was standing beside me. I noticed she had on her yellow dress. 'When I was a little girl, I had a yellow dress,' I said. 'It had big pockets and that's where Nosey Parker used to sit.'

'Can I have something to put in my big pockets?' she asked eagerly. 'Something of my own to love?'

'What would you like?' I watched her animated face.

'A kitten, like Vivien has, with the same colour eyes.'

She looked at the sleeping baby, and then tiptoed across the room.

'We're more lucky than God, aren't we?' she asked.

'Why?'

'Because God hasn't got a sister.'

'No.'

'And He hasn't got a brother neither.'

'No.'

'When will Hayley and me get a brother?'

'One day, when he's ready to come,' I told her.

'I think you have the most beautiful feet in the world,' she said abruptly. 'If I saw your feet sticking up out of the long grass, I'd think they was flowers and I'd pick them and put them in a vase in my nursery.'

And she ran out into the garden.

So the whirligig of time rolled round. Smokey the Siamese cat arrived, and was duly carried about in the pockets of Bunch's yellow dress, just as Nosey Parker had been all those years ago! And the garden seemed always to be full of children crawling under the currant bushes or lying full length in the tickly, sun-warmed long grass.

*

In February 1947 we bought Fernacres, a small manor house near Fulmer, built in about 1800. We first saw it on Johnnie's birthday, the 22nd. The snow lay thickly everywhere, but the sun shone brightly across the sparkling lawns. A little grey house covered with wistaria, nestling between lawns and meadows full of old oaks, and beyond them a small lake covered with ice and surrounded by rhododendrons, we fell in love with it instantly, and bought it. To Johnnie I know that Fernacres was of all our homes, his most beloved. He would happily have never wanted to move again, and though I loved it, particularly in the spring when the wistaria wrapped the house in a lavender cloak, it was still not Polesden Lacey; there was no walled garden, though there were greenhouses and stables and a splendid asparagus bed.

At Fernacres I started writing *Angel*—a play based on the Constance Kent murder in 1860. Binkie Beaumont said he would produce it, and Johnnie was to direct. On the day of the dress rehearsal, our Nanny gave in her notice; she wanted to become an air stewardess and had to catch the nine o'clock train! It was a nerve-racking morning, for Hayley, sitting thoughtfully upon her pot, wasn't in a co-operative mood.

'*Do* hurry up, Hayley!' I urged.

'Can't!' was all she would say, so we were not only late for rehearsal at the Strand Theatre, but we had to take the two girls with us. Bunch was happy enough playing about among the seats in the theatre and talking to herself, sometimes a little too loudly, but Hayley was a different matter. Too young to be interested for long, or able to sit still, I had to put her in charge of one of the lady character actresses in the cast, but during the morning I realized that the lady in question was now on the stage in a scene. I ran round to her dressing-room to collect Hayley, but there was no sign of her. No one had seen her! I asked the stage doorkeeper if he had seen what might have appeared to be a small dwarf, but he shook his head. She seemed to have disappeared and I was distraught with worry and fear. It was nearly an hour before she was discovered. She had walked straight out of the stage door and up the road to the next theatre, the Aldwych. Here she was found sitting on the lap of the stage doorkeeper, chatting away and having sardines levelled into her mouth on the end of a knife! No one, least of all Hayley, seemed in the least concerned.

*

After *Great Expectations*, Johnnie started *Scott of the Antarctic* for Michael Balcon at Ealing. There was, from the beginning, a haunting likeness between Johnnie and Robert Falcon Scott, so much so that when we first met Peter Scott and Cherry Garrard, they were astounded. Cherry Garrard had never fully recovered from Scott's death. He told me that when Scott was eventually found eight months later by the relief party, his body was seen for one moment to be sitting up facing the opening of the tent. His coat had been pulled aside at the neck, and his blue eyes were wide open; on his cheeks were two frozen tears. Johnnie was tremendously affected by Scott. He read everything he could about him as well as many of his personal letters. He would spend hours staring at the photographs of Scott and the various polar expeditions which the studio sent him. He became remote and thoughtful. He told me that he felt he had come to know Scott intimately, and that sometimes he felt a close contact to him. 'Look, he even walks like him,' Cherry Garrard told me.

I followed Johnnie to Norway, from Oslo by train through the red and gold valleys to the snowfields of Finse. I had re-read Evans's *South With Scott*, as I had written some of the dialogue for the film, and although undoubtedly the clothing helped a great deal, it was curious how closely the actors playing the parts resembled the original people. Surely, Bowers himself was never better represented than by Reginald Beckwith, or Oates than by Derek Bond, Wilson by Harold Warrender or the stalwart Evans by James Robertson Justice.

Scott of the Antarctic was a great film. It could have been even greater, had Johnnie and the director been permitted to show Scott more as an ordinary human being, with the human frailties which he must have had. This unreal balance Johnnie found difficult in his portrayal. Even so, he was more affected by the making of *Scott of the Antarctic* than any other film in which he has appeared.

19

THE BOY WITH RED HAIR

In April Roy Saunders told me that I was going to have another baby. April again! From the beginning I was certain that it was to be a boy, that red-headed boy I had seen in the curious dream during Hayley's birth.

'I'd like to call him John after you,' I told Johnnie. 'You and grankapa and Johnman.'

'Let's call him Jonathan, just Jonathan Mills,' he said.

I became a cabbage, a rather dried up old cabbage, without a thought in my head. I used to sit for hours in the two-hundred-year-old Romany caravan that Johnnie had put in the meadow for me, struggling to get hold of an idea to write. Johnnie was producing *The History of Mr Polly* with Ant, and Bunch had a small part in it as the young Polly.

The following weeks were moody and restless. To Johnnie's amusement I was constantly in tears about the most idiotic of things. Then I started being unable to breathe, gasping and clawing for air, and telling myself it was some form of hysteria!

One night the situation became worse and Johnnie sent for our local doctor, who arrived at three o'clock in the morning in a pair of bedraggled pyjamas. 'It's asthma, Mrs Mills,' he said wearily—and every morning for the rest of that week, there he was, in the same pyjamas, with his injection of adrenalin. Sometimes I thought I was dying, sometimes I almost hoped I would, then I remembered that it was April and I was *sure* I would. But I struggled up and down Harley Street to one doctor after another, with no results.

'It's fear,' they told me.

'Fear?'

'A deep-rooted fear that you won't have a son, a fear you are possibly not aware of.'

Fear. This was a facer. It brought me up sharply, in spite of my denials, and I decided that it was time for a little self-analysis, a time to hold the mirror up to my own particular nature. The Romany caravan was the place, and here I repaired to consider myself.

Repeatedly I told myself that my work now was to look after my adorable family, to enjoy them all, and to cease from chasing the rainbow of ambition, 'That last infirmity of noble minds.' Perhaps I should turn once again to Lao-Tze and Buddha for that inner serenity which I had never achieved, for God gives it to few—though I could truthfully say that He had given it to Johnnie in abundance.

'I don't really care about success and fame,' he said to me once, standing by the lake, 'I just want to work hard so that we won't ever be a nuisance to anyone.'

Struggle as I did against it, the restless maggot of childhood drove me on relentlessly, cursing the daily frustrations of responsibilities and the inevitable interruptions, longing at one and the same time for hours of solitude and hours to play with the children, but somehow achieving neither, as the hours and days went swiftly by and out of reach.

Watching Johnnie playing with Bunch and Hayley and Hamlet, I wondered if we would save my daughters from the fears, anxieties and bewilderment of my own childhood, for their futures were in our hands. There is no doubt that we are by process of identification what our parents were before us, catching something of our father and mother, for personality must develop from external impressions and children are quick to notice moods and gestures. It is what we are rather than what we do that is important to them. I had tried to follow my father's ideals, but much of my mother's feeling of inadequacy was stronger. I was, and had always been, full of misgivings, with little peace of mind. The childish feelings of rejection, the 'Outcast Child of the East' that Cousin Rudyard had spoken of, had developed through the circumstances of our family life.

To my parents, the love, warmth and gaiety of our young days had been of paramount importance, but they were born and lived in an age of rigid pride and intolerance, the days of the British Raj. 'The man's a fool' was a phrase too often heard and assimilated, and we as a family had inherited much of that arrogance and intolerance.

Johnnie of course refused to accept this: 'Everyone is made of the same human clay,' he would tell the children. 'The only real Religion that I can pass on to you is never to hurt anyone.'

'We must never allow them to be frightened of anything,' Johnnie said over and over again. 'They must respect themselves—and truth.'

*

In October the burglars broke into Fernacres. 'It's that owl,' the cook told me. 'When you hear that owl you know it's them thieves sending each other messages!'

Night after night, sleepless, and gasping for breath, I lay awake listening to that owl, until I could stand no more, and begged Johnnie to sell the house and move to London where there were no owls.

'I know you love Fernacres,' I told him. 'I feel selfish and loathe myself, but—'

'I don't care where we live,' he said gently, 'as long as we're all together. I wish we could all squeeze into the caravan and just keep moving, for I've married a potty gipsy and I don't think she'll ever settle.'

'I wonder if this baby will ever know what we went through in having him!' I prevaricated.

We sold Fernacres and moved to a house in Cheyne Walk looking across the Thames to Battersea Power Station. There was a sooty fig-tree in the garden, and white carnations which, when you bent to smell them, left you with a black nose. I shall never forget Johnnie's face as we drove away from Fernacres, or the way he turned his head to take a last look, holding my hand steadily as I coughed and wheezed and condemned myself all the way to London. I knew he loved that house, and had it not been for my illness, or my roving spirit, we might never have left it.

I was back at 27 Welbeck Street. Roy Saunders stood over me and Dr Lewis sat beside me.

'Just breathe easily, Mary. Think of reflections in still water.'

Reflections in still water! I wondered if I would die, a possibility which had been suggested by some of the doctors who had wanted to remove the baby. Had I looked for the last time upon Johnnie's and the two eager, excited faces of the girls? Would I see my father and Johnman? Was the baby waiting to be born, the long-legged red-headed boy of my dream? And would I ever see him?

Words and faces swam through my half conscious mind. The solemn peaks of mountains, flashing rivers, sun streaming across the sea at sunset, and distant voices calling my name. . . . Baba! Muggins! The cornflower blue eyes of two children, their hands held out to me as I reached the cave and was swept back to earth again. . . .

'Where's that place where the children are?' I asked Dr Lewis. 'I can't find it.'

He put the mask over my face without a change of expression.

Low clouds, floating near me, so near that I could put out my hand and touch them, and below, a field of marguerites which children were collecting; but they weren't the children for whom I was looking, for they had clothes on, and didn't look up as I called. I was frightened and called out for Johnnie. . . . Johnnie. . . .

Johnnie was standing beside the bed. He was looking down at me and smiling.

'Where's Dr Lewis?' I asked idiotically. 'He's gone away on a barrage balloon until next time,' Johnnie laughed.

I stared at them, not daring to ask. Had I missed the boy altogether? Just because I couldn't find my way back to that place?

Outside the windows I could see that it was dark.

'What time is it?' I asked.

'It's eight-thirty, and it's December the third, and it's nineteen forty-nine,' Johnnie said.

To my astonishment I found myself breathing quite naturally. The asthma had gone, never to return!

'Who . . . is it?' I asked hesitantly.

'Jonathan, of course,' he said, and leaned down, his arms around me, his cheek against mine. 'And he has all his fingers and toes!'

Roy put the baby beside me on the bed. I don't know why I should have expected to see the long-legged red-headed boy of my dream, but for a second I did, and then I realized that that was to be far in the future. For the moment he was a very old gentleman, with the smallest, flattest ears, and unmistakable signs of red fluff on his round bald head. As I took him in my arms the tears ran down my face.

'What a sentimental ass I am!' I laughed at Johnnie, but he only shook his head and turned away.

We took him back to Cheyne Walk. The two girls were interested and delighted, but at that time more heavily engrossed in the white mice which accompanied them everywhere.

'I don't want them mice in here!' Nanny exclaimed with horror in her voice.

'There's nothing to be afraid of,' Bunch retorted, 'they only do a little brown rice from time to time.' She regarded Nanny with some disfavour as she stood against the table, her skirts held tightly to her side. The mice escaped a few weeks later, in Fortnum and Mason's. Bunch found it interesting, she told me, to see all the sales girls on chairs, clutching their skirts in the same way as Nanny had, but mercifully the panic only lasted a short while until the creatures were found swaying happily in the dress preservers of the Model Suits.

As the weeks went by, Jonathan proved to be an overactive old Adam. He was always trying to get up and he would try to sleep lying on his face in his cot, a trait which, curiously enough, he must have inherited from me. Nanny thought it dangerous, that he might suffocate, so she bought some straps and tied him in. As I was opposed to this restriction, when Nanny was away on her holiday I cut the straps and let Jonathan free. It was a night of dismal howling, and until I handed back one of the straps for him to hold, he refused to sleep. These straps were afterwards known as his 'Luckies'. As a baby he was never able to sleep without one of them to pull through his fingers, and I have carried them half across the world and back, and when he went as a boarder to his first prep school, I tied one of his 'Luckies' round the neck of his small tiger, hoping the other boys would imagine it to be the animal's scarf.

All children have a 'friend'—some of them have strange names, some of them live in curious places. Johnman had a 'familiar' who lived in the gutters of Macao, and he was often seen bending down to converse with him. Hayley had a dirty pink blanket which she never allowed to be washed.

'It changes the smell,' she told us one night. 'See, I fred my fingers froo like this. Then I suck my fumb, and I go to sleep.'

Bunch had a disreputable-looking teddy bear, which became more flattened and unrecognizable as the years went by; and Jonathan, the most restless of the three, was surrounded by a tiger with green glass eyes, his 'baby pillow', his 'Lucky', tied round his wrist, and Tiggy the Porcupine. Wherever we went, our luggage had to include this assortment of 'friends', these scraps of comfort for the dark hours when the sun has set. Few children are as lucky as my sisters and brothers and myself, who slept under a wide starlit sky that was never dark, and shared the same Friend.

*

During the hot days of the following August, we took the family down to the sea at Sandwich. The car was loaded with toys, a canary, Hamlet, the two mice, and an apathetic new acquisition in the shape of Pissy, a ginger cat. Although my asthma had disappeared, I was far from well, the doctors refused to allow me to work and told me to take up a new hobby. I started painting, and the curative powers of colour and form, the deep marshes and bowery hollows stretching away to the glassy sea, intrigued me for hours, and the days passed in contented contemplation without any sense of time rushing by.

I stood on the beach, my arm tucked through Johnnie's, watching the children as they ran shrieking with delight along the sea's edge to empty a bucket of water over the baby's head.

Later the same night, when Johnnie and I were walking along the road outside our cottage, Hamlet was run over by a car. He was dreadfully hurt, and though we wrapped him in my jacket, laid him on the sofa, and gave him drops of brandy, he never recovered. We sat up with him all night so that he shouldn't feel betrayed if he regained consciousness, but at three in the morning, with one last flicker of his amber eyes, he stepped out of his faded old overcoat, and left us. It was the first time I had ever seen Johnnie cry.

The next day we had to face the girls with the news. A child's first meeting with Death, if God is merciful, is often in the passing of a beloved pet or an animal. Like those children long ago in Macao, they refused to eat anything, and drifted silently away together. In the evening, Bunch came down from her room with a string of imitation daisies. She stood in the doorway, the light behind her, a small figure in a white nightdress holding a garland of flowers. . . .

'Bunchie—' I started.

'These are for Hamlet's grave,' she said solemnly. 'They're not real you see, so they can't die.'

*

We used to go out to Richmond Park and spend the weekends with Sir Louis Greig. His lovely Thatched House Lodge lay in the middle of the Park. Deer grazed around it, and from a garden smothered in roses and clematis in the tranquil summer sunlight, we looked far over the ancient oaks to Kingston and Twickenham.

'How wonderful to have such a horizon!' I said one afternoon. 'Living in a small world with a small view gives you small thoughts.'

'Why don't you come and live here?' Phyllis Greig asked.

Johnnie looked at me and grinned. I knew what he was thinking. That already I was tired of London's hard pavements and the close proximity to other people.

'Not already!' he half groaned.

'Well—the children . . .' I began. 'It's a bad thing to start your life staring at notices which say "Keep off the Grass"!'

'I must say,' Johnnie said, 'if I thought that there were a house out here, I'd love it—if we could sell Cheyne Walk—but I don't suppose there is one anyway. . . .'

'There is,' said Louis. 'There's The Wick.'

'The Wick?' we asked together. 'What's that?'

'It's a beautiful Georgian house belonging to the Stirlings, and they want to go back to their home in Scotland. It stands high on Richmond Hill, with a walled terrace garden looking down on the turn of the river. All the rooms on the south side, facing the Thames, are oval shaped. There's an old walnut tree, and in the spring great wads of wistaria hang down all over the house.'

'I think,' said Johnnie, looking at me in mock despair. 'I think we'd better see it. . . .'

A few moments later we were in his car crossing the Park and through the gates, past the Star and Garter Home, to draw up in the forecourt of an exquisite little Georgian manor house, guarded by two vast maples. Jack Stirling opened the door to us himself, and suddenly we were standing in the wide, beautiful hall with its cool, stone-flagged floor, curved and unsupported staircase, and ahead of us, the open drawing-room doors showing the turn of the river sparkling in the afternoon sunlight.

I was conscious of a deep sense of joy, of belonging, as though I had been there before. Almost as though someone had folded their arms about me, and whispered 'Stay, oh stay!' As though an old friend peered at me through the delicately curved balcony, and an old voice whispered, 'Why! It's Mary! We haven't seen you for ages. . . .'

I had seldom seen such grace in a room, with its Adam green walls covered with trails of carved wooden flowers, the eighteenth century fire basket and curved white marble overmantle, its high ceiling and french windows leading out on to the slender veranda over the terraced garden.

Polesden Lacey! I found myself thinking. Yet to my mind it was even better than Polesden Lacey, for the commanding view was glorious, with the far horizon of trees away to Leith Hill on one side and Windsor Castle on the other.

'You're lucky today,' Mrs Stirling said, 'for it isn't always that the weather allows us to see the Castle.'

It's been done on purpose, I thought. We're being shown the house at its loveliest, because *they* want us to come back. . . .

'When the property was for sale in 1775, before this house was built on the site,' Mrs Stirling was saying, 'the advertisement in the *Times* read "Surely this parcel of land enjoys the most beautiful prospect in Europe".'

She led us through to the conservatory and down stone steps to the vinery; it had recently been watered and the fragrance of moist earth reminded me vividly of Grandmother Hogg's greenhouse in Shanghai. On the wide York stone terrace I grabbed Johnnie's hand and squeezed it. 'Oh, Baba!' he said, and laughed.

Mrs Stirling's bright eyes met mine. 'It's for sale, you know,' she said.

'I could live here forever,' I murmured.

She smiled sadly, and shrugged her shoulders. 'I shall miss my garden. Flowers grow here as they will, lilies of the valley, wild garlic and fraise du bois all tangled up together. In the spring the walls are covered with forsythia, and aubretia and alyssum creep up the steps and stray about all over the terrace. But it's the age, and the feeling of people here that I love.'

She took me down to the bottom of the garden by the folly where the roses grew.

'Some of these are very old, and quite rare. I was thinking of planting Bourbon roses along this wall. Do you know them? Hugonis, and Moonlight? Hugonis comes from China, you know; there are more than a hundred specimens and most of them come from China. . . .'

'So do I,' I said quietly.

'Then you'll have to plant them, won't you?' she said without turning.

'How do you know we'll come here?' I asked, laughing.

'Oh, you will,' she answered.

Johnnie and I drove back to London in silence, both busy with our thoughts.

'That room at the top of the house, where one of the children could sleep—or all of the children—it's so big!' I said at last. 'It's like living in a lighthouse. What a splendidly beautiful sight for a child to look at, like living in the sky.'

He couldn't help laughing. 'Baba, we've only just finished spending a great deal of money on Cheyne Walk!' he reminded me.

'It's *our* house though, Johnnie,' I insisted. 'I know it is. I've been there before . . . sometime. . . . Just as *you* were familiar—so is the Wick.'

A young man was waiting for us when we got out of the car at Cheyne Walk. He hoped we would forgive his intrusion, but could he possibly persuade us to sell him our house. . . ?

We just managed to refrain from gasping! It was a miracle. A gift from Heaven. We sold the house to him that night, phoned the Stirlings, and next day rushed as fast as the car would take us back to Richmond to buy the Wick.

'I knew you'd buy the Wick,' said Mrs Stirling. 'I'm so glad—and I'm sure that the ghost will like you.'

'Ghost?'

'Lady St Aubyn. She walks up the stairs from the dining-room dressed in a grey Inverness cloak. She built the house in 1775 on the foundations of what was once the Bull Inn. Robert Mylne was the architect and Daniel Pinder the builder; we have their signed drawings, which I'll leave with you. Lady St Aubyn was a great hostess. She loved the arts and all sorts of people came here—George III, of course, and Sir Joshua Reynolds who lived next door and painted from this balcony, Edmund Keane who was playing at the Richmond theatre, Mrs Jordan and Mrs Siddons, Macready, Rossetti, and practically all the pre-Raphaelites. I sometimes think I hear their voices echoing across the garden on summer evenings!'

We moved in three months later. Before she left, Mrs Stirling took down a glass walking stick from the mantelpiece and held it out to me. 'This is a witch stick! It's been here for years, no one knows how many. Each person who leaves passes it on to those who come in, but should you take it with you, you will most surely return!'

I put it back on the mantelpiece behind the Emperor of China's buttons, and that night Johnnie and I sat up late after the children had been tucked up in their beds. We sat by the dying fire in the dark as we have done a hundred times since. The flickering light on the old wig chair and rose velvet sofa cast the strangest of shadows and it seemed at moments that the room was full of the rustle of silk and whispering voices. I have often wondered since whether one day, when another young couple sit beside the dying fire on a winter's night, they too will hear some of the voices that have filled that room in our time.

An enchanted and magical house. A house and a garden which rang with the laughter and shouts of children, and the barking of welcoming dogs. A house that seemed to wilt and grow sad whenever we left it, as if all those whispering voices had become fearful and bewildered; a house which sprang to life again after we had been back a few hours. A house which beamed with joy at Christmas, surrounding the sparkling tree in the hall with a light that didn't come from the candles, and giving the holly berries a dark radiance which seemed to glow from within, lighting up the faces of our three small children as they stood wide-eyed round it. A house which mingled their giggles with its other voices as they tiptoed secretly into our bedroom in the early light of morning carrying their stockings. A house which welcomed with its warmth the church choir on Christmas Eve, to sing 'Good King Wenceslas', and put away a guilty glass of punch when the Vicar wasn't looking.

Yes, a shining, splendid, dominating and bewitching house, which to me never seems empty. We would sit down to dinner in the late evenings of summer, as the squirrels crept up the walnut tree to steal the nuts, and duck swept down on to the lawn from the river, and a little wandering wind gently shook the clematis outside the nursery.

Johnnie's dresser, Jolly, lived in the gardener's cottage at the bottom of the garden, and Mrs Jolly worked in the house. One morning she asked me if the lady had found me.

'What lady?'

'The lady that went upstairs. She was wearing an old fashioned cape, and she went past me without a word.'

The children heard her footsteps by the library, but I did not see her, and I never have.

But sometimes, working alone at night in the library, I have been aware of the door opening quietly, conscious of someone else in the room; or again, on the terrace in the mornings, I have felt a warm wind touch my face, like a familiar, brown, dry hand, and known the awareness of someone standing close to me whom I couldn't see. Was it her? Or was it somebody else?

20

THE GARDEN BY THE WATER

The children grew up in an enchanted world of flowers, trees and water; the house cast its spell over them as it did over us. . . . Bunch, Bags, and Noony! A new set of names from another nursery.

Springs, summers and winters rolled by, and they grew and learned and laughed a great deal, for Johnnie loves children as they love him, and wherever Johnnie is, there is always hilarity. Not only has he the greatest sense of humour, but a glorious sense of the ridiculous.

One Christmas he decided to play Father Christmas to a party of thirty children, who gathered round him wide-eyed in their belief and excitement at meeting the Old Gentleman and hearing him speak to them in his wonderfully curious accent. After he had given out the presents all round, he said that he must attend to his reindeer and made a dignified and solemn exit by the front door, thinking that the back door was open and that he could enter quickly and divest himself of his clothes and beard. But the door was firmly closed, and as he stood there banging on it and getting more and more impatient, a large and amused crowd gathered round. In order to get away from them he fled down Nightingale Lane, hoping to come in through the stables. This time it was the children who saw him racing past, and wild with delight at the chance of seeing him leave in his sleigh, they set off in pursuit. Finally he found refuge by locking himself in the tool shed, and walking in half an hour later to inquire idly if Father Christmas had been, managed to avoid complete disillusionment.

Bunch went to the Vicarage School at the bottom of Richmond Hill. Her reports were excellent, unlike her mother's years before! 'A most enthusiastic pupil . . . a good memory for words in French . . . has made a marked improvement in painting and expresses her ideas with facility as she does in History with her delightfully illustrated stories. Writing neat and well formed . . . spelling excellent . . . her reading accurate and fluent. She is an industrious little girl with great charm and gaiety. . . .'

Later Hayley went to the same school. With great precision and sense of importance she walked steadily down the road clutching her over-large sized handbag. But her reports read mostly that 'She seems to live in a dream world of her own. Her arithmetic is lamentable, her popularity enormous. She is the friend of everyone in the school, but the despair of her teachers, for she sits through classes with a beatific smile and appears to assimilate very little, except in Nature class where she easily excels everyone else.'

At home it was the same. She was the 'Queen of the Ladybirds', and always seemed to have a dozen or more wandering across her shoulders. She also had an affinity with frogs and toads, many of which were found in her pockets, accompanied by worms; she knew an Italian bee from a wild bee or any other bee, and her pony would have let her sleep between her feet had she wanted to. She had a pure singing voice, and if you couldn't see Hayley, you had only to listen, and sure enough the high lark-like voice would indicate her whereabouts.

From the beginning the two girls were the greatest of friends. Bunch took care of Bags like the small mother of eight years old that she was, and Hayley's admiration for her slim, elegant sister with the long corn-coloured hair was shown in the bright affection of her eyes as she regarded her. Between them, they used to get up little 'Shows' for us and friends like the Oliviers or Lionel Jeffries and his family. The characters were often the same, though the theme different, and a typical programme read:

The olde wuman in a cloke	*Hayley Mills*
The Balereena	*Juliet Mills*
The wuman in the high healed shoos ..	*Jonathan Mills*

As he grew older Jonathan graduated to the Electrician, and later the Director, but Hayley was always a character part, a wuman in some sort of cloke, and Juliet always danced gracefully to Swan Lake.

It was an exhilarating and fascinating experience watching them grow up. And their everlasting questions! 'Does a chicken *know* she's laid an egg? Do animals talk to each other? Why do we *have* to sleep? Why can't we pick our noses?—the monkeys do! What is that bird singing about? Where are this frog's ears?'

One night when I was working late, the door of the library opened and there was Hayley in her nightdress:

'What is the matter, Bags?' I asked. 'Aren't you well?'

'My heart's stopped,' she said gravely—and Johnnie carried her pick-a-back to bed, trying to hide his laughter.

As I had been before her, and as most elder children are, Bunch was the Law of the nursery, and many a standup fight took place between her and the reigning Nanny. On one morning she marched up to our bedroom, and said with a drawing back of her imperious little shoulders: 'Will you come and send the Nanny person away?'

'Oh dear, why?' I asked.

'She's just hit Bags with a hair brush, hairy side up if you please!'

That Nanny was out of the house before breakfast had finished, while they stood round me, their eyes wide, their lower lips caught in their teeth with a mixture of guilt and triumph.

'Why do we have to have them. Why can't you look after us?'

I tried to explain that I had work to do, but their accusing eyes drove me into the garden. Of *course* I should have been looking after them. Every woman should look after her own children; maybe this is where the rot sets in, I thought, with Nannies! Undoubtedly Johnnie, who had been brought up solely by his mother, had had a happier, more secure childhood than I. A stranger coming into the nursery is always eyed with distrust; sometimes antagonism leaps up which is never overcome, and conversely even the most adoring of Nannies is inclined to give way to her charges and spoil them. What to do! The maggot in me was still driving, and by now I was on to another idea, and longing for the hours alone. It wasn't so much that I wanted success as that I wanted desperately to be still part of Johnnie's life in the theatre, the fun and the comradeship, the creation, and plans, the smells of grease paint and tallow, the talk and laughter and the stimulation. There was a time in the early years of the war when Terence Rattigan and I were described as being among the young hopes for the English Theatre, but Terry has long ago outdistanced me, and the qualities of Emlyn Williams which I have so much admired have never been within my grasp. Being a woman writer, I tell myself, has its disadvantages, for not only do the responsibilities of being a wife and mother lurk all day in the back of her mind, but there also is the green serpent of remorse and guilt for the time that should be spent with the growing children. Sometimes, I think, in this respect I failed them, living too much in my own world of fantasy, which at that time they were too young to share, except in terms of the children's stories I used to tell them.

*

We watched them growing, in wonder and curiosity; running through the bracken in the Park, to stop abruptly at the sight of a tortoiseshell butterfly; full of questions, even suggestions; sitting on the edge of the Lake at Penn Ponds, their feet dangling in the water, serious eyes upon the advancing swan; lying on their faces in the garden watching a nest of ants. Bunch under the walnut tree, slim, her pale hands reminding me of petals on the grass. Hayley, looking at me with her shrouded cornflower blue eyes as though we shared an enormous secret. I asked her once what it was.

'*You* know,' she nodded gravely, and I nodded back, not daring to admit that my wavelength had gone haywire.

The only quarrels in the nursery were over Jonathan. Bunch and Bags had a feeling that I spoiled him, and so I did, in spite of Johnnie's pleadings. He was a strange, proud boy, with green eyes and dark red hair—much of my father emerged in him, even to the familiar touch of arrogance, which annoyed the girls; but he was humorous, truthful, and courageous. When he was two, he told us one night that he remembered being born, that he had to come down a long black passage from a lovely place on the top of a hill, and that he hadn't wanted to. Years later he dismissed the whole story, and refused to believe that he had ever said it! As a child he showed the most independence and also showed the most prejudices and impatience, with a considerable temper. He was inconsistent, at times even rude, and we have had more than one battle. But today he is an optimistic and confident boy with long lean limbs and erect carriage, full of the joy of living; he has Johnnie's prowess at games, his sense of the ridiculous and his mental and physical equilibrium, together with a great sense of justice and adventure, closely resembling his grandfather's. And he has the dark red mane of hair of Recompense Sherrill!

They were all different in their ways. Of the three, Bunch found life the hardest battle. Dominant and self-willed, capable of biting scorn, she also had deep sympathy and understanding, and a tigerish loyalty to her family and friends. Her letters were always the most loving and compassionate, and almost as soon as she could form her letters, Johnnie and I would find little notes left about the house, from 'your first, moist dificalt and beluvved daughter Juliet'. It was she who first gave me a name that has stuck, 'Mimosa', and Johnnie was always 'Doosie'. She had, and still has, a directness, a singleness of purpose which will not be shifted from her ultimate goal or her conception of life, and as she grew older she developed a serenity which has made it possible for her to accept the ups and downs of her sometimes 'outrageous fortune' with a voice full of infectious laughter.

She wanted to be a dancer, and after a term at Sadlers Wells when Dame Ninette De Valois told me she should be encouraged, she was sent at the age of nine to Elmherst Ballet School in Camberley; oddly enough, an enlarged edition of the kindergarten I had attended when we lived there for a brief time.

Johnnie and I stood with her on Waterloo Station, trying not to see the gulping tears, the ticket and bag held tightly in hands whose knuckles were white with suppressed emotion. It was the same station from which, years before, two other small girls, dressed in the green of Sherborne, had felt that same sickness rising from the stomach . . . only now there were girls in grey capes, though the voices and the words were the same.

'Why do we *do* it!' I gritted my teeth and clung to Johnnie as the train drew away.

'So that she can learn to stand on her own two feet.'

'I hope she won't be as lonely as I was,' I muttered. 'You know how I hated school and all that wretched mob instinct.' Yet I knew too that as Carl Sandberg had said, 'We must learn when to loosen our hands. . . .'

She learned, as I had done, as other children very soon do, that children can be the cruellest, as well as the kindest, of companions. 'And don't think just because you're John Mills's daughter . . .' to a child who had never thought of, let alone expected, any favours because of it, can be the most baffling, cutting, and unanswerable torment. It was to hit all three of them at some time during the course of their education. A malevolent seed of thought which might, in children of lesser character, have developed into a destructive growth of hostility.

On the night that Hayley-Bags joined Bunch at school, I cried myself to sleep, as I had done over her sister. It was the first time her room had ever been empty, and I couldn't bear to look at the collection of abandoned animals. She had however departed in the highest of spirits, clinging tightly to Bunch's hand and smiling benisons on all to whom she was introduced, holding out her pudgy baby hand to the cries of 'That's Juliet's baby sister!'

From the beginning, her great enthusiasm drew people to her, and during the five years at Elmherst, she collected a group of gigglers that followed her unswervingly through many enterprising practical jokes and many over-optimistic ideas; for the most part her mistresses adored her, even so far as neglecting to punish her for the nightly convulsions of laughter which came from her dormitory. Deeply affectionate, gregarious, and with a zest for living that was catching, she slid through five years of reminiscent Reports of 'too impatient to be thorough . . . too much day-dreaming . . . inclined to leap before looking' and 'just a little *too* clumsy for a dancer!'

*

During their days away, Johnnie and I continued our work. I wrote a play for him called *The Uninvited Guest.* Henry Sherek decided to do it and we were lucky enough to have Cathleen Nesbitt, Joan Greenwood and Lyndon Brook playing with Johnnie. It was the story of a man who had escaped from a lunatic asylum, a man with red hair. Johnnie had to wear a wig, and was slightly set back when one of the notices referred to him 'wandering about like a bewildered carrot'. While he looked gloomily at himself in the mirror at the St James's Theatre the following night, Larry Olivier, who was in the dressing-room with him, roared with laughter. 'That makes two of us, Johnnie. It just goes to show how little people appreciate the time and care we spend on our make-up!'

For in one production of *Henry IV*, Larry had worn a titian wig, and as he stood in the centre of the stage, dressed in azure blue, a shaft of light descending from the flies to catch the aureole of hair, Johnnie and I gasped at his beauty.

At his next entrance, he looked even more fantastic, for now he was dressed from head to foot in white. He stood in the centre of the stage, the same bright light on his emblazoned head. Johnnie and I clutched each other's hand at the sight of such magnificence and radiance—and just at that moment, a voice beside us said: 'Oh! 'ere's old ginger again!'

Johnnie was the first President of the Lord's Taverners, a club and society of people who under the patronage of the 'Twelfth Man', Prince Philip, set out to raise money for one of His Royal Highness's favourite causes, the National Playing Fields Association. The first Annual Ball at the Dorchester in 1951 was a splendid, though nerve-racking occasion. Johnnie, as President, dined at Prince Philip's table. The table consisted of Princess Elizabeth and the Prince, Princess Margaret, the Mountbattens, Terence Rattigan, and various ladies and gentlemen in waiting. Johnnie thought that he and I should take something to calm our nerves on such an occasion, something that would relax us. Robert Helpmann suggested Benzedrine. We took it just before we left the Wick, all dressed up, palms sweating with apprehension. As we had never taken anything of this nature before, we had no idea how it would work. Unfortunately, all it did was dry up our saliva so completely that by the time Johnnie met the Princesses, he was almost speechless, his mouth a dried-up gourd!

When Johnnie was dancing with Princess Elizabeth, he was most touched when she asked him suddenly where the television cameras were; when he indicated them and told her which one was transmitting, she stopped and smiled straight into the lens.

'You see, Daddy is at home looking in!' she told him confidently, and she smiled and nodded again towards the camera.

*

Nine months later the King died. We brought Bunch up to the Lying-in-State at Westminster Hall. She wrote: 'I will never forget it—the slow march when they changed guards, the people streaming by while tears like diamonds lit up their faces, so sad and moving. I didn't know whether to laugh or cry, did you get my message written in greasepaint on your mirror, did you have a good house? I think you are the most wonderful actor in the world, you really are all things bright and beautiful. I shall always remember the lying-in-State because Hayley had middle ear infection.'

In his time off Johnnie, encouraged by Prince Philip and Lord Mountbatten, took up polo. He was coached by Billy Walsh, whose polo ponies were stabled at the end of Richmond Park. I was busy on another play, *Foreign Field*, which was bought by Henry Sherek for Ann Todd. It was a busy and exciting time. In the middle of it Johnnie went off to stay with Rex Harrison at Portofino before he started the film *Hobson's Choice*. Unable to go because I was working with Sam Wanamaker on my play, I remained at the Wick. I wanted to be with the children during the day so I worked through the night, but on the night that I finished the last draft of *Foreign Field*, and having eaten my sandwiches, I noticed the light growing dimmer. I realized that it was half-past five in the morning. Finishing off I went upstairs, and exhausted, flung myself fully clothed on the bed. The next morning when Nanny Day, who had come to live with us again, brought in the breakfast, I asked: 'Why have you come in so early, Nanny? It's still dark!'

'It's twelve o'clock, Mary,' she answered, 'and the sun is shining.'

I could see nothing. For ten days I lay in bed with ice-packs on my eyes, blind, and thinking of my father in Canton. Johnnie rushed home at once and sat with me constantly but I wondered whether I would ever see him and the children again. It appeared that the cornea of both eyes had been torn by overwork, and from then on I had to wear glasses to read.

'Oh, Bunny, it makes me feel so *old*!' I told Juliet as she stood by the bed.

'You'll never be old, Mimosa, never, and you're more precious than anything else in the world, even with your horrid old glasses, isn't she, Bags?'

Hayley was busy looking at a magazine. With a saintly smile she looked up at Johnnie and asked, 'Do you like big charlies, Daddy?'

*

One November Johnnie was asked to go down to East Grinstead to light a charity Guy Fawkes Bonfire for Isadore Kermann, an old friend of his. After lighting the Fire, we were in a small pub and a farmer started talking to Johnnie about the glories and challenges of farming.

'There's a good one over Cowden way, Sussex House Farm . . . you ought to look at it if you like farms.'

'A farm!' Johnnie said to me later that night. 'I'd love to have a farm. Bring the kids up with animals, beside a running stream with a view across long meadows and woods. . . . What do you say?'

'I'd love it, too—so long as we don't have to leave the Wick,' I answered guardedly.

The next morning we went to look at the farm. There was a thirteenth-century farmhouse with what was once a chapel under the dining-room, black and white plaster and clapboard, mullioned windows, and a wealth of old beams and wide open fireplaces. Below the house rolled a five acre field with a stream at the bottom, and all around, woods and meadows cut us off from the world.

'D'you like it?' Johnnie asked enthusiastically.

'Love it, so long as—'

'No, no, just for holidays and weekends. One hundred and sixty-five English acres! A herd of Guernseys, pigs, chickens, and an empty attic under the rafters that would make the most wonderful bedroom for us.'

I was carried away by his enthusiasm. 'They can live as you lived without any shoes, without much clothing, learning about life from the fields and woods, animals and birds. Run wild, as you did.'

We bought Sussex House Farm. Every weekend we left the Wick with a fully-loaded car, Nanny's canary, Charlie Staircase the poodle, and a new Hamlet, a black and white cocker spaniel.

The children were transported by the farm. To every child at some time, round a corner, on some crossroad will come instantly the sight of a beloved house. For me it had been the old place on the wall in Macao surrounded by my mother's marguerites. To them, it was undoubtedly the farm, where an ivy greaved church stared down from the wooded rise of the hill, and on Sundays, bells rang over the meadows as bells had rung for me across the fields of Dorking. Here the floors were worn to the smoothness of lard—ducks bobbed on the pond and bees swarmed round the garden clinging to the honeysuckle; cherry blossom, and later on every imaginable kind of rose, poured its heavy scent through the casement windows.

Many years later when Bunchie took her own small son to the farm to look at it she wrote: 'It was a funny sad sentimental journey for me, memories flooded back, laughing voices, Christmasses and summer evenings, church bells across the fields, the smell of hay and a talk to a lovely lady in the raspberry bushes, with the sound of Doosie's trumpet summoning us to supper, fantail pigeons roaring overhead, and people, lots of people who were once part of the pattern of our lives and who now have for one reason or another slipped away. We so loved that farm. You handled your family very well, didn't you, darlings? And whatever it cost you in terms of money, none of us three would exchange those blissful haymaking years together, for anything in the world.'

Haymaking years! Far from ugliness and hard pavements and people with desperate faces.

But the day came when our accountant told us that we could not live in two houses at once.

'The ruddy taxation won't let you!' he almost shouted. 'You have to decide between the farm and the Wick!'

'But you promised me that we wouldn't have to leave the Wick!' I wailed.

'It's not me, it's the ruddy tax inspector. No one could *really* afford both,' he said. 'You definitely can't.'

For hours Johnnie and I deliberated, pacing the terrace at the Wick, and later the floor of our bedroom.

'We must weigh the pros and cons,' he said—a favourite game of his. 'The kids love the farm, and there's no doubt that it is wonderful for them at this age.'

'I wish I'd never seen it!'

'This garden is glorious, but it's not really a place to play in when you're six, ten, and fourteen,' he reminded me.

No, I thought. Perhaps it is a bit too formal. No secret places for children.

'After all, you had it in Macao, the freedom to roam, I mean,' he smiled, touching the top of my head. 'They can ride and fish, watch the corn turning gold and help to gather in the hay.'

'Yes—'

'We'll build on, make a terrace on that old bank, turn the attic into a bedroom and bathroom for *us*! Make a swimming pool, have a tennis court! We'll take the caravan down to the river and you can write undisturbed by anything but birds and cows!' He talked excitedly and I knew he wanted it.

I stared at him dejectedly, my spirits sinking; walking to the window I looked dismally out over the moon-flooded garden. The remembered scent of Bourbon roses drifted towards me, and I sighed.

'It would be an exciting thing to work for, to buy more land, have another herd, create something out of it, for them and with them,' he said gently.

I gazed down at my garden. It was true that it wasn't *quite* the garden and it wasn't *quite* the country for children either; the polo which excited us wasn't such fun for a child who couldn't do anything but watch. I could see them suddenly ranging through the meadows and woods, collecting bluebells and firewood, rearing rabbits, sloshing about in the mud of winter, drying their clothes before the huge open fireplace.

'But there's no *real* garden there,' I began. 'Except for the Kanzan cherry, it's just all that grass where sheep have stamped through the centuries, and someone has bunged up the fireplace with a modern horror—'

'Make one!' he urged. 'Tear the fireplace out.'

'I could . . .' I mused. Then I turned to him. 'All right, Johnnie! The pros outweigh the cons.'

He started planning. The whole project excited him and the children, but for me it was difficult. I found myself brooding over my pet trees and plants; I couldn't work, and had a sort of colic from pure nervous tension. How strange, I thought, what bricks and mortar can do to you, for it had been a love affair from the start between me and the Wick.

'I don't want you mooning round the house like a lost ghost!' Johnnie said. He put his arms around me. 'I'm sad too about leaving the Wick, but you'll love the farm. The summer will make it all right, when we've planted something. . . .'

I stood in the hall watching the last of the wooden crates being carried out by the removals men. Half were to go to the farm, and the other half to store, for we would have to have a small flat in London as well, to work from. The children were all waiting excitedly to get into the car, Hamlet and Charlie Staircase, Nanny's canary, and a collection of toys. Memories of other packings, other wooden crates and other children flooded back into my mind. I walked out onto the balcony and looked down at the garden; already an ashen sadness seemed to have shrivelled it, the leafless trees were holding out their bent limbs to me—and there were no birds singing. . . .

'There will be another ghost here now,' I whispered, and turned back into the empty drawing-room. Empty, except for one thing. On the mantelpiece lay the glass witch stick. Slowly, I walked up to it, picked it up, and holding it carefully in my two hands, walked out of the front door, closing it behind me.

Johnnie caught my eye—and grinned.

21

OVER THE DIM BLUE HILLS

In the next seven years we did all that John had suggested. We built the extra wing at one end of the farmhouse, turned the great attic under the sloping eaves into an enormous bedroom and bathroom. We tore out the modern fireplace and discovered another one behind it that looked straight up the chimney to the sky. Helped by Edward Roberts, the farm manager, and his sons, we built a swimming pool with our own hands; but for days men worked and battled with the mud to get the terrace right.

'It's a bloody great grave!' I sobbed, my head against the windows watching the streaming rain, while Johnnie rolled on the sofa with laughter. But before a year was out the York paving looked as if it had been there a hundred years, and the Kanzan cherry threw a pink haze in all the rooms. Roses were planted everywhere, yellow, pink, and mauve, climbing the house and peering through the windows, and the old herbaceous border was restored to law and order. Johnnie put up a greenhouse in the vegetable garden, and we planted herbs, raspberries and strawberries. All grew in abundance, until one night the whole herd of Guernseys swept through a gap in the hedge and left us nothing but cabbage stalks.

'That's farming,' Johnnie said.

'That's life,' Bunch added, philosophically.

'That's cows,' said Jonathan practically.

The sunflowers and hollyhocks grew against the wall in what had once been a bull ring, and the azaleas brought from the Wick flourished and flowered prolifically.

Johnnie's polo ponies were transported from Richmond Park and the children rode them around the farm, but Cobré, a chestnut mare in foal, developed ringbone and the vet suggested that she should be put down. Hayley's enormous eyes met mine with horror.

'Couldn't she have a baby? Just stay in the fields and have a baby? Oh do let her, then we can race it!' Her eyes were bright.

The foal, christened Sean, was born in the tool shed one September night, by the light of a hurricane lamp.

There was in those years both a sense of time flying, and yet a timelessness, for nowhere is one more sensitive to the feeling of the cycle of creation and re-creation, than on a farm. The sowing and the reaping. The iridescent fields of summer under a lapis lazuli sky; the same fields, iron grey in the grip of winter, when nothing stirs, and the nostrils are full of the scents of pine fires, rubber boots and mouldering leaves. Then it is spring again with the first burst of primroses under the hedges, and the intoxicating joy from the throat of a blackbird; and those which had been calves and lambs are now heifers and sheep, and the legs of little girls flashing through streams are somehow longer; the child and the foal, no longer babies but growing apace, standing together in a field studded with buttercups; the snub-nosed, freckle-faced boy and the roan, curiously alike in their colouring and hobbledehoy, coltish movements. We could almost *see* them growing, and with a sense of shock were aware one afternoon of this barefoot boy with a fishing rod in one hand, rushing into the room where the Vicar was having tea with me and snatching up the telephone.

'Jonathan! You haven't said good afternoon to the Vicar—'

'But Mummy! Edward told me to ring up the Artificial Insemination people 'cos Love is bulling!'

A hurried glance to see if the Vicar comprehended, and the lame explanation: 'Love, is, a cow. . . .'

'Are you glad I was born to you?' Bags asked, as we sat among the raspberry canes.

'*So* glad! Why, you might have gone to somebody else!'

'But Mummy! I chose you out of all the world. I could have come sooner.'

'I could too,' said the boy, 'but I thought I'd wait a bit.'

'You could have been the oldest,' said Bunch, scooping a handful of raspberries into her mouth.

'I wasn't quite sure I wouldn't rather be a bird,' Hayley said gravely, 'then I could have flyed.'

'Why *can* birds fly, Mimosa?' The boy's round eyes were as green as grass.

'Because they *believe* they can,' Bags told him.

'I believe I can too,' he answered.

'You believe you believe, but you don't, not really,' Bunch told him, and realizing he was in deep waters, the boy changed the subject.

'There's Edward going to shoot rabbits. Can I one day?'

'Poor rabbits, . . .' Hayley murmured.

'They're used to being shot at,' Jonathan told her with manly authority. 'D'you like the new cook's face, Bags?'

'Never look at her face, only her teeth.'

'Why?'

'They frighten me.'

'She looks like Palethorpe sausages—'

'If her corn hurts it always rains, always,' said Bunch.

Johnnie sitting on a hill with me looking down at the farm. 'I want to buy all this extra land round us, but now it seems *Hobson's Choice* is a failure. I haven't been offered a job in weeks. They say I'm box office poison!'

'Oh, no! It was one of your best performances.' And almost at the same moment Bunch blew Johnnie's trumpet from the terrace, summoning us to a telephone call from Ivan Foxwell, who wanted him to play in *The Colditz Story*—and the world was again suddenly full of the fragrance of the earth after a storm.

When Johnnie was playing in *Figure of Fun* at the Aldwych, we took the three children to see it from the Royal Box. It was a tricky afternoon, for Jonathan soon became bored and retired to the royal lavatory where he interested himself in a constant pulling of the chain, to the convulsed amusement of Cicely Courtneidge, who sat in the stalls below us. Bunch and Hayley watched hypnotised, and when Johnnie appeared in an intoxicated condition in one scene, and staggered drunkenly down a flight of stairs, Hayley's clear voice rose from the box: 'Oh, Daddy, *really*!' and laughter rippled through the theatre, as once more from the precincts behind us, the vigorous pulling of the exhausted chain drowned Johnnie's words. But it was while we were sitting there that Leslie Henson spied Bunch and decided she should play Alice in *Alice Through the Looking Glass*.

'Can I, oh can I? I want so much to be an actress.'

'What's it like to be an actress?' Hayley asked. 'What do you need?'

Johnnie smiled. 'You need to learn a lot of lessons,' he said. 'You need to learn that it's the jungle, and there's no use going into it unless you can accept criticism and defeat, and not let them beat you to your knees. Truth, sincerity, charm. All these things you need—as well as a certain talent to start with!'

On the night that Juliet opened at the Chelsea Palace, Binnie Hale put her arms round Johnnie and said, 'She'll be a big star if she gets the luck.' Bunch overheard her, and leaning over the back of the stalls, she looked up at Johnnie with excited eyes. 'What makes a star, Doosie?' He looked at her for some moments in silence, and then said: 'The audience, darling. It's whether they like you or not.'

They all painted, and they all wrote. Hayley recorded her thoughts and experiences in a secret journal tied up with red ribbon that no one was allowed to read.

Bunch wrote poetry, which she showed me, smiling shyly from under the thick fringe of dark lashes. 'Not even a poem, darling, just a thought,' she told me.

The scent of a closing rose
White wings of a sleeping dove
The glow of your scarlet clothes
Your hand, your heart—my love.

Jonathan also wrote poems. These were never produced, but he didn't try to hide them, and I used to come across them on scraps of paper in his trouser pockets, mixed up with string and stones and tickets and air gun pellets—with no punctuation.

When the snow was thick
And everything was like a trick
The air was thin and cold
But everyone was bold
When the clouds rolled away
When the sky didn't sway
When the frost was so crisp
And the wind so wisp
Which is done by the cretur
Which is just like nature
When the snow lies deep
And every animal is asleep

*

In 1957 Bunch decided that at the age of sixteen she wanted to leave school and go into the theatre. She arrived at our flat in Berkeley Square at eleven-thirty in the morning, tears running down her cheeks as she held a drooping bunch of daffodils clutched in her hand, the parting gift of one of the younger children at school.

'Oh, Mummy! Isn't the end of anything sad!'

'Dry your tears, darling, and put the flowers in water. You're going to an audition at five o'clock for *Five Finger Exercise*. John Gielgud's producing it at the Globe.'

Instantly everything changed, and the flat was full of whoops of laughter, shaking hands and a rustling through my cupboard for the right thing to wear. We chose a knitted navy blue suit that had a pleated skirt and belted jacket. It was a suit that was at some time or another worn by both Bunch and Bags for interviews and auditions, and hangs in the cupboard today, alongside the nasty striped pinafore dress with the brown zipper that I was wearing when I first met Johnnie at Ant's flat!

Hayley and I accompanied her to the Globe Theatre. In the stalls were Binkie Beaumont, Terence Rattigan, Adrienne Allen, who was playing the leading part, the author Peter Shaffer, and John Gielgud. Hayley and I, hands clenched together, sat at the back with pounding hearts.

In the first scene that Bunch read, she wasn't very good; she was nervous and it wasn't a scene that helped her to show what she could do. The old familiar line rang up from the stalls.

'Thank you very much. We'll be in touch with you.'

Hayley and I met her at the pass door; her eyes were full of tears, for she knew she had failed, and already someone else was reading the scene. I couldn't bear it for her, but the old trouper in Hayley Bell, the actress who had pursued Seymour Hicks into a taxi and shouted at Leon M. Lion from the stalls, exerted itself. Taking their hands I crept up to the circle, and listened to the comments from below.

'I liked the Mills girl,' Adrienne was saying.

'I didn't think her comedy—'

'Oh, come on! She didn't read a comedy scene!'

'What about the girl with long black hair?'

'Definitely not, Binkie,' said Adrienne. 'I think the Mills girl should read the funny scene with Brian Bedford.'

'But she's gone!' said John Perry.

'Oh, hell!'

'Call her back!' Adrienne was firm.

At this moment I snatched their two hands and started up the passage to the street.

'Play it calm and cool, darling,' I said to Bunch. 'Oh, *look*! Here's a picture of the Moscow Arts Theatre. *Stare at it.* . . .'

We stared at it steadily as we heard the running feet of John Perry tearing up the stairs.

'*Lovely* picture, isn't it, Hayley?' I asked.

'*Lovely!*' she said in a high voice, a trifle too loudly.

John Perry's feet came to a sliding halt beside us. 'Oh, I'm so glad I caught you,' he panted. I looked at him in surprise.

'Why, John?'

'We want Juliet to read another scene, a comedy scene.' He cleared his throat.

'Goodness!' I laughed easily. 'What a bit of luck that Hayley wanted to look at this picture. We were just about to get a taxi!'

'Will you come back, Juliet? Sir John would like you to read another scene.'

Calmly, very relaxed, Bunch walked back with him as Hayley and I followed. At the pass door she stopped, looked back at us and gave a broad conspiratorial wink. Hayley and I sat in the stalls holding each other's hands again as we watched her reading the scene with Brian Bedford. She was completely different this time and took her opportunity with both hands.

She opened six weeks later at the Comedy Theatre; the audience loved her and Johnnie and I were so proud that we couldn't stop grinning at each other. It was only as we left the theatre that I remembered that this was where I had been in *Tony Draws a Horse*, and where Johnnie and I had said goodbye to each other under the lamppost when he went to join up at the beginning of the war. We stood holding hands and laughing.

'It's incredible, isn't it?' I asked. 'Who would have guessed all those years ago that we would be standing here, while the Bunch is taking off her make-up in the same dressing-room.'

'I wonder what lies in store for Hayley and Jonathan?' Johnnie said quietly as we went through the stage door to find her. . . .

We soon found out for one of them. In September that same year, 1958, Lee Thompson came to Sussex House Farm for the weekend. We were sitting on the terrace in the evening, watching the sun go down over our fields, when there was a burst of raucous laughter from the pool.

'What's that?' he asked.

'Oh, it's Hayley entertaining some kids,' I replied.

'What does she do?' he asked.

'She does an imitation of the advertisements on television all run together,' Johnnie told him. 'It's really rather funny.'

Lee crossed the lawn and watched her from the shadows as she went through soap powder advertisements, milk, bread, and deodorant advertisements; then he came back and sat down.

'I've had an idea, Mary. I'm going to make a film called *Tiger Bay*. It's about a chase after a murderer which develops round a small boy who assists the man to get away. Strangely enough, I came down here to ask Johnnie to play the detective, but now I've seen Hayley, I know quite positively I want to change the boy into a girl, into Hayley. What do you think? Could she do it? Would she?'

We talked to her about it that night, for we were to meet Lee at the Ritz the following morning, stopping off on our way to stay in Portofino with Rex.

'The girl is supposed to be nine and you're nearly twelve,' we told her. 'So you may be too old!'

We met Lee in fact on the corner opposite the Ritz, and when the lights turned and we started to cross he touched me on the arm and pointed to Hayley, walking ahead with Jonathan. Shoulders hunched, and knees bent, she seemed no taller than her seven-year-old brother.

'Why does she walk like that?' he asked in some consternation.

'She's afraid she's too big and might not get the part!' I laughed.

Encouraged by this, Lee spent the whole lunch telling Hayley the story, while she chewed her way through one course after another, never taking her eyes off his face. Jonathan on the other hand kept referring to the large clock on his wrist. He was clearly in terror that the longed-for holiday was going to disintegrate, for it wouldn't have been the first time that plans had been made only to be cancelled for a film or a play.

'Don't forget she peels,' he started.

'Well, what d'you think, Hayley? Like to try a test?' Lee asked.

'Now?' she squawked, her eyes going quickly from one to the other of us.

'Don't forget she *peels*!' Jonathan raised his voice. 'In the sun,' he added lamely.

Lee laughed. 'When you get back,' he said, and gave Jonathan a wink which brought an answering smile of relief from the boy.

Two weeks later Hayley made the test with Horst Bucholtz. Lee was ecstatic. 'It's the most exciting thing I've seen in twenty years.'

Completely at ease, and never ruffled either by long days of shooting or long nights of waiting, Bags took the whole situation completely in her stride. Never appearing to be learning the lines, for she has a most curious photographic memory, she was always word perfect; her rendering of the part was completely her own, truthful, amusing, and often touching. It was as though she had been acting for years, and yet at the same time it was so fresh that I often had to remind myself that I was looking at my own daughter—that I hadn't come into a Welsh field, suddenly, to catch sight of a strange child on a white pony, whom I had never seen before. In her childish way she had her first feelings of love for Horst Bucholtz, for the film clearly emerged, as David Lean said later, as one of the most tender of love stories.

As soon as she and Johnnie had finished the film, he was offered *The Seventeenth Doll* in Australia, and went on ahead, making the three-day journey alone while I rounded up the children to follow him. That journey took us seven days! From the outset, when we had to jettison fuel over the sea outside Prestwick in Scotland, the plane never landed anywhere without engine trouble. In New York we were held up at the International Airport, and Hayley and Jonathan discovered the joys of television in the bedroom and a bidet in the bathroom, where they sat with their feet in the water. At San Francisco, it was an all night wait. 'If there weren't so many of us I'd get off this plane,' I told Bunch, who had been allowed two weeks holiday from *Five Finger Exercise*. We seemed to spend the whole night eating or going to the lavatory, until at last, tired of spending the few dimes that I had in my purse on the latter, the two girls and I decided to crawl under the door and not pay anything, only to be caught in the act, all three of us, by an outraged cleaner. Emerging red-faced and a little fearful, we found that Jonathan had disappeared, and after a long search discovered him sitting on a bench beside an American soldier to whom he was endeavouring to sell half-a-crown in exchange for a dollar. Repeatedly the man refused, even getting up to walk away, but such was the boy's persistence that finally and wearily, longing to be rid of the red-headed, spindle-legged boy, he handed him a dollar note.

'I said a *silver* dollar,' the boy remonstrated. 'If I give you a silver half-crown, you must give me a silver dollar.'

'Son, I ain't *got* no silver dollar,' the man said desperately, and it was at this point, full of apologies, that I rescued the man from the irate boy.

*

Back in England, *Tiger Bay* had opened in London. Most of the reviews were rhapsodies of praise and enjoyment. Nancy Spain wrote in the *Daily Express* that '*Tiger Bay* is dominated from first to last by this wonderful child Gillie . . . one of the most memorable performances of the year. You believe in every moment because you believe in Hayley Mills. I hope she grows to maturity with her talent and her enchanting little mug unspoiled. In Hayley we have a new Star for Britain. . . .'

Unfortunately producers and directors in Britain are slow to realize the potentiality of many of their actors and actresses. Thus it was with Hayley, and it was the great Walt Disney who took her away and made her a star for America.

It wasn't an easy decision for us. After all, she was only a child. Johnnie and I discussed it for hours on end. 'Would it be the right thing for her?' he asked. 'She has a *right* to be a child. What about her education? Will it spoil things for her in the future? If we turned the chance down now and she wanted later to be an actress, would she hate us for the opportunity we didn't take?'

'She's only a *baby*!' my mother wailed.

'What do you think, Hayley?' she asked.

'Will we all be together, or would I have to do it alone?' was all she said.

'I can promise you some of us will always be with you,' I told her.

'Then I'd like to do it,' she said simply.

So our life was arranged. For five years she was to make one picture a year for Walt Disney, starting with *Pollyanna*. To my mother's undisguised pleasure David Kilmuir, who was the Lord Chancellor, came to dinner and dropped a bomb onto the dining-room table by saying: 'Oh, but she can't possibly go. Don't you know there's a law in England that no child under the age of thirteen can leave the country for gain!'

In the end, however, it was decided that she could go to America to make the film on the understanding that she was paid no money! And that when she became thirteen Walt Disney would be allowed to start on his five year contract. At the same time he asked Johnnie to play the father in *The Swiss Family Robinson*. So we set off, with Jonathan, but temporarily and sadly leaving Bunch in London at the flat in the charge of our herdsman's wife Soxie, for Bunch was still in *Five Finger Exercise*. The tearful parting at the airport was to be one of many that we have since had to experience, to which we have never been able to accustom ourselves.

*

A small cottage came up for sale in Cowden village, near the farm. It had a walled garden and some of the most glorious lilies of the valley I had ever seen. I bought it, intending it for my mother, partly out of the meagre returns on a novel I had written called *Avolena*.

'You can garden here, have your grandchildren to stay, and lie out in the summer in a long chair,' I told her. 'All this, and over one field to Sussex House Farm.'

Gently, she put her hand on my arm. 'Thank you, my darling, but I won't have it. It's almost too late for me to start in a new house. I prefer my little flat with all of you bobbing in and out, and I should miss my St John's Ambulance work. . . . I hope it's not too much longer before I can join the other two.'

*

'You can't ever see people from the sky, Mimosa,' Jonathan told me in the plane. 'It's because they're too small and unimportant.' And the sad waters of separation were borne in on me with Hayley's voice singing:

> Over the dim blue hills strays a wild river,
> Over the dim blue sea rests my heart ever. . . .

At Los Angeles there was heat and the smell of tarmac and engines, a flustered battery of sweating cameramen with deadpan faces dripping with moisture, with a fat little man springing ahead of the others: 'This way, Hayley. Smile. Say cheese! Please John. All together now. Hey! little boy, you! Look at your sister! All look at Hayley! One more please. . . .'

'This is the beginning of hell,' I said to Johnnie as we fell into bed several hours later.

For four months we stayed in Hollywood while Hayley made *Pollyanna* and success rolled up to her and took her in its arms, as the surf rolls up the beach. We made a great many friends, the greatest of whom was Walt Disney himself. Idolized by his crew and staff he was to be seen striding daily through his great studio, a strange little smile of pleasure hovering on his face in everything he saw. An undemonstrative man, he would suddenly throw his arms round Hayley and hug her, or stand watching her playing a scene and burst into a guffaw of laughter. Though he was such an enormous figure, neither Hayley nor Jonathan was ever afraid of him, and would unsolicitedly tuck their small hands through his arm to ask him a question on cowboys or hamburgers, or when they were going to Disneyland.

Johnnie went off to Tobago to make *The Swiss Family Robinson* and the three of us stayed on till *Pollyanna* was finished.

We arrived in Tobago four days after Bunch had joined Johnnie from England. The meeting was boisterous and there were no flustered, sweating cameramen, only the cool jade green of the jungle, water lilies like plates, birds in bright colours, and boys with hand-made reed baskets full of pomegranates and avocados, standing at the airport in the early morning. Bunch, her eyes full of tears of excitement, had a taxi manned by the giant Maxie-Spence-of-the-Downtown-Taxi-Stand ready to take us to the little house hidden by palms on the edge of the sea, where pelicans flapped the livelong day.

'Faery Queen' the house was called, and inside, Mrs Batiste, a Negro lady with stiff black pigtails, a mouth full of shining, smiling white teeth, a red commando beret covering her head at all times and a singing voice, looked after us. Her daughter Eileen was full of shy giggles, and 'Mistress' Phillips did the laundry. We lived on a sea-green island in a sea-green sea, surrounded by coral and great seas beating against Bucco Reef. Yellow sugar birds sat down to breakfast and helped themselves casually from the papaya on the plate, and the scent of the frangipane sent the senses reeling.

We stayed there four months. The children grew as wild as I had once grown, years ago in Macao. Tearing through the surf on milk white beaches, wandering through coconut groves and consuming freshly caught red mullet with Mrs Batiste's rice, the best cooked that I have ever had, even in a Chinese village.

How the children loved that little marvel of an island! Their wonder increased daily, for never had they hoped to see such birds as those that lived near Faery Queen. Bizarre brown pelicans, dignified and slow; great black-and-white Men o'War birds with their long pointed tails and angular wings, hanging motionless in the Caribbean sky; the bitterns, the parrots and scarlet migratory ducks. . . .

'Look, Mummy, look!' With shaking fingers they would point out yet another. 'What are they? What are they!'—and I was forced to rush to the public library, my favourite refuge anywhere, and learn about the local birds so that I could join in their excitement. . . .

To me, in some curious way, it was almost a return to my childhood. Seeing them running along the beach, it seemed sometimes that I was looking at the retreating form of myself in Hayley with her long wet hair and bare brown legs, and the small red-headed boy running beside her . . . was that Johnman? And who was the slim creature who ran on ahead, flinging herself into the sea with cries of delight . . . ?

To them the island had an extraordinary magic; Johnnie, being immersed in *The Swiss Family Robinson*, led them into a Robinson Crusoe life of days in the tree house built for the set in an enormous Immortelle, with orchids growing out of its crotches. Below them was a world of animals imported for the film from America: Ostriches, tigers, a baby elephant, monkeys, and giant turtles.

It was a dream world, of sudden tropical storms like Doré's print of the world's end, of early morning birds and flowers lit with an abrupt brilliance and heady fragrance, as the children ran through sparkling waters onto prune-coloured rocks to throw out their arms to the flapping pelicans. So the long lovely summer of childhood settled like a gossamer cloak of happiness about their young shoulders.

'But you have to have some kind of education,' we told Hayley and Jonathan. With noses wrinkled in disgust they agreed; anything was better than going back to England. I had an interview with the Head Master of the Negro school and we arranged that Hayley and Jonathan should join it. On the morning that I was driving them over the hill, Hayley suddenly seized me by the arm.

'Hey! I've just thought of something!'

'What?' I asked, avoiding a dog.

'Nobody in the school is white except us, right?'

'Right.'

'S'posing it's Little Rock the other way round! S'posing all those coloured children don't like us?' Jonathan's eyes widened.

It wasn't Little Rock the other way round, or anything like it, and though they didn't learn very much, Jonathan at least learned how to play soccer in bare feet.

The time came when Juliet had to join *Five Finger Exercise* in New York. An air of gloom filled the Faery Queen and memories of my loneliness in that great city came back to me. 'Oh, Mimosa! I shall miss the lovely breakfasts with papaya and limes.' Now nearly seventeen, yet with the untouched face of a child, I would see her sometimes sitting alone, thinking, and I knew what she was going through, the growing pains so well remembered, the problems of youth, passion, poetry and truth, all mixed up with the sound of chirruping crickets.

I went with her to Trinidad, to Piarco Airport across the Bay. The other two children and Johnnie stood waving, and my heart was wrung with the knowledge suddenly that not only was it the end of her childhood as it had once, many years before, been the end of mine, but the knowledge that it was always going to be Bunchie who would be left behind on a hundred airports. And so indeed it has been.

We had dinner together, and then went early to bed, for her plane was coming in at three o'clock in the morning.

'How I loved living in that feathery great salad bowl of palms with you all,' she said. 'And although in a way I'm looking forward to playing in New York, I'm kind of scared.'

'It's wonderfully exciting for you,' I told her. 'This chance, at your age. Take it with both hands, darling; you'll make lots of friends, and one thing leads to another, one torch lights another. We're so proud of you, Daddy and I.'

As I spoke I realized how like my mother I must be growing in my possessiveness of the family, that old hangover from China! I reminded myself that I must see to it that I didn't think all my geese were swans, not confuse Love with possessiveness, but give them strength, courage and understanding, and then open the door to the World and let them go out.

'What are you thinking about, Mimosa?' she asked sleepily.

I laughed: 'My mind was running away with me! I was looking into the future,' I replied.

'Hope you don't see anything nasty in that old Irish witch ball,' she said, and there was a giggle from the other bed.

'It all looks wonderfully bright to me. Just take care of yourself and don't become enslaved to any false things that aren't really *you*, and remember whatever happens, if you ever want us we'll be there, and on your side whatever it is!'

It was still dark when the plane landed to carry her away. She trudged off with a little wave of her hand and that characteristic walk; small steps, as though she carried the weight of a long bushy tail, so different from Hayley, whose stride is long and often difficult to keep up with.

I stood watching the plane from the runway, taking off like a great grey bird on the wings of the wind, its red eye winking farewell until it was lost to sight high in the Caribbean sky. There are some pictures that remain clearly imprinted on one's mind forever. This one was significant to me, for I knew that the first of the three doors had opened, and that Bunch had stepped out into her World.

*

It took us two weeks to decipher a cable from our agent, Lol Evans, which was handed to Johnnie one morning as he sat in the top of the tree house. He read it and threw it down to where I was sitting.

'Really! What next?' he laughed. I opened it up and read: 'Liz and Phil decorators offer you the part of Charlie Birdseed Esquire Palace follies Jan one.'

'What does it mean?' I asked. 'Hammersmith Palace? Victoria Palace? Follies?'

'Tear it up,' he answered. I put it away and forgot it until later when, in New York with Bunch, I telephoned Lol about something else. 'Lolly,' I said. 'What on earth was that other cable about some palace follies?' There was a long silence, then Lol spoke with a groan.

'Oh, my God! Haven't you done anything about it?'

'What should we have done? We couldn't make head or elbow of it,' I replied.

'Liz and Phil . . . *Liz* and *Phil*!' he shouted down the phone.

'Liz and Phil? Who are they?'

'Decorators . . . *Decorators*, darling!' he shrieked.

'What do we want with—oh!—' My voice trailed away.

'*Liz* . . . *Phil* . . . Palace . . . January . . . got it?'

'You mean, the Queen?' My voice was trembling.

'Of course! Charlie Birdseed Esquire . . . got it?' His voice kept fading under the Atlantic Ocean.

'C.B.E.' I spelt out the capitals. 'Commander of the British Empire.'

'Yes!' he yelled. 'For God's sake *do* something. The answer should have gone off two weeks ago!'

Johnnie received my cable from New York on the same morning that Hayley, asleep, stark naked under her mosquito net, was awakened to see two jet black Government House soldiers from Trinidad staring through her window. Clutching the net round her she stared at them wild-eyed.

'Hey, hop it,' she said.

'No hoppit,' one of them replied solemnly.

'Must hoppit, too early, no clothes on.' She grinned weakly at them from behind the rumpled safety of the mosquito net.

He shook his head. 'No matter no clo's, must give impotent letter to sah.'

'Sah is asleep. Throw it on the floor, I give him later.'

'No, man. I give letter sah now, no hoppit. . . .'

This intellectual exchange went on for some time according to Hayley, as the white-coated, fez-headed soldiery leaned through her window, until at last she was forced to leave the bed, 'like an uncooked chicken in a meat safe', her winding sheet of mosquito netting tucked securely round her. She advanced towards them, bringing the whole net down from the ceiling, and causing such ear-splitting laughter that Johnnie was woken up. He rushed into Hayley's room to come across the oddly assorted picture of the all-but nude figure of his younger daughter enmeshed in clouds of mosquito netting, and two huge Negro soldiers guffawing in the window.

'What the hell's going on?' he said, struggling with his own disarrayed sarong. The men leapt smartly to attention, saluted, and one of them handed him a long official envelope.

'Impotent, sah,' he said. It was from the Governor of Trinidad, requesting Johnnie's presence that afternoon.

*

We left Tobago two days before Christmas. Mrs Batiste, Eileen, Mistress Phillips, Maxie-Spence-of-the-Downtown-Taxi-Stand and most of the Mills were in tears, the stentorious wails of our Tobagan friends pursuing us to the steps of the aeroplane as they bombarded us with flowers.

'We'll come back,' the children shouted. 'Don't cry, we'll come back soon.'

But tears were forgotten at the miracle of the New York skyline, and Bunch's jubilant face flushed with excitement.

'Hullo, old fruit!' Jonathan yelled.

'How are you, Snodgrass,' she bawled back, and once more it was a tangle of arms and legs, endless baggage, straw hats and the usual unsuitable paraphernalia that people bring with them from a tropical island to a country where the temperature is forty degrees below freezing and there is snow on the ground.

It was a joyous and rowdy Christmas. They saw Bunch in her play and flew up and down Fifth Avenue buying everything they could afford, spending more on the coloured paper and string than on the presents, and before they had time to realize what had hit them, they were roaring round the farm again to the howls of welcome from Hamlet and Charlie Staircase, and suddenly, we were into 1960—and Charlie Birdseed Esquire went to Buckingham Palace to be given his Gong.

*

Johnnie was in Spain making another picture, *The Singer Not The Song*, when I was woken suddenly in the early hours of one morning by Hayley, standing beside me like a ghost in her long white night-dress.

'What is it? Somebody ill?' I asked, struggling up through the mists of sleep.

'It's the telephone, it goes on and on. It's Aunty Wyn and she says it's important.' I glanced at the clock and snatched up the phone.

'It's Mummy—' Wyn said.

'Oh!' A flutter of apprehension: 'Yes?'

'She's had a heart attack.'

'Oh no!' I swung my legs out of the bed as the hobgoblin horror of childhood ran before me. Wyn and I as children in Macao—leaning over her in the night to see if she was still breathing. I was conscious of Hayley standing beside me.

'Go to bed, darling, it's all right,' I told her.

'I think I'll just pop in here with you in case you need me,' she said, and lay down in the bed beside me.

'She'd been standing all day,' Wyn was saying. 'She went with her St John's Ambulance people to meet de Gaulle at some wretched station, and later there was this garden party at Buck House.'

'Yes?'

'She was coming out of that gate at the Hyde Park entrance with a friend and collapsed in that Archway, you know the one, with the chariot and all those horses. . . .'

'Where is she now?'

'St George's Hospital. I'm here now. Don't worry . . . she's asleep.'

'It's poor Granny,' I told Hayley as I crawled back into the bed beside her. 'She's very ill.'

'Oh, Mummy, she won't die, will she?' she whispered.

'No, darling, no,' I assured her.

'When we were very small, Bunny and I used to be afraid you and Daddy would die in the night, and we used to come into your room and listen to see if you were breathing,' she confided to me in the darkness.

'Did you?' I put out my hand and held hers. 'Did you really!'

'Are you glad I'm here in bed with you?'

'Very glad,' I said with some feeling.

'It's nice to have a good influence with you when you're worried,' she said, and almost at once was asleep.

I lay awake for a long time, thinking of my mother. I saw her down the years as in a kaleidoscope, the pieces moving from picture to picture. I saw her bending over us at bedtime, the stars twinkling through the cloud of her hair; I remembered the scent of her perfume and Nanny in a white starched apron in the background. I saw her running ahead of me along the Bund in Shanghai, a young woman with a large hat and a tight waist kicking a ball. I remembered her leaning over my first school trunk, packing little surprises to bring joy and comfort, but which in fact brought the slow, searing tears of loneliness. It wasn't only incidents that rolled before me, but a gallery of mute pictures, of her hats, her tiny boots and long velvet dresses, her young voice calling at the window of a train in the station: 'Write me every thought, Baba, gay or sad. I want to know everything.'

The next morning found me back in that familiar hospital with its smell of iodoform, and the sound of busy wheels echoing down long passages. She lay asleep, her face on her hand, a wistful bird imprisoned in one of the hospital's over-large flannelette nightgowns. Beyond the window, the world went by as it always will, cars and people moving towards the start of another day's work under a cloudless spring sky—and with a stunning blow, I realized that it was April again.

For two weeks she lay staring at the luminous sky over the park, but her subconscious mind had mercifully taken her by the hand and led her back down all the paths she had loved as a young woman. Eyes bright with an inner fever, and with the eager words of a girl, she rambled back through the days of her life, while Wyn and I sat, fearful and numb, two children tearing backwards unwillingly, through the country of childhood, on a school train. . . .

'Alice looks lovely in that Chinese vermilion, but why are those flowers in her hands. . . . I shall ride Hayley's horse and we'll have a picnic at the Jade Pagoda. Mama, does our darling monkey have to stay in the Zoo? His hair has gone white and the Keeper says. . . . Now Beako, hold Beatty and Johnman's hands, the sea is so rough. . . . How sweet they are, the children, Hayley. It's sad to think that one day they'll be grown up and then there'll only be you and me—like in the beginning.'

There was never any doubt in my mind that she was happy, surrounded as she seemed to be by familiar and laughing faces, sometimes smiling, sometimes humming quietly to herself. . . .

'Listen, that's Papa playing the organ,' and her voice, suddenly clear and sweet as a child's, singing in Sunday school:

Now the day is over
Stars begin to peep
Birds and beasts and flowers
Soon will be asleep.

I was packing Jonathan's school trunk, adding the 'surprise' packets of goodies that I knew would please him, just as she had done for me all those years ago, knowing that he would probably not be reduced to tears as his sentimental mother had once been—when the telephone rang from the hospital. It was the Matron.

'I'm so sorry. She's gone. Just slipped away in her sleep. . . .'

I walked out into the garden, across the field to my caravan. How was it I couldn't have *known* that moment of passing. . . ? How could the being who gave me life walk out of it without my knowledge? Had we failed her? Why was none of us there to hold her hands as we had been for the others?

The sky was beginning to grow grey, a few rooks cawed over me from the tall trees; the unrelenting spring had laid cruel, frosty fingers on the cherry blossom, blighting its prime, and a little wind stirred through the young leaves of the trees. The singing of new sap rising in dead boughs, the constant renewal of life's creative force. . . . April.

Incongruously, I found myself in the kitchen, eating out of a tin of baked beans with my fingers, and caught by my son to whom it was a forbidden dish.

'Mummy! You're eating baked beans!'

'Sometimes,' I told him, 'when something makes you unhappy, you do queer, unreasonable things. Granny died this morning, and somehow these beastly baked beans are a comfort, a stuffing up against being miserable. Maybe it's because once when I was very poor and sad, I lived on them.'

'I love them!' he said happily. 'Eat them all the time at school.' And we sat down together and demolished the tin.

Years later, he was to catch me again, only this time it was in my room in the attic at the Wick when my writing was going badly. He'd been asleep and his hair was ruffled and on end. He stood in the doorway grinning.

'Caught you!' he said.

'I get so hungry,' I replied. 'A bar of chocolate or a tin of baked beans stimulates the fading fagosites!'

He started turning over the pages of some of my notebooks, picking things out that he liked.

'I'm a bad example to you all really,' I told him. 'I'm just a messy Irish writer of little promise, banging my head against a wall, happy to live on a bowl of soup. My room is a mess of banana skins, papers, black coffee and cigarette stubs.'

'I've got a book of stuff written. I'll show them to you if you don't laugh,' he said, admitting to an interest I had known for years.

They were mostly poems, full of the promise of fulfilment, for he was not yet sixteen, and I got very excited.

'There's a long line of writers behind you,' I told him. 'Who knows, you may be the best of them all in the end!'

It was a night when we were very close together.

22

WHAT SHALL WE DO TOMORROW?

The years of Hayley's contract with Walt Disney were not always easy. The waters of separation that divided us were full of dismay, with Johnnie in England finishing a picture, Jonathan at school, Juliet in New York, and Hayley and I taking off for long flights to 'Horrorwood'. For the most part we were lucky. What money we had we spent in fares so that at some point we could all be together in some strange house with its inevitable pool. But we were all aware that behind us somewhere the farm stood empty and disenchanted, the horses out to grass, bicycles propped forlornly up against some old shed, forgotten and growing rusty, dogs waiting endlessly, their eyes on the gate for people who never came.

'We don't belong to these chicken coops,' Hayley said once. 'It's only all right when the sun shines. . . .'

Privacy was a thing of the past, and prying eyes and dishonest pens wrote the kind of articles in magazines that would have been libellous in Europe.

'As for giving parties,' someone once said to me, 'just don't. You can knock yourself out and half the people are too ill-mannered either to show up or send a good excuse. They just sit around waiting to see if something better turns up, for they're the greatest snobs in the world, and if they think they can get to a more successful party, you've had it!' I found this to be only too true. Manners in Los Angeles consist of a man knocking the table over to light your cigarette, but walking through a door in front of you to leave it to swing in your face.

I regarded the Hollywood mother with alarm. I dreaded being part of that gang of ambitious parents standing guard with unctuous smiles over their well-scrubbed and unsuitably clad children, and one of the most considerate things Walt Disney ever did for me among many was to give Hayley a 'guardian' at the studios so that I didn't need to sit eating my heart out, listening to endless discussions of money, body odour, money, dandruff and money, watching the poor little pampered mites working hard for their supper with their waved hair and nail polish, while their mothers stepped out of their Cadillacs and sat ingratiatingly in their luxurious mink coats telling any who would listen that their children's salaries went to the 'good of the family'.

'Oh Bags,' I said to Hayley one night. 'I hope we didn't make a ghastly mistake coming to this awful place. Perhaps we should have left you at your school in England, to grow up with friends of your own age. It's so bad for you here with this false sense of values and endless talk of money.'

'It's all right as long as you're here, Mimosa. Nothing can hurt me as long as I have you and Jonathan.'

And truly, Hollywood never did hurt Hayley. She was impervious. Natural and spontaneous, completely unselfconscious, she lived her life as she would have lived it anywhere, and for that reason was loved. To her, acting was only an enlargement of the 'imagining' games she used to play at the farm, by herself or with Bunch and Jonathan. The adulation and applause she received never for an instant turned her fair head or gave her a moment of conceit, whether it was placing her hands and feet in the cement next to Shirley Temple's at Grauman's Chinese Theatre, or being met at Tokio Airport at midnight by three thousand children waving flags with her name on it.

'Gosh,' she exclaimed, tugging my hand. 'Somebody important must be on the plane.'

She sang her way through the day from the bathroom back to the bedroom, and wherever she went she was followed by a horde of laughing children. She was Walt's delight, and I can see him now standing a little apart to watch her at Disneyland, holding his arms out to her as she came up to him with her eager face full of excitement.

'You really *are* the Pied Piper of Hamelin,' she told him. But when he turned to look at me his eyes were full of tears.

'Don't grow up, Hayley,' he said to her. 'We need people like you in this world.'

She has often been accused since of staying too young for too long. In many ways, this was due to Walt, for he believed that she had so much to give the children of the world before she was swept up into adult films.

'What's the hurry?' he replied to a columnist who demanded when she was to be allowed an adult scene.

'Don't let her do Lolita!' he begged me. 'She's a child of fourteen! And an English child at that. Don't let them press her into being some nasty sex symbol! All those poor little creatures have always been the unhappiest, for by the time they have really awakened, childhood has fallen away from them forever without any of them having been able to enjoy a moment of it.'

She had the ability and virtue of being able to go back to the farm and take things up from where she left off. Her pony and her animals became the centre of her life; she was unconcerned with the fact that three secretaries in Hollywood were dealing with a fan mail of 7,000 letters a week, that every imaginable type of present was arriving at the house under the sweating figure of the local postman, from mink jackets and expensive guitars to the promise of palomino ponies and otters to keep in the bath. Once when I asked her to endorse a cheque for some merchandising royalties on Pollyanna dolls, she wrote hastily on the back of it, 'Yours sincerely Hayley Mills'. For a long time that cheque was in Walt Disney's study at the studio.

She missed much of her schooling, for often the terms were cut short and before she could take her exams she was back in Hollywood; and sadly the school trailer where she worked on the lot with the other children never afforded her much education.

'How can I get these sums right when I'm thinking about how to cry in the next scene?' she asked me.

Finally there came a time when, reluctantly, she had to leave Elmherst. It wasn't fair to her or the other girls, so we decided to send her to Switzerland so that at least she could be fluent in French.

Her year at the school in Switzerland was her unhappiest, for by now she had a feeling that she no longer fitted in. Girls who were told by the Headmistress that 'Hayley Mills is to be treated like an ordinary child' were inclined to go too far in the opposite direction and leave her to herself, though even during this period (apart from dying from some varying imaginary diseases) she wrote some very funny letters:

'I'm growing into a beefy type, tweeds and brogues, possibly a cavalry moustache and pipe. Have taken up mountain climbing—what a laugh. The sheer drop of the cliff face, and this *rather* indecent harness we have to wear, round our middles and between our legs, but it's thrilling to do something with danger in it, swinging from one foot hold to another. Madame says I am a hooligan and will never be a "jeune fille" eh bien, too bad! I do get homesick, and wish I was with me mum in bed talking heatedly in the pitch dark as we used to in "Horrorwood!" I do miss the darling parent birds and Snodgrass. Open a horse show? How nerve-racking. What do I do? Crown the star horse with a swift upper cut with a good old bottle of champas?'

And to her brother: 'Hullo old Snodgrass, I wish I was with you at the farm. Stupid being homesick at my advanced age of fifteen, practically on the shelf with my horse books. There's still some snow on the Vidamanette, it looks like an enormous white dog with mangy patches and a bald head. We haven't been able to ski and I look like a spotty English rose with twin sets, pearls, and a roaring cold. Must fly to prep, old fruit. I'm not the school type, any more than Mimosa was.'

*

'I'm a moaning bleeder I know,' I wrote Johnnie, 'but I don't like this lonely place without you.'

Hayley and I were in a rented house in Hollywood waiting anxiously and rapturously for the family to arrive. We had filled the place with gardenias, turned on all the garden lights, placed Champagne and caviar on ice, and generally made it all look as glamorous as Hollywood is supposed to be. It was one of those typical Mills family airport welcomes of tangled legs and arms and exclamations of delight, when suddenly Juliet threw a large stone into the tranquil family waters by telling us she was in love. It was a shock because it was not only sudden, but we didn't even know the name of the man, and I realized with a pang how much she had grown up and away from us in those days alone in New York.

'No one will *ever* be good enough for Mummy's girls,' Johnnie laughed. 'The one she will have for you in her mind's eye will be the one that she would have chosen for herself!'

'That would mean you, Doosie!' Hayley laughed. 'I'd settle for that; in fact, that's what I shall probably be looking for!'

'Then you'll be accused of having a father complex!' I told her.

'What were *you* looking for, Mimosa?' she asked.

'I suppose if I'm honest I would say that I was looking for someone whom I could admire as much as I did my father, and yet at the same time someone who relied on me as a son. Very complicated,' I laughed.

'Maybe I'm only looking for the son bit,' Juliet smiled.

Russell Alquist, the first stranger into the magic family circle, was a tall slim boy, with fair hair, clouded eyes of blue shyness, and a hurt smile.

At first we battled against it. She was too young, we told her, how could she know her own mind? Russell wasn't quite sure where he was going. He wanted to be a singer, a song writer. There was much of the adolescent about him still, he was a bit of a dreamer, but I couldn't condemn him for that, for what else was I? That Juliet loved him there was no doubt, and she fussed over him and protected him like a little mother. He was good for her too, for I have never seen him in a temper or a fit of sulks. He took life as he found it, and he found everything in it that was good. We had to like him for there was never anything to dislike, and above all, he loved and cherished her deeply.

They were married in our village of Cowden, a few days before Johnnie went off to New York to play Lawrence of Arabia in Terry Rattigan's play *Ross*. The church and village were crammed with sightseers, smiling and waving and throwing flowers. Hayley was a bridesmaid and Jonathan an important and hard-working usher with an enormous and errant white carnation in his buttonhole.

The familiar figures in the choir, their voices rising as surely seldom before in 'Praise to the Holiest'; the October sunlight streaming through the stained glass windows above the altar, colouring Juliet's white veil and alabaster face; Hayley plucking at the flowers in her bouquet, and Johnnie's calm, untroubled eyes upon the black and white robes of the Rector, Eric Hart Dythe, while down the aisles behind us were the happy faces of Cowden folk who had come to love her, and her life's friends.

The Reception took place under the drifting chestnut leaves over the cow yard, now covered with blue and white bunting and golden and red chrysanthemums; and with eyes alight with happiness she went off to Paris, pursued by a hail of rice.

'I wonder who I shall marry,' Hayley pondered as we sat in front of the crackling log fire that night.

'Wonder who I'll marry first,' was Jonathan's reply as he crammed yet another slice of Juliet's wedding cake into his mouth.

*

Young people streamed through the farm in those days. They loved

Hayley's gaiety and sense of humour and love of life. The rooms echoed to the sound of music of one kind or another, a great deal of laughter and the thumping of rubber boots. Of them all, the memory of Judy and David Birkin's son, Andrew, remains the strongest, probably because he had first danced a 'square dance' with Hayley at the age of six at some charity performance. He was long and coltish even in those days, but the years had added to his stature in more ways than one, and he followed her everywhere like an overgrown faun.

'I look upon Andrew as my best friend,' she told me. 'I can say anything to him, tell him everything. It's like Rupert Brooke said about friendship: "Love without its wings".'

One of my closest friends, then, and now, was our secretary of twelve years, Kay Forward. She has seen Johnnie and me through many upheavals, success and failure, illness, worry about money, and my own frustrations and irritations over household responsibilities when deeply immersed in my work. To wake early in the morning and know that her cheerful and uncomplaining face will greet me at ten o'clock has been as cosy as knowing that the mother of my childhood was in the next room. The picture of Kay leaning against the bathroom door to see me sitting in the water in floods of tears after some rejection slip or other had been received in the post and saying, 'Well, you'll have to start another today, but not before you've interviewed a couple of would-be cooks!' has been repeated many times.

Long months of absence in various countries had left Sussex House Farm cold, lonely, and deserted. Springs and harvests had come and gone without us, and now with Juliet married to her Russell and living ina mews in London, Hayley inS witzerland, and Johnnie at school, the place seemed sad, and many weekends passed without Johnnie and I even wanting to return to the empty rooms and forgotten toys. I was more than ever aware of how my mother had felt all those years ago when as children we were all separated.

Dickie Attenborough and Bryan Forbes had bought my story *Whistle Down the Wind* to make with Hayley and a young actor called Alan Bates, and we spent the spring of 1962 up at Burnley in mud and biting winds. But when we came back in early April, Johnnie wasn't at all well. He had bad insomnia, and I used to lie beside him night after night in terror, remembering it to be April again.

'If anything ever happened to you,' I told him, 'I wouldn't be able to go on living. I would kill myself as soon as I knew the others were all right. I could never live here without you because I'm so unhappy when you're away, the place is so full of you. I can see you everywhere, digging up potatoes, mowing the lawn, bringing in wood and sitting on the tractor at haymaking. You're more dear to me than I could ever have believed anyone possibly could be. Life is so simple and direct with you, and though I know I must have often driven you mad with my meanderings, you've never shown me anything but your strength.'

He leaned over and kissed me. 'It's a funny thing, darling,' he said. 'But every night now, for weeks, I have been thinking of the Wick.'

'The Wick?'

'I can't get it out of my mind. Night after night I see it lying in the sunlight, or early in the mornings when the birds are chattering in the forsythia.'

I didn't answer directly. I knew how he and the children loved Sussex House Farm. I had made a mistake once in taking him away from Fernacres, and though I had often thought of the Wick, particularly when I was in America, I had mostly kept those thoughts to myself.

'I wonder, I just wonder if there's a chance to go back,' he said quietly.

'Leave the farm! It's impossible,' I cried.

'Why is it? Nothing is impossible. For all you know they might want to sell it again. Anyway, I have to find out.'

'What I mean is, that it's impossible to leave the farm. Not now, it's too late. We're as interred in this countryside as if we'd been planted in the garden. It's not fair, not to you or the kids or the farm people.'

'I don't agree with you,' Johnnie replied. 'We've nothing to reproach ourselves from the farm's point of view; we've done everything to improve the place, cottages and all, and as for the children, I think they've outgrown it.'

'Can one ever go back to anything?' I asked tentatively. 'Isn't there a chance that it might destroy a happy memory? Nothing is ever *really* the same. . . .'

'The Wick will be the same,' he insisted. 'And by the way, Baba, where is the witch stick!'

'Quite safe'—and I couldn't help laughing.

'What made you bring it away?' he asked.

'I'm not quite sure, but I knew I had to. Perhaps it was just a nasty streak in my character that didn't want us to be forgotten.'

Outside the windows the first violet light streaked through the curtains, and the dawn chorus of birds started from the cherry tree. I thought of the Wick, the muffled chime of the clock in the hall, the shaking birch leaves outside the windows, the puff of breeze that rose from the river and the blackbirds on the lawn.

'Let's have a cup of tea,' Johnnie was saying, 'and I'll phone Gabby Bowman tomorrow.'

*

'Of course you must both come over to the Wick,' Gabby said. 'I've asked you many times but you always refused!'

'I want to lay a ghost,' Johnnie told her with a smile at me.

With Hayley and Jonathan we drove up the long, familiar Queen's Road for the first time in seven years, and drew up to the house as we had done a hundred times.

'How small it is!' Hayley cried. 'I can step over these little railings. I always thought they came up to my waist!'

We stood shyly in the big hall, remembering that it was no longer our house, tiptoeing from room to room and recognizing all the old corners. Hushed and cool, the fragrance of the flowers in the conservatory brushed our faces as it had done fourteen years ago.

'What a fool I was ever to leave it,' Johnnie said quietly.

'Why don't you come back?' Paul Bowman asked.

'Come back?'

'Yes,' he said sadly. 'I really have to go to London to live. The old place is for sale. . . .'

It was a high price. And many of our friends thought we were mad to go back now the children were growing up.

'Money means nothing,' Johnnie said. 'Happiness is everything.' He snipped a flower as we walked round the garden. 'I know this is the place you love, Baba, and I love it too, and one day if we can't afford to live here with staff and gardeners, we'll just live here! This is our castle on the hill surrounded by flowers and water. . . .'

'But the farm . . .' I began.

'Obligations, responsibilities—that's what you're thinking of. It's a form of moral cowardice, the fear of facing faces. Our only responsibilities are to the children, and before you realize it, they will have flown away,' he said.

'Then there'll be only you and me—like in the beginning.' My mother's words came to my lips quite easily. Full cycle. The noiseless foot kicking the dying leaves in the lengthening sunset.

It wasn't as easy as he said, for moral coward as I am, the eyes of the good, kind friends who worked at Sussex House Farm followed us everywhere, and the trail of would-be buyers made me angry and my heart ache as they poked about in private corners. The farm looked good now, but it had been a struggle to make it so, although for the most part there had been only lovely times. The children had been happy there. The good air, the trees and meadows, the sluggish river, spring and harvest; it had given them something never to be forgotten, no matter what their fortune. For us, for Johnnie and me, the time was over. The Wick beckoned. The glass stick, the witch stick, shone brightly.

When the day came to go, neither the roses I had so lovingly planted, nor the second Hamlet's grave, the noisy, bobbing friends upon the pond or the shimmer of the distant bluebell wood had any longer the power to hold us back. My eyes were on my retreating caravan as it rumbled uncertainly on aged wheels down the lanes ahead of us on its way back to Richmond. Richmond! The very name, now that I could say it, gave me a shudder of delicious joy, and as we swung past the hedges that would soon be sprinkled with honeysuckle and morning glory, I knew I was going home at last.

The doors of the Wick were wide open. The empty house waited with open arms to receive everyone and everything back in its place—totally forgiving.

A small collection of people stood in the forecourt: 'Glad to see you back, sir . . . missed you, ma'am. . . .'

Around us stood the huge pantechnicons full of furniture and china, their white-overalled crews watching. John had told Kay that no one was to enter the house before I did.

Bubbling over with enthusiasm, Hayley and Jonathan clambered out of the car, pursued by the dogs. Johnnie laid his hands on their arms.

'Wait,' he said. 'Baba, you go in first,' and he grinned at me to show that we shared the secret.

With great deliberation, I brought out the glass witch stick. The men in white watched with some interest. I crossed the wide, empty hall into the oval room overlooking the river in the morning sunlight, and laid the witch stick on the marble mantelpiece.

'We have come back,' I said in a loud voice. The Unseen people in the room seemed to rise to their feet, and it was no longer empty.

I turned and saw Johnnie and the children framed in the doorway behind me. He was smiling.

'What shall we do tomorrow?' Hayley asked, without knowing what she was saying. . . .

*

Severally, and together, we have been all over the world since that day, but no beckoning fingers of tropical islands, mountains of Africa, or the dearly loved scents of the East, have the same power to call us back like migratory swallows, as that house of enchantment standing serenely on the top of Richmond Hill looking across the Thames to Windsor.

The Wick. Two hundred years old, but the same as we first knew it eighteen years ago, for it is only we who count the flying days. Each year the garden recreates itself anew. The Bourbon roses now rise eight feet, and the azaleas which were child high are nearly the same; lilies of the valley riot where they will, and the long tendrils of the wistaria clutch more of the balustrade along the veranda. Everything is the same. Unchanged.

There is only one hurt for Johnnie and me. The rooms are empty. For they, whose laughter echoed across the garden and down the corridors, have all grown up.

Blue Harbour,
Port Maria,
Jamaica. 1967.

The Wick,
Richmond,
England. 1968.